Third Edition

Learning for the 21st Century

by:

Bill Osher, Ph.D.
&
Joann Ward, Ed.S.

 KENDALL/HUNT PUBLISHING COMPANY
4050 Westmark Drive   Dubuque, Iowa 52002

TABLE OF CONTENTS

ACKNOWLEDGEMENTS

There are many people who have helped us with this book. While, none of them is responsible for its shortcomings and errors, each has helped to make it better than it otherwise would have been. *We are grateful to all who have helped us.* Special thanks are in order for the following:

Linda Cabot, for serving as unofficial and unpaid editor

Katy Landers, for providing information regarding students with disabilities

Michael Sheldon and Ed Broach, for providing information about campus computing

Bill Flanagan and Stuart Tross for assisting in the development of the College Adjustment Inventory

The staff of the Office of Information Technology for helping us in many ways

Julie LaPointe and Whitney Shephard for designing an eye-catching cover

Paul Bryant and Tobias Stanelle for their library research

Cathy Wiggins for proofing, copying, administering, and helping us out in countless ways

PREFACE

I'm (Bill) in my office on campus, reading my e-mail. This morning I posed a question to Future Work, an interest group I access through the Internet. I want to know how best to educate people for the future.

Arthur tells me Tomorrow is already here. We all must approach our careers like entrepreneurs. Arthur was an executive who got downsized after many productive years because his corporation was struggling to stay competitive. Now he must fly by the seat of his pants as a self-employed career consultant. This is the wave of the future, he says. A relevant college education must prepare people to navigate through uncharted waters.

Jack is a Silicon Valley engineer who lives in Ireland. Or maybe he's an Irish engineer who telecommutes to California. He enjoys a relaxed schedule with friends in the local pubs and keeps up with work by e-mail and phone. He's convinced his way is The Way for most people in the future.

Several days ago, a researcher from the Rand Institute agreed to send me a report on educating people to work in the global economy. It arrives today. I thumb through it and learn that American colleges aren't doing such a hot job. Our graduates don't know other languages well, nor do they understand other cultures. No wonder our businesses are struggling to stay competitive. There are, happily, several strategies enterprising students can follow if they really want to be ready for the next Century.

Ian, from the other side of the world at Aukland Institute of Technology, stresses creativity and life-long learning. Fred, a university chemist who has started up a bio-tech company, tells me that students need to read voraciously so they can learn to write well. Communication will be key. Even though he's a scientist, he never spends time in the lab. He's busy traveling the world, trying to persuade people to invest in his ideas. He adds that students also need to be comfortable with mathematics -- whether they're scientists or not.

My computer beeps. I've got new mail. My sister and brother-in-law have had a good stay in Prague and are on their way to Israel. They'll be coming through Atlanta in a couple of weeks. Maybe their layover will be long enough for us to get together.

Back on the Internet, I fumble my way to government documents. (When it comes to surfing the Internet, I do well to hang one or two. I'm not sure I'll ever be able to hang ten.) I'm looking at the U.S. census reports for **demographic** trends for college-age men and women in the year 2,000. Suddenly, it dawns on me how different my work has become in the less than ten years ago that have passed since I wrote the first edition of this book at home on a very slow personal computer I shared with my wife. I did not have a computer at work, nor was I hooked up to the Internet. I couldn't do business by e-mail, nor was there voice mail on our campus. We didn't have a College of Computing, nor could students major in a separate major called Computer Engineering. There was no List managed by the American Association of Higher Education on education and technology. There wasn't an entire section in the local newspaper each week devoted to personal technology. And students didn't have more computing power in their wrist watches than scientists did on super computers twenty-five years ago.

And so it's only natural that I change the title of this book from <u>The Blue Chip Graduate</u> to <u>Learning for the 21st Century</u>.

I'll tell you a secret (shhhhh). I (Joann) am the one that encouraged Bill to surf the net. I told him about the interest groups and we took the class on the World Wide Web together. As I reflect on my time at this institution of higher learning, I have evolved, as has the institution. It grew and so did I. I had to go back to school to facilitate my evolution. And schools, colleges and universities are evolving too. While I contemplate moving toward a Ph.D., I hear of an accredited, respected program for distance learning, that includes a program in Psychology....on the internet!

With slightly different interests than Bill, I have researched mental health issues, student development concerns and even Freshman Year Experience programming through the internet.

One thing I see happening in our society, is people are increasingly overwhelmed professionally and personally by the volume of information that must be assimilated and digested. I also see people, an "animal" with strong need for affiliation, seeking one another out. No longer do they stroll the sidewalks of small town America in the balmy summer dusk. Now, in a society with increasing pressure to perform, to achieve, to excel, more people are getting together via electronic means. The internet, undernet and e-mail have us gathered in electronic groups to "chat" and discuss our common ground. I have to ponder how this affects the human animal? Will loneliness become more problematic, or is this sufficient to meet our social needs? Did you know that loneliness is the first most common reason that freshmen leave college? Will accessibility to computer friends **mitigate** this loneliness? Will it decrease student participation in on-campus social opportunities? There is no doubt that while I was re-making myself by returning to college, and while the campuses of today are being influenced tremendously by technology, there are larger questions that have to do with our society as a whole.

I believe that nothing will replace the reassuring touch of a mentor's hand upon the shoulder of a student. I believe that the opportunities for this newest generation, yours, are just as fraught with opportunity and controversy as Galileo Galilei's What will be different is the tension to learn to balance our scholastic, family, career and personal needs in a society that will increasingly make more and more demands on the individual; not less. Our challenge is to make our Selves efficient in the process of digesting this diet of impossible proportions, and to learn to thrive and grow in environments that challenge us to find balance and personal growth amongst an avalanche of data. It is not all just learning, it is also part of the human journey called life. I believe we all need to take in the understanding in this book, but I challenge each of you also to make your journey as exciting, worthwhile and as truly fulfilling as you can. I ask each of you to read chapter 17 and take in the values discussed there. You are an important and critical cog in the machinery known as the universe. Make your moments here worthwhile.

You *ARE* Indiana Jones, and this is your adventure. What will it be? Remember, Indiana Jones was a professor before he was an adventurer. He took his knowledge with him, just as surely as he took his bullwhip and pistol. Perhaps the modern day Indiana Jones will become a professor and then find electronic adventures armed with computer and technology? Use this book to help you first of all, obtain the knowledge necessary to become the foundation for your life adventure.

Georgia Institute of Technology
April 30, 1996

CONTRACT

We want to give you the highest Quality education we can. We must work together as a team in order to accomplish this lofty objective. We as the lecturers agree to deliver the following:

TEACHERS

1.   We will start class on time.

2.   We will be prepared to teach.

3.   We will attempt to administer fair tests and score them fairly.

4.   We will give reasonable assignments.

5.   We will field student questions with respect.

6.   We will attempt to deliver a class that will ensure your survival, promote your success, and encourage your excellence.

7.   Barring emergencies, we will keep any posted office hours.

8.   We're trying to find out exactly what interests and traits predict student success. We'll be using some career and attitude inventories to do so. Your individual scores will be kept confidential.

9.   If you show any signs of being an at-risk student we will contact you and explore ways to increase your chances of success.

10. We will consider and try to adopt any reasonable suggestions for improving this class.

Faculty Survival Tips	Student Survival Tips	Things I Plan to Do To Ensure My Survival At GT:

Faculty Survival Tips

1. Your full-time job is to be a student. Do this job full time: that is eight hours a day. When not actually in class, use your time, just as if you were on a job and study, work on papers, do projects, etc.

2. Set goals and prioritize them everyday.

3. Review and organize class notes the same day you take them.

4. Join or form an effective study group.

5. Use campus resources, such as the Counseling Center, Career Services, Math Lab, STEP Program, Freshman Experience Tutors, campus ministries.

6. Don't wait to be rescued. Get assistance if needed.

7. Use a systematic method of reading your textbook.

8. Do homework problems the day they are assigned.

9. Get enough rest, relaxation, recreation, and exercise.

10. Don't just memorize. Try to understand.

11. Review every day.

12. Set-up a budget. Stick to it.

13. Always attend class. Your grades can be correlated directly to attendance.

Student Survival Tips

1. Find where your classes and other essential resources are.

2. Know what your computing resources are, where they are, and how to use them. Get access to them as soon as possible.

3. There is Stinger bus service available to you. The Stinger bus service will take you not just around the campus, but up to the local MARTA stations, and even a local shopping center. Get wise about how to use this resource.

4. Find out where to eat off campus and where to get groceries.

5. Learn how to register for next quarter's classes.

6. The grading system here is different than high school. Curves are more common, so don't get ulcers over test grades that are lower than what you're used to.

7. There are all sorts of campus organizations. The Student Government Association has a list of them. Go find out about the many interesting social and community service opportunities available.

8. Know what you have to do to manage your way through Financial Aid. Know what the deadlines are and be sure to respond promptly.

9. Focus on what you want for a career. Get whatever campus resources you need to help you make your decisions.

10. Find somewhere that you can study effectively.

Preparing for the 21st Century

Time travel. The very concept fascinates us. Imagine wading through a steamy swamp, the musky smell of the **primordial** ooze envelops you. You feel as much as hear the giant footfalls nearby. You are drenched in sweat as you peer through a stand of giant ferns into a Jurassic forest to watch enormous dinosaurs lumber past, foraging for food. Or consider traveling forward in time. What direction will history take in ten years, or twenty, or twenty thousand? Can humans sustain a viable environment? End warfare, disease, and poverty? Will there even BE a human race in the future, and would you want to be a member of it?

Will humans ever be able to travel back and forth through the years? Who knows? But one thing we can guarantee is that YOU will travel into the 21st Century. True, you won't be thrust forward through time as rapidly as someone in a science fiction novel. But, if you're a college student today, barring death, you will live, love, work, and play in the 21st Century. You can't avoid it. What will it be like? And how can you prepare for this journey?

The calendar is, of course, a human artifact. There probably will be very little in the course of history that changes between midnight December 31, 2000 and 12:01 AM January 1, 2001.* The 21st Century, however, will be the first century in which the computer is king. It will be the first century in its entirety to belong to the Information Age. Because of that, it will be different than any century preceding it. If you understand and prepare for the challenges ahead, you can seize the opportunities they hold. If you ignore those challenges and wander casually into the future, you may be one of the casualties. Do you really want to be roadkill on the Information Highway? We bet you don't.

This book will tell you how to use college to prepare for the 21st Century. It is your personal guide for succeeding in the Information Age.

THE INFORMATION AGE

Every year, thousands of college students travel all over the world. For some, it's a Study

---

*Technically, the 21st Century doesn't begin until a moment after midnight on December 31, 2000. Therefore, the start of the new millenium is in 2001. For the sake of convenience, we will talk about it beginning in the year 2000. While technically incorrect, most people will, we believe, look at it similarly, excepting Arthur Clark (author of *2001: A Space Odyssey*).

Abroad program. For others, it's an international internship. Some get involved in service projects. Many travel on a shoestring with friends, their possessions in their backpacks, hitchhiking and staying in youth hostels. One thing virtually all of these travelers have in common is a guide book which advises them on the country where they're traveling.

A well-done guidebook is an indispensible resource. It will tell you how much the hotels and restaurants cost, transportation options, and what to see and do. It will also say something about the terrain and climate and what to wear at different times of the year. A guidebook will tell you something about the history and culture of the country you visit. It will probably have phonetic spellings of key words and phrases.

Visiting a foreign country for the first time, you would want to know all of these things, and that's just if you were visiting. Well, you're moving permanently into the 21st Century. You'll be setting up house in the Information Age for the next fifty or so years. (Obviously, if you're an older student, you won't enjoy the scenery as long, but it's still in your interest to know the territory.)

So, you'll be spending the rest of your life in the Information Age. What's it going to be like?

You may already have heard of futurist Alvin Toffler. His best selling books include *Future Shock* and *The Third Wave*. He and John Naisbitt (who wrote *Megatrends*) are probably the two most widely read futurists who write for the the general public. Toffler argues that civilization can be divided into three **epochs**: agricultural, industrial, and informational. (Toffler follows Daniel Bell's three ages -- preindustrial, industrial, and postindustrial -- which were **posited** in *The Coming of Post-Industrial Society*.)

The Agricultural Age

Toffler states that up until about 8,000 years ago, humans lived a tribal, nomadic existence. Our hunter-gatherer ancestors were perennially on the move, following the animals which provided the food. As humans began to farm instead of forage and herd instead of hunt, a radically different society evolved. Farming required permanent settlements so crops could be tended. Settlements grew into cities, and society became more diverse and complex. While there were warriors and priests, artists and craftspeople, kings and scholars, most humans worked the soil. The question, "What will you be when you grow up?" would have puzzled most people. They would spend their lives struggling to survive by planting crops and harvesting them. The history of civilization has been predominantly agrarian.

The Industrial Age

The agricultural age began to decline in the 17th Century when people began to make products in much greater quantities. Eventually, the power of steam was harnessed which led to factories capable of mass production. As the Industrial Revolution spread throughout most of the globe, the way in which fundamental societal institutions were organized changed. The change was often painful. Human muscle could not compete with steam power and gears, and many workers lost their jobs. John Henry, the steel driving man, lost his life, the ballad says, because he couldn't keep up with a machine. Eventually, most men toiled in factories or in the mines which provided the fuel to power the factories. Mass production permitted the accumulation of much greater wealth.

The Information Age

In 1955, white-collar workers surpassed the number of blue-collar workers in the United States. For the first time in history, more people earned their money pushing pencils behind a desk than pushing parts on an assembly line. The significance of this is the pencil pusher manipulates information instead of machinery. Since 1955, the number of information workers has grown; the number of machine operators has declined. Increasingly, the Information Age is built upon the computer. It permits the power harnessed in the Industrial Age to be wielded much more effectively and productively.

From plow to machine to computer. From farm to factory to office. From farmer to machinist to expert. Work is changing. Government, families, and communities are changing. Society is changing as we rush forward into an Information Age already begun. We believe there are seven features that characterize the Information Age. These seven principles will permeate every aspect of 21st Century life. Ignore them at your peril!

The Seven Principles of the Information Age

1.   **Knowledge is power.** In the Information Age, strength and power are related to knowledge. The strongest countries are those with the best educational systems who produce the best scientists, technicians, and managers. Japan, for example, is a small, crowded island nation with relatively few natural resources. Yet, its economy is very strong because its educational system produces technically skilled citizens with very few falling through the cracks. When compared with Japan, the United States high school dropout and illiteracy rates make it very difficult for us to compete industrially as a nation. The strongest corporations are those which attract and cultivate intellectual talent and know

how to nurture its expression. Currently, it is considered vital for any business enterprise to be "a learning organization."

In the Information Age, the height of your career ladder will be largely determined by the depth and breadth of your knowledge. College is probably the best chance you'll ever have to strengthen and lengthen that ladder.

The implications of this truth are profound. If you want to prosper in the next century, you must do it with your brain. That means attending college and getting one or more degrees is more important than it has ever been. The 1992 U.S. Census reports the following correlation between education and income:

Educational Attainment	Housefold Income
Less than 9th Grade	$13,300
9th to 12th Grade	$17,300
High School Degree	$29,000
Attended College	$35,300
College Degree	$49,500
Master's Degree	$57,900
Doctorate	$70,100
Professional Degree	$84,900

Education has been related to success for many years. Its significance today is even more profound. Russell Jacoby observes in *Dogmatic Wisdom, How the Culture Wars Divert Education and Distract America.* that in the 1970's white college graduates earned only 18% more than white male high school graduates. By 1989, the difference had shot up to 45%. For women and blacks the difference is even more striking. By 1989 the white women college graduates earned 75% more than their high school graduate counterparts. In that same year, African American female college graduates made 92% more than their high school graduate peers.

Of course, education is about much more than getting a string of degrees. What really counts is learning how to learn and becoming a continuous learner throughout your life. Ed Cornish, in the January/February 1996 edition of *The Futurist*, predicts that education may become compulsory for adults as well as young people.

The computer chips of 1971 calculated in "additions" per second, at a rate approximately proportional to the period at the end of this sentence.

A decade later, the computer chips of 1982 calculated in "additions" per second are approximately proportional to the block below.

Not quite 25 years since that "period" at the end of the sentence above. our present computer chips calculate "additions" per second at a rate approximately proportional to the screen of this computer.

Why do you care about additions per second? Because the volume and speed of the computer has increased the volume and speed of the work world. And when you get out of college, the work world you enter will require more hours, more efficiency, and a higher level of educational sophistication than people in previous decades. And, as the volume and speed of computers increase so does our capability as a society. The flip side of that coin is, how does it eventually affect our humanity?

2. **The pace of life will accelerate.** If any thing characterizes contemporary society, it is speed. Time is already money in today's world. Meeting deadlines, working overtime, doing business in a "New York minute" -- these are common practices today. Federal Express was build on the need of businesses to deliver fast. This trend will only increase in the 21st Century. Letters used to take months. Now they take only a few days, but that's still not fast enough. That's why people now use e-mail instead of "snail mail." The phone and the FAX carry information at the speed of light. One way to represent the speed that characterizes contemporary life is through the speed with which computer chips process information. The October 1995 *National Geographic* devoted an entire article to the Information Revolution. That, in itself is revealing: cyberspace has in a sense become the geography of our time. Among the observations made was the breathtakingly rapid increasing speed of computers: In 1971, a chip could perform 60,000 "additions" per second; in 1974, 290,000; in 1979, 330,000; in 1982, 900,000; in 1985, 5,500,000; in 1989, 20,000,000; in 1993, 100,000,000; in 1995, 250,000,000 "additions" per second. In twenty-five years, the speed of computers has increased four thousand fold!

    As smaller chips are manufactured with more circuits, computers get faster and smaller. As computers become faster and smaller, they become more portable and more affordable. As portability and affordability increas, so does the speed with which business and industry is conducted. We are traveling into the 21st Century with the foot of society firmly pressing the accelerator to the floorboard.

3. **Change will be pervasive.** Technological innovation will constantly alter our lives. In the early days of the television industry, three networks broadcast programs to a few thousand viewers in one country. With cable television there were dozens of channels pumping out information to millions of customers across the world. Soon there will be hundreds of channels. Nations, industries, and companies rise and fall. Those who best cope with constant change will endure and prosper. Joel Baker in *Future Edge* recounts the following true story of the challenges and opportunities associated with change. In 1968, Switzerland dominated the watchmaking industry worldwide. They made the best watches. They worked unceasingly to improve them. It was understandable then that they would garner 80% to 90% of the industry's profits worldwide. Yet, by 1980, the Swiss' profit share had dropped to less than 20%. Why? Because they did not adjust rapidly enough to change.

What happened? The Japanese adopted and developed the electronic quartz movement, and that became the benchmark of the watchmaking industry. What makes this story so ironic is that it was the Swiss themselves who invented the technology. Their corporate leaders, however, did not anticipate the changing demands of their customers and so rejected this technological innovation. Japan now leads the world in the sale of time pieces.

4. **We will be overwhelmed with information.** Derek Price charts in *Little Science, Big Science* the phenomenal accelerating growth of scientific knowledge in the last few hundred years. In the middle of the 17th Century there were two scientific journals. One hundred years later there were ten. Fifty years after that there were 100. Fifty years after that, 1,000. By 1963, there were approximately 50,000! Presumably, there are over 100,000 scientific journals regularly published as we approach the 21st Century. This means that scientific knowledge doubles every few years. Petersen, in *The Road to 2015*, guestimates it doubles every 18 months. It's extremely difficult to keep up with all the advances in any one field. It's impossible to keep up with the advances in all fields. There's even a term for this state of affairs. It's called information overload.

Petersen further observes that a person who reads an entire copy of the Sunday *New York Times* would take in more information in one afternoon than the average citizen in Thomas Jefferson's day would within a lifetime. There are many implications to the problem posed by information overload. Which information do we regard as essential to pass on to the next generation? What core knowledge must college students master? How can you as a citizen stay informed? How can you as a professional keep abreast of your field?

5. **Diversity will dominate.** We live in a global economy, buying, selling, and trading with every part of the world. The planet will continue to shrink as transportation grows faster and instantaneous communication networks reach all areas of the globe. It is highly likely that you will work outside of the continental United States at some point during your career. You will be called upon to do business with people whose culture, language, and beliefs differ from yours. The composition of the American workforce is also growing more diverse. By the year 2,000, the percentage of white non-Hispanic men, historically the largest segment comprising our labor force, will shrink, while the percentage of African-American, Asian, and Hispanic job holders will rise. Women of all races will

account for almost half of the labor force in the U.S. Your colleagues will be of African, Hispanic, European, and Asian origins, as well as mixtures thereof. Historically, career women could choose between nursing and teaching. Today, women are entering science and engineering, law and medicine, management and the executive suite. You will work for and with women.

Ired Forum, a publication of the Geneva based Development Innovations and Networks captures the flavor of the future by creating an imaginary village of 1,000 people to represent the **demographics** of the entire planet. In this village, there would be:

> 564 Asians
> 210 Europeans
> 86 Africans
> 80 South Americans
> 60 North Americans

There would be:

> 300 Christians (183 Catholics, 84 Protestants, 33 Orthodox)
> 175 Muslims
> 55 Budhists
> 47 Animists
> 210 without any religion or atheist

While the planet as a whole has always been characterized by racial, cultural, and ethnic diversity, this variety has a much greater impact upon us today because telecomminications and transportation have eroded most of the national and geographical barriers that historically have separated us. I (Bill) live in Atlanta, Georgia, a scant few years ago the heart of the deep South. When I finish this chapter I will drive to The Dekalb International Farmers Market which serves a thoroughly international customer base and is staffed by employees from every continent. Each wears a name tag indicating the various languages that individual speaks. I can buy collard greens, pork chops, and catfish. I can also buy squid, jicama, and lemon grass. This Farmers Market is a snapshot of the future demographics of the United States.

6. **The secure, lifetime job will be a thing of the past.** Employees won't work for a giant corporation over a thirty year career that culminates in a retirement dinner and a gold watch. People will have many jobs and a number of careers. Some would say that the traditional job is an endangered species. Downsizing has become a way of life in the corporate world, affecting blue-collar and white collar employees alike. More and more people will manage their own careers, selling their expertise to a variety of individuals and organizations as self-employed entrepreneurs.

7. **Enormous challenges loom ahead.** As the world population grows on a planet that doesn't, there are numerous obstacles to peace and prosperity looming on the horizon: overpopulation, environmental degradation, violence, disease, and poverty. Any one of these issues could fill a book if not an entire library, but that is beyond the scope of this text.

So there it is. You are closing in on the 21st Century. You will face a strikingly different world than your parents faced. Can you keep up with rapidly changing technology? Will you flounder in an ocean of information? What will the world of work be like? How will you manage your career? Will public schools be good enough to educate your children? Will your confidence in our government and its elected officials continue to plummet? Will your streets and neighborhoods be safe? Will you want to live behind walled and gated communities? Change is often frightening and painful. It ushers in tremendous challenges, but it can also offer unprecedented opportunities. Will you be prepared to meet the challenges and seize the opportunities? Read on. This book tells you how to go through college and graduate ready for what's ahead.

Implications and Applications

The purpose of this book is to make you a better student, a better citizen, and, some day, a better professional. Ultimately, however, education is not just about how to make a better living. It's about how to make a better life. You can use your college experience now to live better later. This book can help you do that, not because it is Revealed Truth, but because it contains much that is true. The truths it contains, however, won't take you very far if they are only answers to tests. Therefore, it is crucial that you question, consider, and contemplate the message of *Learning for the 21st Century*. And even that's not enough. To get the maximum benefit from this book you must see how it applies to your life and use it to plan a better one. Throughout the book there are exercises, experiments, and invitations to make commitments and take actions. We recommend you engage in every one. Starting now!

Seven Principles of The Information Age:

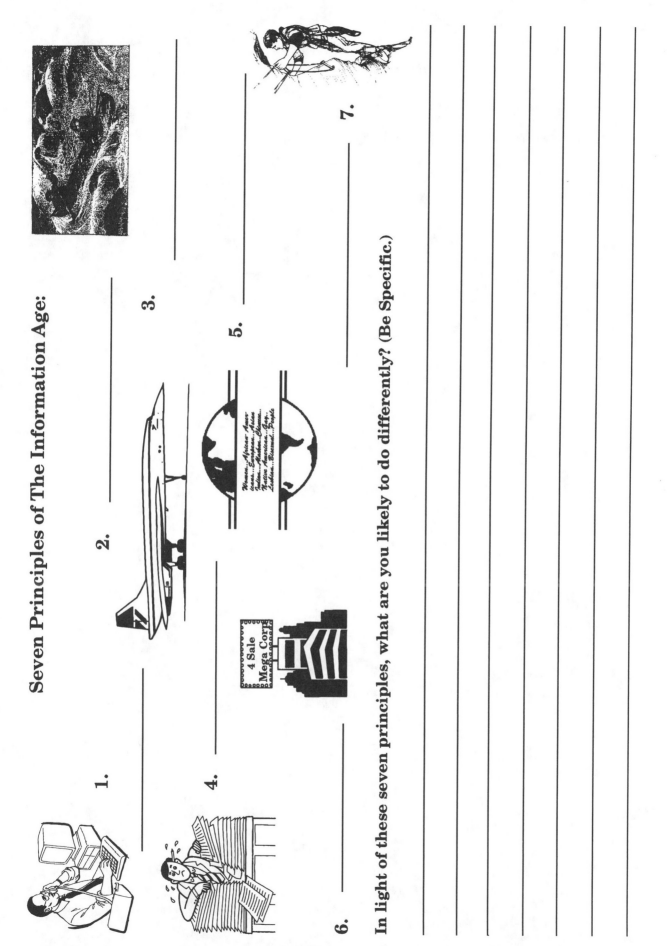

1. _____

2. _____

3. _____

4. _____

5. _____

6. _____

7. _____

In light of these seven principles, what are you likely to do differently? (Be Specific.)

_____

_____

_____

_____

_____

_____

_____

13

2010 CALENDAR

Who Am I Tomorrow?

My Name is: _____ .

Today is January 1, 2010, I'm _____ years old.   I'm (circle one) single/married/ divorced, and have _____ children.

I've accomplished the following personal goals: _____
_____
_____

My parents are: _____
_____
_____

I reside in: _____
_____

I'm working presently for: _____
_____
_____

I have plans to: _____
_____
_____

I feel my career is: _____
_____
_____

I wish that I had: _____
_____
_____

The things that give my life meaning today are: _____
_____
_____

My annual income is about $ _____. I am satisfied/dissatisfied with that sum. I hope to invest $_____ per year, so that I can retire with an annual income of about $_____ . I have about _____ years left to work before I retire.
The thing I most want to accomplish before I die is to: _____
_____
_____

Religion figures into my life in the following way(s): _____
_____
_____

Someday when I look back at this, I hope I will have: _____
_____
_____
_____

2
Ready for the 21st Century

Chapter 1 outlined what we believe the 21st Century will be like. Will you be ready for it? To help you answer this question, we ask you to take a look at two graduating seniors. Graduation might seem like eons away right now, but it's not. You have just four or five years before you launch your career. Here's what you can expect.

JOE/JANE RECRUITER

Every year corporate recruiters scour college campuses, looking for talent. As more companies downsize in an attempt to stay competitive, their numbers shrink. They call on fewer colleges. They interview fewer students. Nonetheless, the screening interviews conducted in college placement centers remain an important avenue for securing employment. In the future, more of these interviews will be conducted live via video conferencing. At Georgia Tech, a few students already are doing "remote" interviews.

There will also be more job searching done on the Internet. Already, many college placement centers provide advice, tips, and strategies electronically. Already, students are surfing the net for job leads. Ultimately, however, there's got to be a meeting between employer and candidate. Let's watch a recruiter assess two prospects.

The recruiter spends his day in a tiny office not much larger than a closet. It's furnished with a modest desk and two or three chairs. The offices and furniture are interchangeable from one placement center to the next. Sometimes it seems to him that the candidates are interchangeable as well. Dressed

We share an office building with a number of departments, including career services. Since that department schedules job interviews on our campus, we see a steady stream of dressed-for-success college students scurrying with book bags to meet with one or another corporate recruiter. Recently, a grim-faced senior announced on the elevator to no one in particular that he had just learned that the company with whom he had just finished interviewing planned to talk with 75 candidates before they made an offer for the one position they needed to fill.

Sam Dresden

Campus Box 1000   Atlanta, Georgia 30332   (404) 894-1970

Objective: A challenging and responsible position with a chance for advancement in a growth industry.

Education: Fulton University
Atlanta, Georgia   GPA: 2.8/4.0
   B.A. Psychology   6/96
   Minor in Business

Merrimac College
Dawsonville, Georgia   GPA: 3.1/4.0
   Sociology Major   9/92-12/92

Middleton Junior College
Atlanta, Georgia   GPA: 3.3:/4.0
   A.S. History   9/90-6/92

Coursework: Abnormal Psychology, Industrial Psychology, Management, Marketing, Accounting

Work History:

Waiter	Dugan's Restaurant 6/95-Present Responsible for servicing lunchtime shift for mostly capacity crowds
Bus Boy	Set and cleared tables, helped in kitchen. Promoted to waiter after two months
Delivery Boy	Pizza Hut 6/93-12/94
Cashier	Burger King 6/91-12/92

References: Furnished upon request

conservatively and armed only with his questions and powers of observation, he pulls out a stack of resumes from his briefcase. He knows he will talk with many more candidates than his company has jobs to offer.

He takes a sip of coffee from a styrofoam cup and looks at the resume of the candidate he's going to interview in a few minutes, Sam Dresden. This is how he appraises it.

Objective: A challenging and responsible position with a chance for advancement in a growth industry.

The JOB OBJECTIVE tells him nothing. What kind of challenging and responsible position? What sort of advancement?

Education:	Fulton University	
	Atlanta, Georgia	GPA: 2.8/4.0
	B.A. Psychology	6/96
	Minor in Business	
	Merrimac College	
	Dawsonville, Georgia	GPA: 3.1/4.0
	Sociology Major	9/92-12/92

Our recruiter moves on to EDUCATION and frowns. Sam has a fair GPA and has a minor in business, but he seems to lack focus. If this resume had come in the morning mail, he would have dropped it in the wastebasket under his desk within ten seconds of picking it up. But he has an appointment with the candidate, so he quickly reviews the rest of the resume.

Work History:

Waiter	Dugan's Restaurant	6/95-Present
	Responsible for servicing lunchtime shift for mostly capacity crowds	
Bus Boy	Set and cleared tables, helped in kitchen. Promoted to waiter after two months	

| Delivery Boy | Pizza Hut | 6/93-12/94 |
| Cashier | Burger King | 6/91-12/92 |

At least Sam has a WORK HISTORY. He may even have put himself through school. That counts for something. But Sam doesn't relate his work to marketable skills or to a career path -- unless he wants to work in the company cafeteria. Joe Recruiter frowns and heads for the waiting room.

A few minutes later Sam is seated in the small office facing the representative from Coca Cola. "Tell me about yourself," the recruiter asks.

"I grew up in Dawsonville, Georgia. I have two older sisters. My Dad is a plumber and Mom keeps the books for him. As I got older I helped him some, but I never really liked the plumbing business. I did the usual stuff as a kid -- little league, hunting and fishing. I played in the band for a couple of years, but I honestly wasn't much of a musician. I did OK in high school. I got along with everybody.

"Summers we'd visit my uncle's family in Atlanta sometimes. That was quite a big deal to me after growing up in a small town. You could go to any movie you wanted to, and there was the zoo, and a couple of times we went to see the Braves play. That's why I wanted to come to Fulton University -- so I could live in Atlanta. It took me a while to work it out, but I finally got here. I've had to work part time, but I've made some good friends here.

"Let's see, I still like to fish. I still like to watch the Braves. And I still like Atlanta. If possible, I'd like to find work here."

The recruiter nods and asks him what his professional goals are. Sam knew early on that he didn't want to be a plumber. He'd thought about teaching, but he figures business is what he'd like to do. He wants to know what sorts of opportunities Coke has available. The recruiter asks about Sam's strengths. He says that he is hard-working, ambitious, and a good communicator. He doesn't offer any evidence to support his claim, so the recruiter asks him to elaborate. Sam says he has helped to pay his way through college. He has worked as many as twenty hours a week while being a full-time student. He wants something better in his future. He discusses how hectic his college years have been. The recruiter nods and begins to appreciate Sam a little more. He does get the feeling that Sam isn't afraid of work. And while his answers aren't well organized, he has a relaxed manner about him.

When asked to discuss his weaknesses, Sam draws a blank and makes a nervous joke about not really having any. The recruiter remains silent, giving Sam a chance to collect his thoughts. This only makes the candidate more anxious, and he begins to ramble on about how restless and bored he gets when he has to write papers. The recruiter notes that Sam certainly hadn't anticipated the question. Plus the answer he gave was very negative. Would he have the patience to fill out his reports? Would he meet his deadlines?

The recruiter asks what Sam has learned from his various jobs. Sam replies that he knows now that he doesn't want to be a plumber, and he doesn't want to work in the fast food industry. Again, he fails to elaborate what else he learned -- about teamwork, leadership, or customer service. The recruiter is forced to conclude that Sam may well not have learned much.

The recruiter asks Sam to describe an obstacle that he encountered in the last few years and how he handled it? Sam frowns, obviously stumped by the question. Finally, he mentions his work with Pizza Hut. He didn't like his manager. In fact, he thought he was a doofus. He was glad to be done with that work and start work with Dugan's. Again, the recruiter notes that Sam has cited a situation which many people have experienced, but he doesn't appear to have handled it particularly creatively. Neither does he appear to have learned much from it.

To the question about his reading habits, Sam answers that he reads *Sports Illustrated*. He mentions no business reading, no trade journals, nor anything that would stretch his mind.

In answer to the question about his computer skills, Sam says he uses Word Perfect and that he had to "do some spread sheet stuff in one of my business classes." He does not appear to have mastered the number one tool that will dominate the 21st Century.

The recruiter has pretty well already eliminated Sam. He gives him one last chance. "What could you contribute to our company, and why do you want to work for us?"

Sam says that everybody knows about Coca Cola, and he's always wanted to work for a major corporation. He has nothing more to add. Just as the recruiter suspected, Sam hasn't done his homework. He doesn't know any more about Coca Cola than the next person on the street. Maybe less. He doesn't seem to know marketing from research from the fifty-yard line. He's not a bad kid, but he's out of his league. He doesn't know what he wants. He doesn't know what Coca Cola wants. So naturally he can't sell himself.

Corporations pay recruiters to screen out weak candidates, not to provide a job placement service. An interviewer has no obligation to help lost applicants sort out their confusion. Yet Sam acts like he came for career counseling instead of a job interview. It's

SALLY SCHEIN

Campus Box 1234   Atlanta, GA 30032   (404)894-1234

Objective: Design and write multimedia.

Education: Fulton University   GPA: 3.2/4.0
                   B.A. Communication   6/96
                   Minor in Computer Graphics

Coursework: Film History, Animation, Advertising, Multimedia 1 & 2, Technical
                   Writing 1 & 2, Public Relations, Public Speaking 1 & 2,
                   Conversational Spanish I & II

**Honors &
Activities:**   President, Student Multimedia Society, Award: First Place in Senior
                   Multimedia Design Project, Entertainment Columnist for THE Fulton
                   ECHO (CAMPUS NEWSPAPER). Selected as member of Emerging
                   Leaders. Friend of International Students Association.

Skills:
Multimedia Design: Designed award winning Training Module to teach Fulton
                   University freshmen how to use the library. Did Internship with
                   Coca Cola, worked with various vendors on developing training
                   material. Familiar with Corel Draw, MicroGrafX Illustrator,
                   Storyboard Live, Persuasion, Power Point.

Technical Writing: Wrote first drafts of training material for vendors while
                   interning at Coca Cola.

Leadership: Started Student Multimedia Society. Secured faculty sponsorship,
                   coordinated creation of charter and by-laws, built membership,
                   and was elected first president. Secretary of Emerging Leaders at
                   Fulton University.

Public Speaking: Presided over Student Multimedia Society meetings, led
                   orientation groups of parents and students at Fulton University,
                   made A's in Public Speaking 1 & 2. Gave speeches to Rotary Club,
                   and Temple Beth El in Marietta, Georgia.

Experience:
                   Coca Cola International: Intern during Summers of 1994 and 1995. Assisted in
                   development of corporate training and marketing materials.

                   The Fulton Echo: Paid staffer -- Features writer, film reviewer, and entertainment
                   editor from 1991-1994.

interesting that the recruiter thinks of Sam as a kid. Sam is, in fact, twenty-four. He thinks and acts like a kid though.

Sam leaves the interview with a headache. He has a sinking feeling he's not going to hear from Coca Cola, and, of course, he won't.

SALLY SCHEIN

Sally is eager to speak with Coca Cola. She knows a lot of people there and was very pleased with her internship experience with Coke. She knows big companies aren't hiring scads of new graduates to be permanent full-time employees like they were ten or twenty years ago. She also knows that Coke (as well as many another large corporation) hires lots of independent contractors to do project work. She has worked with several small companies who do work for Coke and has already discussed working for a couple of them. Still, she wouldn't mind working for the big corporation itself. It would be more good experience, more good contacts, and a nice additional credit on her already impressive resume.

Meanwhile, Joe Recruiter has just completed his interview with Sam Dresden. He doesn't bother making any notes because he knows that Coke has no place for Sam until he acquires a lot more experience, direction, and maturity. He picks up the resume of his next appointment and nods his head. She looks a lot more promising.

Objective: Write and design multimedia.

Joe knows that Coke uses a lot of technical writers and multimedia designers. Coke has to train its thousands of employees all over the world, and they use computer assisted instruction to accomplish this task cost effectively. Coke also needs people who can develop top quality slides, transparencies, and special effects for marketing presentations and the like. His eyes move on down Sally's resume.

Education:

Fulton University	GPA: 3.2/4.0
B.A. Communication	6/96
Minor in Computer Graphics	

Coursework: Film History, Animation, Advertising, Multimedia 1 & 2, Technical Writing 1 & 2, Public Relations, Public Speaking 1 & 2, Conversational Spanish I & II

Honors & Activities: President, Student Multimedia Society, **Award:** First Place in Senior Multimedia Design Project, Entertainment Columnist for *THE Fulton ECHO* (CAMPUS NEWSPAPER). Selected as member of Emerging Leaders. Friend of International Students Association.

He notes that Sally's coursework and activities complement each other. Plus she's gotten involved in some leadership activities. She's won an award for designing a multimedia program. She's written for the public. She's been active -- no, she's been a leader -- in a relevant professional society. And she appears to have some appreciation for the international dimensions of today's business world -- she has studied conversational Spanish and has interacted with international students.

Skills:

Multimedia Design: Developed award winning Training Module to teach Fulton University freshmen how to use the library. Did Internship with Coca Cola, worked with various vendors on developing training material. Familiar with Corel Draw, MicroGrafX Illustrator, Storyboard Live, Persuasion, Power Point.

Technical Writing: Wrote first drafts of training material for vendors while interning at Coca Cola.

Leadership: Started Student Multimedia Society. Secured faculty sponsorship, coordinated creation of charter and by-laws, built membership, and was elected first president. Secretary of Emerging Leaders at Fulton University.

Public Speaking: Presided over Student Multimedia Society meetings, led orientation groups of parents and students at Fulton University, made A's in Public Speaking 1 & 2. Gave speeches to Rotary Club, and Temple Beth El in Marietta, Georgia.

Sally's skills mesh with her schoolwork which meshes with her career plans. She's good at doing what she wants to do professionally: create effective communications for others. Writing, speaking, multimedia development, another language, and a potential leader. Plus she's already interned for Coke. Joe Recruiter smiles. He's looking forward to this interview.

Experience:

Coca Cola International: Intern during Summers of 1994 and 1995. Assisted in development of corporate training and marketing materials.

The Fulton Echo: Paid staffer -- Features writer, film reviewer, and e n t e r t a i n m e n t editor   from 1991-1994.

Sally's experience completes the picture. She's worked on campus doing something pertinent to her own career. She has worked with Coke in her field of interest. Joe gets up and heads for the waiting room. He's eager to meet Sally. When he gets there a small woman in a navy blue dress folds the newspaper she's been reading, stands up, and offers her hand.

As he escorts Sally down the hall, he's thinking that she's already making a good impression. An infectious smile, a firm handshake, and good eye contact. She said she looked forward to meeting the representative from Coca Cola, and it felt like she meant it. He invites her to sit down and takes his own seat. They chat for a few minutes about the Atlanta Braves. He knows some of the people she interned with. She seems quite at ease, so it's time to get down to business. He asks her to tell him a bit about herself. Sally has anticipated this question. She uses her answer to show how her personal history has led her to this interview.

"As a kid I was fascinated with movies and wanted to be a movie star. Next I wanted to make movies -- be another Steven Speilberg. Then I got interested in cartoons and wanted to work some day for Disney. My parents were supportive of my dreams. They got me a computer and sent me to computer camp. They encouraged me to fool around with a camcorder. They gave me art lessons. But they also were practical. Most people don't get to direct Hollywood movies. Most people don't end up working on *Pocahontas*.

"I've always loved to read, and I've always kept a journal and played around with creative writing. But not that many people make a living writing fiction. My Mom knew somebody who knew somebody who actually got me a phone interview with Pat Conroy. He was extremely gracious and encouraged me to write if I really loved it. He also said he was a lot luckier than most writers, and that very few novelists make any real money. I worked on the school paper from middle school through high school and college. So I thought for a while that maybe I'd be a journalist. That's sort of what I was thinking of when I started at Fulton. It was a real eye opener for me to learn early on that the newspaper business was undergoing so many changes. There are fewer newspapers each year. I just didn't think I wanted to risk going into a field that was shrinking.

"So I was working on the Fulton University paper and loving it, but I couldn't really see how that was going to prepare me for the future. Then I took my first Technical Writing course, and I really liked the professor. He was very enthusiastic about the field growing in the future. Some of what technical writers do doesn't interest me, but there really is a lot that does -- developing materials for presentations, writing audio visual scripts, and designing multimedia. I've done these things for classes here at the Fulton. I've done them at Coke. I like doing them, and people tell me I'm good at what I do.

"Although I love working on my computer on a big project, I'd have to say that I'm a 'people' person. But that's another thing I've liked about working on multimedia projects -- it's a team effort. That's part of why I thought my internship was so exciting. We'd get together and brainstorm ideas for hours. My ideas counted too even if I was still in college.

"And the whole idea of dealing with all kinds of people. When I was in High School, we started getting a lot of Hispanic students and Asian students. At first none of us knew how to relate to them, and they very much kept to themselves. Then our Temple sponsored some immigrants from Russia and I started to learn about how they had to adjust to American culture. I could see some parallels with the new kids at school. I started talking with them, and found out I love finding out about other people. I've continued that at Fulton by living in a language house one year which was such a great experience. It was difficult at first, but by the end of the year I was dreaming in Spanish. I got involved with the International Students Association and I loved that too. I really felt like I was doing something when I could talk with students from Venezuela and Panama in Spanish. I even thought about getting into the travel industry, but I figure I'm better off doing something I'm good at for a company that does business outside of the United States -- which is another reason I'd love to work for Coca Cola."

Joe Recruiter smiles. He's engaged by Sally, and he's impressed. She has many interests, but she has woven them into a whole that hangs together. He asks about her strengths. She pauses thoughtfully and mentions three: she considers herself to be a good team player, a hard worker, and a leader. Then she backs up her statement with facts from her personal history. She talks about committees she's served on with international students, the school newspaper business meetings, and her work with Coca Cola. Communications was a natural major for her. She loves working with people. But she also likes getting things done, and she'll do what it takes to finish a project. She described the hours she put in on her multimedia projects -- and the satisfaction she got when they turned out so well. Naturally, it was necessary for her to be well organized to juggle all the things she has done -- school, newspaper, International Students Association, and the Multimedia Society. She's headed up a number of committees and projects, but she believes starting the Multimedia Society best demonstrates her ability to lead.

When the recruiter asks her about her weaknesses, she says she has to watch herself or she gets impatient with others. She likes things to be done right, but she's learning that different people contribute in different ways and at different speeds. She adds that working with people from different countries has also taught her to be patient enough so that everybody understands what's going on.

It is obvious to the recruiter that Sally has thought out her answers to the standard interview questions. He's already convinced enough of her potential to offer her an interview with someone in the Coke building downtown. Still, the skeptic in him wonders just how thorough she really is. He asks her his final standard question. "How do you think you could contribute to Coca Cola, and why would you want to work for us?"

"I honestly believe I can contribute in many ways. I've worked for Coke on an internship, and I fit right in. In fact, I've listed Ms. Gomez as one of my references. She was the project manager, and I thought she was great. I'm a good writer and designer. I'm a team player. I speak Spanish fluently and wouldn't mind relocating in Latin America. I know you're opening some new markets in Venezuela. I'm not afraid to work hard. I'm confident I can contribute wherever I end up working, but I'd like it to be Coke. Why? Coke is a very good, very successful company. My professors kept telling me to think globally. Well, you don't get any more global than Coca Cola. So, when do I start?"

They both laugh. He knows Sally doesn't expect a job offer at this point, but he also knows they both enjoyed this interview. Sally may well work for Coke. If not, she'll be a strong candidate for one of the many smaller companies that are bursting onto the scene. He tells her she can expect further contact from Coke and thanks her for an interesting interview. If more candidates were like her, his job would be a lot easier.

WHAT THE EXPERTS SAY

We've taken you through two fictional job interviews. Were they realistic? Is that the way recruiters really think? In order to make sure, we asked a lot of people.

We asked recent graduates who were still going through their own job search. Ralph, an engineer who has had to settle for underemployment for almost a year now, says that every recruiter goes over three things: grades and courses, extracurricular activities, and work experience. "I was weak in all three areas, and I'm having to pay for it." Lajuana told us that she really was asked about her reading habits. Fortunately, she had some. She landed a good job with a growing software company.

We asked recognized authorities what students should be doing while in college to get ready for the job market. Ken Blanchard, coauthor of the phenomenally successful *One Minute Manager*, had this to say: "One of the things that's in vogue now is entrepreneurial thinking. I think it's exciting for interviewers when students can talk about some aspect of creating their own business and the initiative it took to start it. Or if they had some kind of position where they actually had subordinates.

"I would say to young people, 'Your lifeguarding and all your fun summers are fine, but it will cost you on your initial entry into a job. What employers would rather see is what kind of real-world issues you've had to deal with. What's your experience in selling and getting turned down? How do you deal with that? What kind of people have you supervised? Have you had to deal with any older employees when you're the young upstart?'"

We talked with a number of corporate recruiters. They said things like "career-related experience. Those who have it learn much more from their courses." Another emphasized obstacles and setbacks. "How do students handle them? And if they tell me they haven't had any, I'm not interested because it means they've never taken any risks. These are challenging times. We require 'Can do' people." Leadership came up a lot. Companies are looking for people who can persuade and motivate people. They're looking for people who can work with all kinds of people. And learning was mentioned time and again -- "not necessarily 4.0 GPA, Harvard professor learning, but intellectual curiosity, openness to experience, and the desire to keep up with your field. People who don't want to learn are going to have a hard time in tomorrow's workplace."

So what must you do to be ready for tomorrow? You must develop skills, cultivate attitudes, and acquire experiences that aren't necessarily in your curriculum. You must be able to communicate, collaborate, organize, and lead. You should be able to write a clear, concise memo and deliver a knock 'em dead speech. You must be comfortable with information technology. You must cope with change, tolerate differences, and love to learn. You should have contacts and work experience. How do you develop all this in four or five short years? Turn the page, because that's what the rest of this book is about.

3

Learning: The Cornerstone of Success

If you're preparing for the information age it seems pretty obvious to us that acquiring knowledge must be at the heart of your preparation. While every one of the Seven Principles implies the importance of learning, there are three which literally shout your name:

1. Knowledge is power.
2. Change is rapid.
3. Information overload can drown us.

If knowledge is power in the 21st Century, who would choose to enter it weak? You wouldn't really want to go off to battle without a weapon, would you? Well, you'll be entering the next century unarmed if you're not well educated. To prosper in the Information Age, you must know how to acquire, process, and use knowledge. The best jobs will require knowledge. Do you really want to condemn yourself to a series of low paying, menial jobs without security that lead nowhere?

We must, however, be crystal clear about one thing. There is too much knowledge for you to master in four short years of college. Moreover, because change is rapid and new knowledge is constantly being created, you'll soon be an **anachronism** -- unless you make a commitment to life-long, continuous learning. Cultivating that mindset should be your number one priority. Consider the fact that most colleges and graduate schools have deadlines within which degrees must be completed. If you don't finish within ten years, they start deleting the first classes you took. We wouldn't be surprised to see the ten year time frame reduced. Knowledge changes rapidly in the Information Age. Ten year old knowledge may be quite out of date.

You must keep up with advancing knowledge in order to be a player in the Information Age, but it is very easy to drown in it. (Getting a degree from a competitive university today has been likened to getting a drink of water from a fire hose.) This Information Overload implies at least two things:

1. You must be capable of learning rapidly. Otherwise, you'll be left behind. For example, just a few years ago our management majors were graduating without knowing how to do spread sheets on their computers. While they were getting their degrees the technology changed and required a new skill of them. The best ones made it a point to learn spread sheets on their own or from a friend. Some sat in on classes they had already taken so they could learn the new software which was by this time a course requirement.

2. You must be selective in what you learn. No matter how rapidly you acquire new information, there is too much to keep up with all of it. You must develop learning strategies that permit you to stay abreast of key trends without drowning in a sea of information.

The Rand Institute recently conducted a study of what college graduates need to know to be ready to compete in the global economy. They asked academicians from leading universities and managers from multinational corporations. Both professors and corporate leaders agreed the number one requirement was what they called general knowledge. They meant by this that the graduates had learned how to learn, how to think critically, how to solve complex problems, and that they had acquired the habit of ongoing learning.

> In a time of drastic change, it is the learners who inherit the future. The learned find them-selves equipped to live in a world that no longer exists.
>
> ~~Eric Hoffer

Several years ago, the nation's governors met to articulate a set of educational goals for the United States. Arguably, the most important goal of *America 2000,* their manifesto, was that our country would develop into a nation of life-long learners. What does it mean to become a life-long learner? Two things: The DESIRE to learn and the ABILITY to learn. The most important attitude you can acquire while you're in college is a love of learning that will inspire you to grow intellectually as long as you live. We believe the most important skill you can learn in college is how to learn. If you master this skill, you will have acquired the number one life skill to carry you successfully through The Information Age. You can begin to cultivate the ability to learn and the love of learning in how you approach your classes.

There is another of our Seven Principles that underscores the importance of knowledge. The problems of society are going to be enormously challenging. They will require a thoughtful, informed citizenry to address them. Just think about the issues that will confront you: ethnic and religious conflicts, the American (and international) underclass, an inadequate educational system, energy resources, pollution, and on and on. An educated populace has always been a requirement for democracy to work. In The Information Age, this requirement is more important than ever.

WHY GRADES ARE IMPORTANT

Whether you're in engineering, nursing, or accounting, grades are considered a direct measure of your technical expertise. Boeing doesn't want somebody who barely squeezed by in design class developing their airplanes. You can make up for low grades with superior design class developing their airplanes. You can make up for low grades with superior performance in other areas, particularly if you plan to go into sales. But many companies hire new accountants and management trainees who have solid academic records. It is very common at Georgia Tech's office of Career Services for employers to specify a minimum GPA that students must meet before their recruiters will even consider them for employment. In a competitive job market, employers can be more selective. For many years, the cut-off was 3.0. In 1996, more companies are demanding a 3.5. You can't even get your foot in the door to talk about a job without an outstanding academic record.

If you want to be a physician or a lawyer, you've got to have good grades. Otherwise, no medical school, no law school. Graduate degrees will increase in importance, and without the grades you'll never get into graduate school. MBA programs are also selective, so keep your options open. Make a real effort in your classes.

Are grades a direct measure of your value to society? Clearly not. Do mediocre or poor grades doom you to perpetual failure? Again, the answer is no. Nonetheless, you will have a distinct advantage if you earn top grades.

AIM FOR THE TOP

Imagine for a moment that you're an outstanding tennis player. Your burning ambition is to be a top pro. To that end you've signed up for four extended instructional camps. It will cost you plenty of green, but, you're convinced it will eventually pay off. This camp has top-flight instructors and outstanding facilities. There's a library of instructional films. There are grass, clay, and hard surface courts. There are other players to hit against, ball machines for perfecting your strokes, strategy sessions conducted by last year's Wimbledon champions.

Most novice athletes would drool over this kind of chance. Yet, when you get to camp, you discover that some of the campers couldn't care less about being there. They spend most of their time playing video games or cards. They watch endless hours of MTV. Some get drunk every other night. They don't get enough sleep, and they don't eat right. They avoid the drills that would enable them to perfect their strokes because drills are too boring for them. When they play matches, they play against the weaker players so they can be sure of winning. They leave the first camp in not much better shape than when they started it. Between camps they don't practice at all. They enter a few minor tournaments and don't do well in those. And this goes on for four years.

Crazy, right? They'll never make it to Wimbledon. Yet this is a pretty good description of how a lot of students waste four years of college. Their chances of success in the Information Age are no better.

But wait a minute. Most students don't goof off ALL the time. They know that Beavis and Butthead are losers with no future, not role models.

We'd have to agree with you. The typical college student is neither as goofy nor as self-destructive as the two cartoon clowns on MTV. But then the average undergraduate is not on the high road to success, either. Nor are most college students carefully planning for the 21st Century.

To go back to our tennis analogy, most students do go to a fair number of their classes. Most practice their strokes from time to time. And that's about it. They might make it past the first or second round in a typical tournament, but they rarely get any further. They're never going to make it to the big leagues either. Wimbledon will remain just a fantasy.

That's the way it is with most college students. They get by. They don't cause anybody all that much trouble. But they're not really going anywhere. When they graduate, they'll face unprecedented challenges and opportunities in a high tech world characterized by diversity, complexity, speed, and constant change. Putting it bluntly, they'll have to settle for leftovers. If you want better than second-rate, you need a competitive edge. As John Naisbitt and Patricia Aburdene put it in *Re-Inventing The Corporation*, the key to success in the 21st Century is TLC. You must be able to **Think** critically; you must **Learn** how to learn; you must be able to **Create**.

READING

Reading well is a key ingredient for anybody's success in the Information Age. It's not just for history and lit majors and aspiring writers. You may have been raised on Big Bird, computer games, and MTV, but you will probably spend a good deal of your professional life reading. Reading reports, memos, proposals, business letters. Reading research and background material to keep up in your field. Besides, reading is an integral part of any intelligent person's entire life. How else will you remain an informed citizen of the world you live in. It's an unlimited means of personal enrichment and pleasure. Obviously, reading well -- rapidly, with comprehension and retention -- is a big advantage.

In 1961, as I (Bill) approached graduation from college, my mind was filled with questions. I wasn't sure what I wanted to be when I grew up. (Professor? Writer? Minister?) I wasn't sure what my next step should be. (Graduate school? Professional school?) I had doubts about the value and practicality of my college degree. (I'd majored in philosophy.) I spoke to a professor whom I trusted and respected a great deal. He listened carefully to what I had to say. Then, after a long pause, he smiled and told me that what I had learned in college was how to read. At first, I was angry at his response. I'd known how to read since the first grade. What had I learned in four years of college that would make a difference in the rest of my life?

The professor was, of course, right. I HAD learned to read. I had learned to read in a way that I hadn't known before going to college. I'd discovered writers and topics and issues I'd known nothing about. I had been exposed to journals and documents that just a few years earlier had been totally foreign to me. I had learned that just because it's in a book, doesn't mean it's true. I was then just starting to learn that there were many different kinds of reading. Part of my education would consist of mastering as many as possible.

Before I went to college, I possessed one broad skill I called reading. I used it to read any and all material -- textbooks, comic books, and the sports page. I had one speed (slow), one level of concentration (spotty), and one mission (get it over with).

But a truly skilled reader has as many reading styles as an olympic athlete has running speeds or a broadway dancer has steps. I'm still developing my own. For example, I subscribe to several newsgroups on the Internet. If I'm away from my computer for a few days, I can have over a hundred messages, some of them several screens in length. I've had to learn to scan messages and discard them in a second or two. Otherwise, I will drown in a sea of information, much of which I can't really use.

As a student, of course, you must contend with textbooks. You must read them with reasonable speed and still comprehend what you've read. You must also retain textbook material for tests, determine its relevance for other areas of knowledge, and store it in your permanent bank

of information for use throughout your life. You'll probably be required to read some literary classics while you're in college. Literature requires time out for reflection. What does this chapter mean in the context of the entire novel? With poetry, you may need to read the same passage a number of times for meaning, rhythm, and symbolism. There is the newspaper -- you should be able to scan a big one in less than a half an hour. There is reading for pleasure -- restaurant reviews, humor, and light fiction.

If you do not read well, we recommend getting some basic assistance from your campus Learning Resources Center. In some schools reading effectiveness is taught by the English department. We won't guarantee that you'll be able to read *War and Peace* in five minutes, but that sort of speed isn't relevant for your collegiate reading.

Another possibility is that you have some type of learning disability. Dislexia, hyperactivity, and attention deficit disorder are all conditions that can affect your reading performance. Federal law requires colleges to provide you with some assistance if you qualify. See your campus department for students with disabilities to learn more.

How do you know you need assistance with your reading? A low verbal score on the SAT is one indicator. A distaste, bordering on loathing, for reading is another. Poor grades in history and literature can be a tip-off. Probably the clearest sign that you don't read well is the fact that you struggle daily with reading your textbooks. Or at least whenever you try to study one. You may have the experience of reading and rereading several pages without remembering what you've just covered.

Because reading and understanding textbooks is so crucial to being an effective student, we will focus our attention on helping you do it better. Be advised that there are other forms of reading that will be required of you during your career. But if you can handle your textbooks, you've got a leg up as far as college goes.

STUDYING TEXTBOOKS

There are many useful systems of reading textbooks. One thing they all have in common is an active approach to the text. You might think of effective reading as attacking the words and what they mean. The reader is an investigator, constantly in research mode, trying to pry facts, theories, every shred of meaning out of the printed word.

Typically, most reading systems start out with the big picture. Perhaps you scan the book or chapter and reflect on its significance. Next, you read the document. Finally, you digest its meaning and relevance.

The system presented here, then, is not the only one. It may not even be the best one for you. It seems to work for those who use it. Give it a try.

Power Reading

There are three steps to **PoweR R**eading: 1. Preview; 2. Read; 3. Review. Each is essential if you want to maintain maximum efficiency.

Preview. Failure to preview a chapter before actually reading it is probably the most common error that students make. Without previewing material you don't give your mind the chance to establish categories for storing the information you're about to receive. A good public speaker first tells you what he's going to say, then he says it, then he tells you what he said. Previewing gets you ready for what's going to come so that you can catch it, digest it, and store it. If you're ready for it, your mind will tend to wander less from the subject, and you'll soak up more. No more reading the same page five times without remembering what it is that you've just read.

We recommend four previewing steps:

a. Read the introduction, the summary, and any study questions.

b. Read the headings, the captions, anything in boldface.

c. Read the first sentence of each paragraph.

d. Reflect on what you've previewed. How does it relate to what you already know? What relevance does it have for you or for the subject you're studying? What questions come to mind?

This has taken you only a few minutes, and you already have a good overview of the chapter. (As a budding Information Age aficionado with growing organizational skills, you're not likely to fall behind in your classes very often. But if you do and you have very little time to study for a test, your best bet is simply to preview all the material to be covered. You may retain enough to pass the test.)

Read: You're familiar with the chapter. You know what to expect from it. Now you're ready to read it .

We recommend three reading steps:

a. Read the chapter through from beginning to end. Don't underline yet or make any notes.

b. Underline or highlight the key points of what you've just read.

c. Distill the key points into your own words in the margin or onto a study sheet.

Because you previewed the chapter before you actually read it, your reading has been more effective than ever before. Because you read and understood the material before you underlined it or made any notes, you will have underlined only the important concepts and facts. Your notes will be pertinent. You will also discover that this sort of active reading forces you to learn the material. This chapter is now yours. You will probably never have to read it word for word again. Instead, you have a manageable amount to study the night before the test; what you've underlined and your notes.

Review: Professional musicians still practice their scales. Professional tennis players have to practice their strokes. And you have to review. This is because of a phenomenon called the Curve of Forgetting.

You start forgetting as soon as you stop learning. One psychologist found that in only twenty minutes he forgot about half of the syllables he had rote memorized. In another experiment students forgot almost half of the textbook material they had learned within twenty-four hours. Both these experiments illustrate the disctinction between short-term and long-term memory. Short-term memory can evaporate in seconds. Long-term can last a lifetime.

The problem is how to get information transferred from short-term to long-term memory. The solution comes in two parts. First, you retain what you understand much better than what you simply commit to memory. So, do your level best to grasp the underlying principles of each subject. Try to fit the facts into the overall scheme of things. Second, you must practice regular review. If you have read your textbooks the way we have suggested, you have already distilled what you need to know to a manageable level. Now, review it regularly.

> *Students often confuse reading their textbooks with studying.*

An especially powerful way to improve retention of material is to recite it. Often. Oral recitation is effective because it allows you to check whether you really know the material or not. It's one thing to be able to recognize something as familiar. It's quite another to be able to recall it and state it on your own. Since you speak much more slowly than you think, you also give your brain the necessary time to establish firm memory traces.

Students often confuse reading their textbooks with studying. Nothing could be further from the truth. Reading something just once means you'll forget most of it. Reading it several times takes too long. An effective reading system prepares you to review. *Reviewing is studying.* So review. Often.

Come test time, no more all-nighters. No cramming. No last minute confusion and panic. All you do is study what you've underlined and your notes, get a good night's sleep - and knock the top off the test curve. Preparing for the 21st Century can be kind of fun.

More on Study Skills and Strategies for Academic Success

One of the things that I do (Joann) is to work with students on an individual basis to help them learn how to study effectively and to increase their performance (get better grades!). What I tell students about studying is this: "What would you be doing if you weren't in school? Would your parents allow you to sleep in late and watch TV all day?" The usual answer is "No! I don't think so!"

"So, what would you do?"

"Well, I guess I'd have to work," is the typical answer.

"How much?" I ask.

"Well, I guess most people work about a 40-hour work week. I guess that's what I would have to do," students reply. Usually with a puzzled look on their faces.

"Well, if you will look at school as your job, and work on your studies 40 hours a week just like you would a job, I believe you'll make good grades."

Now this may sound like too much to some of you. "I can't spend 40 hours a week doing nothing but studying! I'll never have time to date or talk to friends or hang out!" But think about people who do work. They still have time to date, participate in religious activities, attend Rotary meetings, and meet friends for lunch or shopping. I am not suggesting you become a monk or nun. What I am suggesting is that you structure your life around your studies in such a way that you promote a higher likelihood of success. And, I know my system works. Students who work with me, see their grades improve. I know it works because I did well in school *late in life,* and these are the strategies I have used. School is your job.

Not only is it your job, but just like finding the right road to work in the morning, the one that doesn't get you held up in traffic everyday, you have to find the right road to your study skills success. It is a creative process. You can't try a new skill for one day and then proclaim, "It doesn't work!" You must try it for several weeks and then if it's not working, adapt it, bend it, mold it, make it your own. Keep trying another and another study skill until you find the compliment of tools in your study skills tool box that will successfully see you through to your academic goal.

Here are some of my best suggestions on how to approach study so that you can succeed academically.

Study Skills Tool Box

Study in an environment where you can *concentrate*. Find a spot somewhere. Be creative. It can be the library, an unused classroom, all-night-study, a learning center, your car (with the doors locked), but stay out of your room. It's too comfortable there.

There's the phone, the TV and all the stuff you like to do around you. Friends stop by and it's easy to impulsively go out for pizza or stay up half the night playing *Spades*. So go somewhere else quiet and and safe to study.

Structure time to study into your schedule (see your planner). Are you a morning person? Study in the AM. Some people actually do well if they go to bed early and get up at 4:00 AM to study. Night owl? Be disciplined enough to structure your time and not be tempted to go off with your buddies all the time.

When reviewing your notes, use a highlighter to indicate possible test questions. This will expedite studying later.

Take the iniative and form a study group. In class, look around you for the people taking thorough notes. Those are the serious students. Then two weeks before the first test, ask at least five people if they'd like to join you for a study session (probably only three will show up). Review your notes. Take turns. You will be surprised at the things you missed in your notes that someone else has picked up, and they will benefit from what you have in your notes. Additionally, you can take turns asking one another possible test questions.

In classes like Biology, Geology, Chemistry, foreign languages, etc., where you have lots of individual facts to remember, try this. About a week before a test, transfer the main points from your notes onto 4 X 6 index cards. Carry the cards with you everywhere you go. Whenever you are standing in line, waiting at the drive-through, in the John, etc., review what's on your cards. Have your boy/girlfriend/roommate quiz you. Say the material to yourself out loud.

If you are an aural learner, say what you have to learn into a tape recorder and listen to it over and over.

Make your own mnemonics. The sillier the better (to remember them by). Hang one mnemonic off of another until you have whole "trees" of mnemonics. (What's a mnemonic? Remember Roy G. Biv -- the colors of the visible light spectrum?)

Put a sequence of words to music. For instance, some foreign language rules can be set to *Twinkle, Twinkle Little Star* or *I've Been Working on the Railroad.* You can "hum" it in your mind without disturbing others in class.

Anything an instructor says twice, put a star beside it in your notes. This has a higher likelihood of appearing on a test.

Difficulty with the material? See if the professor has a test bank of old tests you can use to help you review. Go to any pre-test study sessions the professor gives. These are invaluable. Professors don't waste their time at night. Students attending such sessions always get "pearls" dropped in their laps.

Plan ahead. Use your planner to see when you will have test conflicts. Study early for one, so that you have time to study for the other. Have a big paper due on Thursday? Allocate part of each day between now and then toward completion of that project. Don't bunch it up into one night of frantic activity.

Don't doodle. Doodling in your notebooks can absorb you to the point that you forget to take notes. You may be great at drawing Goofy or F-16's by the end of the quarter, but you flunk because you haven't gotten down the facts.

Some people have discovered that taking notes on engineering pads works well for them. If you're having difficulty structuring your notes effectively, give it a try and see if it works for you.

Don't hang around the hall/room where the test will be given. The people in there talking are in "panic mode" and didn't study, and didn't get the facts. Listening to them will just muddle your mind. Go into the test room just as the instructor does.

If you over prepare, you are more likely to ensure your chances for success. You will give yourself more confidence, and by putting the material into long-term memory, you have more of a chance of retrieving the material later. A small detail now, might be the key to a Physics problem later. Additionally, you will reduce the test-anxiety you might otherwise feel if you tried to cram. Studying effectively is also good student stress management.

Improve Your General Reading Ability

Did you know that top executives generally have very large vocabularies? If you're aiming for upper level management, a "Dick, Jane, and Spot" level of reading comprehension is a definite handicap. One way to improve your vocabulary is by reading with a dictionary at hand. Of course, this works only if you use the dictionary.

We recommend reading a variety of material. An occasional thriller or romance ups your speed. More literary fare increases your vocabulary. And also, we believe, your wisdom. Read the newspaper, a good one. Read a weekly newsmagazine. Read the *Wall Street Journal.* Read *Esquire* sometimes or *Fortune* or *Inc.* or *The New Yorker.* Try *Harper's* or the *Atlantic. The Economist* is regarded by futurist Peter Schwartz as "the single best source of information about what is happening in the world." Take a look sometimes at professional magazines and find out what's happening in your field. We have found that reading the weekly *New York Times Book Review* section is one of the most efficient ways to keep up with new ideas and trends. This is the Information Age. If you expect to keep up with it, you'd better read.

Reading the Newspaper

We believe Information Age people need to stay informed. With the advent of CNN, there are other ways than the newspaper to learn about the world around you. Some issues require a depth of analysis, however, that requires the written word. For this reason, you should regularly read a good newspaper or at least a good weekly news magazine. With practice, you can get what you need from one in just a few minutes.

During the American Civil War, news from the front was sent to newspapers by telegraph. At that time, the telegraph wires were often cut, perhaps in the middle of a reporter's transmission. For this reason, the reporters always put the most important news in the first paragraph. If the readers got only that much they would still know who won the battle and how important the engagement was.

To this day, if you read the headline and first paragraph of every important story on the front page of a major newspaper, you'll have a pretty good idea of what's going on in the world around you. You can scan the first paragraphs of the front pages of the other sections of the paper and know what's going on in the world of sports, business, your local community, and the arts. When you see something that particularly engages your interest, you can read it more carefully and in depth. With practice, you can increase your general reading speed AND increase your store of information dramatically. You'll also find that you'll soon be familiar with most of the issues and players that dominate the news. Before long, you'll be able to stay current by spending a few minutes a day with a newspaper.

Learning and Neurology

Well informed people are able to acquire new information more readily than poorly informed people. In the world of knowledge, it's a matter of the knowledge-rich getting richer and the knowledge-poor getting left progressively farther behind. In recent years, scientists have significantly advanced our understanding of the human brain. They have discovered the physiological basis for the fact that knowledgeable people are able to learn more readily than less knowledgeable people. People who are active learners have many more pathways connecting their neurons than people who know less. More pathways create more possibilities for acquiring new knowledge. Throw some information at an active learner, (s)he'll have lots of facts to relate to the new information. An inactive learner will have a harder time connecting the new information to anything.

As active learners age they are likely to stay mentally alert longer than inactive learners. If Altzhiemers Disease impairs some of the brain's pathways, the active learner has many more pathways to call on.

Putting it bluntly, dense people have a hard time acquiring knowledge. As they age, what little knowledge they have will erode. Not a pleasant prospect. So, make a commitment to be a skilled, life-long learner.

Learning in Class

The same principles that help you conquer that thrilling page turner, *Economics in theory and Practice*, by I. M. Boring, can help you soak up knowledge like a sponge in class: 1. **P**repare; 2. **O**bserve and **R**ecord; 3. **R**eview.

Let's take each principle in turn.

Preparing: You have to be ready if you expect to be effective. We suggest three components:

(a) Have a tough, no-nonsense attitude. We don't mean that you should take every word uttered by your professors as infallible. Far from it. Just don't feel too sorry for yourself because your biology teacher is not as easy to follow as Mr. Rogers. You'll probably have some great professors and some who aren't so hot. Just remember, you don't have to like teachers to learn from them. Figure that your tuition is helping to pay your professors' salaries. Try to get your money's worth.

(b) Review your notes from the last time the class met.

(c) Read any material in the textbook that is related to what will be covered in the lecture. Be ready with questions on anything you don't understand.

Observing and **Recording**: Sit front and center. In general, the highest grades come from the first three rows. We know it sounds corny, but it's true. Sociologist E.J. Walsh and Howard Schuman discovered this bit of practical wisdom in a series of studies conducted over a ten-year period. Maybe it's because it's harder for you to doze off with Professor Grim hovering over you. At least you can hear what he is saying. Maybe it's because he thinks your enthusiasm for Renaissance literature earns you the benefit of the doubt, come grade time. Probably it's because you'll learn more in spite of yourself when you sit at your professors' feet than when you sit on the back row of a large lecture hall, staring out the window, contemplating the pain of unrequited love. And the more you learn, the more fun college becomes. Or at least it's more tolerable.

Sit upright and breathe deeply. No, we are neither your mother nor the Marines. It's just that decent posture improves your breathing, which maintains the proper level of oxygen in your bloodstream, which feeds your brain, which keeps you awake and alert. Participate. Ask questions if you don't understand. Volunteer for demonstrations. Take risks.

> # Students who make the best grades attend class more often than those with poorer grades.

And take good notes.

Obviously, taking good notes requires your classroom attendance, but it's worth the effort. Another finding of the Walsh/Schuman studies is that students who make the best grades attend class more often than those with poorer grades.

Experiment with the Cornell Method or with Mind Mapping.

In the Cornell Method, you make a vertical line about three inches from the left edge of each sheet of paper. You take notes from the lecture to the right of that line. The left side of the line is reserved for key words and concepts that organize the material on the right. You can then use the keys in this column as flash cards when you review. See if you can recite the points on the right by looking at the concepts on the left.

In Mind Mapping you begin in the middle of the page with the main point and jot down subsidiary points on the rest of the page. Eventually you connect the points with the lines and arrows and add sub-points. Some people use different colored pens to indicate differing levels of importance.

(Our example of Mind Mapping comes from the process you might employ to do your informational interview. The example of the Cornell Method is typical of notes you might take in your English composition class.)

Reviewing: Clarify and organize your notes as soon as you can. Stay a few minutes after class and do it then, if possible. The Forgetting Curve applies to lecture notes the same as to textbook material. If you wait a long time, you may well find that what your looking at reminds you of secret code more than the class lecture. It's especially important to bring order to your notes before you go to sleep if you really want to capture the main points in the original lecture. Then review your notes periodically.

Seven Tips On Taking Effective Notes

1. Develop your own abbreviations.
2. Write concepts in your own words.
3. Write key terms in prof's words.
4. Copy from board.
5. Use only one side of paper.
6. Label, number, and date all notes.
7. Use white space. Don't crowd.

Acing Tests

Taking tests is the easy part if you have gotten organized. The techniques we have suggested for digesting your textbooks and lectures are nothing more than organized study.

Think of yourself as the Chief Executive Officer of your own knowledge business. Grades are an index of your earnings. Naturally, you want to manage your business to show a profit. You work as efficiently as possible because time is money. And so is energy, so you don't want any wasted effort. Even if you're not the most dedicated or the brightest student in your class, studying systematically gets better results than studying haphazardly.

What's the Good Word?

Try to look over old tests if you can get your hands on them. Some fraternities and sororities maintain test files affectionately referred to as "The Word." Some schools require the library to keep copies of old tests so that non-Greeks will not be at an unfair disadvantage. Increasingly, these old tests are on electronic reserve. One good use for such tests is to consider them a practice test. We do not recommend that you limit your study to the old tests.

As soon as you know when a prof is going to give a test, ask him what sort of test it will be and what material will be covered. Don't prepare for the wrong test!

Ok, so you've studied systematically. Naturally you want to maximize your results on the actual tests themselves.

MIND MAPPING STEPS TO AN INFORMATIONAL INTERVIEW

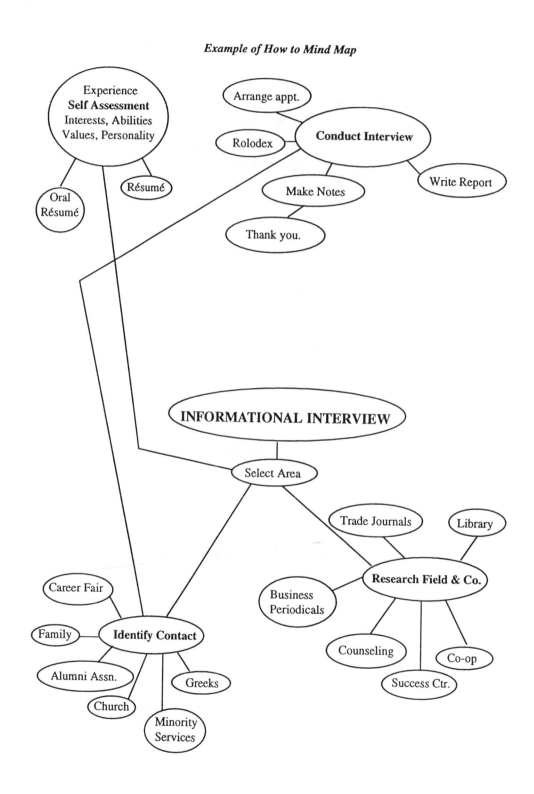

Example of How to Mind Map

44

CORNELL METHOD OF NOTE TAKING

	English Composition
Purpose of	Comparison -- how things are similar
c/c writing	Contrast -- how they are different
	Discussing 2 items together =
	better understanding of both
Divided or	Discuss everything about item A, then everything about
block method	item B; easier for writer, harder for reader;
	sometimes forget or lose sight of thesis; works best on
	pieces
Alternating or	Discuss first point for A & B, then move to second
point-by-point	point for A & B, and so on; harder for writer, easier
method	for reader; forces stronger thesis and sharper organization;
	works better on longer pieces.
Teacher's	Probably best to use alternating method for most
Preference	assignments
Similarities to	Always need strong argumentative thesis; lots of specific
other kinds of	details to support main points; make sure points are in
writing	best order to support thesis; keep organizing principle clear

Hints For Taking Any Test

1. Be on the offensive. Think of a test as an opportunity to show your professor how much you know.

2. Show up on time or a few minutes early. Be sure to have all necessary equipment (pencils, pens, bluebooks, etc.) at hand. You don't want to start your test harried and flustered. Arrive comfortable. Don't come in hungry, thirsty, or wearing clothes that bind or shoes that pinch.

3. Scan the entire test. Attack the test according to the value of each question, problem, or section. Devote 50 percent of your time to the part of the test that is worth 50 percent of the credit. Don't waste twenty minutes on a question worth only two points.

4. Read each question slowly and carefully. Then reread it. You won't get much credit for a great answer to a question your professor didn't ask. Ask the teacher to explain any question you find unclear.

5. Answer the easy questions first. Then work on those that are more difficult or less familiar.

6. Check your answers. If you have time, check them again. You don't get bonus points for finishing early and being the first to leave the room.

Guidelines For Essay Tests

1. Pay careful attention to the directions in the questions. Make sure you really do "compare and contrast" or "explain" if that is what is asked of you.

2. Think through your answer first. Outline it on scratch paper before you start writing your final answer.

3. Support your answer with facts.

4. Review each answer. Your grade will be based on what you actually wrote, not on what you intended to write.

5. Leave space between your answers so you can add to them if you recall forgotten material later on.

6. Put something down for each question. Partial credit is better than no credit at all.

7. If you run out of time before you have finished the test, quickly jot down outlines for answers to remaining questions.

Suggestions For Problem Tests

1. Review key formulas until the professor asks you to clear your desk. Then, jot them down on the back of the test as soon as it's in hand. If you write out your formulas on another sheet of paper, the professor might mistake this for a "cheat sheet."

2. Don't get hung up on a difficult problem. Come back to it after you have finished others you can do more easily.

3. Show each step. Box and label your answer.

4. Check your solutions if you have time. If possible, use different steps. For example, add up instead of down. It's very easy to make arithmetic or algebraic errors.

5. Even if you know your answer is wrong, turn it in. You might get partial credit for taking some of the right steps.

Tips For Objective Tests

1. Read each question carefully. Read it like a lawyer.

2. Watch out for negatives and double negatives and qualifiers. One word can change the meaning of a statement from true to false.

3. Unless specifically told that wrong answers bring extra penalty, guess if you don't know.

4. Watch out for tense, number, and gender. The right answer should agree on all counts.

Getting Your Test Back

One of the keys to being a top student is learning *from* your tests as well as for them. You may be tempted to toss a test, especially if you did poorly on it. Don't do it! Carefully review every returned test. Find out where you went wrong, and make up for any gaps in your knowledge. Get help from a friend or the professor if you need to. File every test for review before the final exam.

USING THE LIBRARY

Living in the Information Era (see Chapter 6) means expertise will probably be a job candidate's most marketable asset. And expertise today has a bewilderingly short half-life. In 1982, John Naisbitt noted in *Megatrends* that scientific and technical information doubles in less than six years. In 1995,

the half-life of such information is even shorter. The future belongs to those who can keep up with this mushrooming amount of knowledge.

As we have suggested throughout this chapter, you can own a piece of the future by developing basic intellectual and learning skills. Reading, writing, and mathematical reasoning are the foundations. Next come computer literacy and mastery of the library. Increasingly, these two go together.

Knowing how to research the causes of World War I effectively doesn't enable you just to write a good history paper. It means you'll also know how to investigate a field of study when you choose a major. It means you'll know how to find out about a corporation or agency when you go job hunting in a few years. It means that you'll be able to keep up with the Twenty-first Century throughout your life.

A necessary step in staying informed in your field is to read a respected professional journal regularly. If you're really serious, the best way to keep up is to refer to a book of abstracts in your field.

Even the library at the smallest school has more books than you would ever read in a lifetime. So how do you find the right book? Or how do you find out whether your library has information on a particular topic?

You probably already know how to use the card catalog or the microfiche system employed by your school or public library. Most colleges and many public libraries have switched to electronic access to catalog information at terminals in the library or accessible remotely from computers with network passwords. In many cases, you can locate books in other libraries at other schools on the internet. Every book (and most other media, such as maps, computer discs, or videotapes) in the library may be searched by: 1. Author; 2. Title; 3. Subject.

If you don't know the author or title, try the subject approach. Broad areas, such as biology, electrical engineering, or journalism, will be subdivided to help you find more specific topic. For example:

BIOLOGY - Dictionaries

BIOLOGY - Methodology

BIOLOGY - Study and Teaching

In libraries with electronic catalogs, locating journal articles has become easier. Databases to groups of journals may be used instead of printed periodical indices. You can then verify the library's holding of journals by returning to the electronic catalog.

Many of your library's holdings may circulate. You can check them out of the building. There is also a goldmine of reference material that stays. You should know about it as well. Becoming familiar with the major reference books for your subject area should be a priority.

If you have problems finding something, ask a *librarian*. Remember, they're working for you. Make sure you get your money's worth. This doesn't mean you should expect them to do your research for you, but they can and will help you get started. And they probably know about the sources of information you haven't even dreamed of.

Most colleges offer courses on using the library. Consider taking one. One of the main differences between high school and college is that you'll have to read much more material in college and write many more papers. If you master the library early on, you will save yourself countless hours. You will also be able to come up with facts and sources that impress your professors.

Make your life as a student easier. Make yourself more competitive. Know how to use the library.

WRITING PAPERS

Most professional jobs require writing skills. You don't necessarily have to be a Shakespeare or even a Stephen King, but the ability to write clear, convincing proposals and concise, readable reports will raise your stock in just about any company. Ironically, being a professional writer is not a high-paying job. But writing well in combination with other skills can only add to your portfolio of marketable Information Age skills. It also makes college easier and means higher grades.

Some suggestions: If you have a choice of topics, pick one that interests you. The better your motivation, the less painful the task. You will probably also write a better paper. Sometimes it's helpful to pick a topic that will increase your expertise in an area relevant to your career. This may be difficult your freshman year. Knowing the causes of the Civil War isn't usually a particularly marketable chunk of information. But as you get into your upper level courses, it will pay you to research something that will some day make you a better engineer, accountant, or city planner.

We know of graduate students who made it a point to write every term paper in such a way that it could also be published in a professional journal. By the time they graduated, they had a string of publications that increased their professional standing. This is a good strategy for undergraduate journalism and advertising majors also.

A word of caution here. Don't be practical all the time. We say go after a topic sometimes just because you're curious about it. How else will you get a larger view of the world? You're not only going to have a career after you graduate. You're also going to be a citizen, a friend, a lover, and probably a parent. And also, we hope a well-rounded human being.

> **The first steps in writing a good paper are managing your time efficiently and collecting good information.**

The first steps in writing a good paper are managing your time efficiently and collecting good information. These are the same steps that you can some day use to write a winning proposal. Start with the date the paper is due and work backwards from there. If a major paper is due on Friday, November 16, you want it finished a day or so before. That means the final editing and proofreading should occur on Wednesday or Thursday. You write the paper a few days before that. And so on, back to your research of the topic.

Suppose on October 1 you are assigned a major paper to be turned in on November 16. You would schedule something resembling the following deadlines:

1. 10/1-10 Research general area to find interesting and/or professionally enhancing topic.
2. 10/11-28 Research topic. Duplicate key articles. Check out key books.
3. 10/29-11/5 take notes. Could be on index cards or on a computer disk.
4. 11/6 Make out bibliography on index cards.
5. 11/7 Organize notes and outline paper.
6. Write body of paper.
7. 11/8-9 Write introduction & conclusion. Title it.
8. 11/12 Reread and edit, first for content, then for style.
9. 11/13 Type it.
10. 11/14 Proofread and correct errors. It's a good idea to have a friend proof it as well.
11. 11/15 Take in a movie while your roommate is embarking on a migraine-producing all-nighter to finish his paper.

"You're crazy!," you might be thinking. "I'd never want to work that hard for that long on one lousy paper." But wait a minute! What we're recommending is actually the *easy* way. Remember, it's your roommate who gets the headaches. And probably the bad grade. You, on the other hand, work at a leisurely pace with minimum strain and maximum results. All we can say is "Have you tried it?" Once you do we predict you'll be a convert. And you'll also be preparing yourself to hit the floor running when you land your first challenging job after graduation.

A few more words about steps 3, 4, and 5. By entering each reference on an index card, you can easily arrange them alphabetically and type out your bibliography. Similarly, by keeping your notes on cards, you will be able to arrange them in a "tree" or pyramid. From there, it is easy to develop a tight, logical outline. Alternatively, you can create a computer database to accomplish the same thing.

Taking Advantage of Your Professors

You read the heading right. We don't mean taking "unfair" advantage. We don't recommend that you try to deceive or manipulate your professors. Nor should you try to get them to do what you can do for yourself. But don't forget: your tuition helps pay their salary. They're working for you just as much as you're working for them. Get your money's worth.

Too many students look at the relationship between students and faculty as adversarial - it's us against them. Professors are the barrier between me and a degree and a good job. We think a much healthier outlook is to view your teachers as your consultants and guides.

You're investing a lot of time, money, and energy in your college education. You'd like to get established on your career path, gain some general knowledge about the world, and acquire some wisdom as well. The more help you can get from your professors on all counts, the farther along you'll be. Granted, the expertise and commitment of your professors will vary considerably. Some are burdened with too many classes. Many have enormous workloads - research, administration, writing, and committee meetings all distract them from classroom preparation. You want them to help you get ready for the real world, but you've got to be insistent to get their attention.

When you take tennis lessons, you wouldn't be satisfied with a coach who never drilled you or expected you to practice. Why pay for instruction that doesn't improve your game? Does it make sense to expect any less of your professors?

The problem is not that your profs work you too hard, but that they're too busy to teach you all you need to know. So be persistent. Ask them questions. Participate in class. Visit them during office hours to pick their brains. Be assertive. Insist on getting all you can from them.

Most of your professors chose college teaching because they love it. Show a little enthusiasm for learning, and they'll almost always be cooperative. And when you discover which faculty members on your campus are particularly dedicated and talented, sign up for every one of their courses that you can.

SUMMARY

1. We live in the Information Age: You'll have to keep learning throughout your life if you want to stay current and marketable.
2. A college education is expensive. Get your money's worth.
3. Better grades get better jobs. You must have good grades to get into graduate school.
4. Reading and writing well make college easier and prepare you for professional work.
5. The three main steps to PoweR Reading are: Preview, Read, and Review.
6. The three main steps to learning in class are: Prepare, Record, and Review.
7. Use a systematic method of note-taking such as the Cornell Method or Mind Mapping.
8. Be familiar with the different types of tests and prepare accordingly.
9. Master the library.
10. Develop a series of deadlines on your calendar for every major paper or project.

If your stockbroker squandered your hard-earned investment dollars, you'd be angry. Be certain the investment of your lifetime, college, pays off for you. Just as the stockbroker educates him/herself about the market, studies corporate profiles, and researches what other traders are doing, you must become a mature and astute broker of your own destiny by meeting the challenge of college.

PoweR Reading

There are three steps to PoweR Reading: Preview, Read, Review. Use PoweR Reading to learn the material in the Paul and Wilson article: *Accelerating Change, the Complexity of Problems, and the Quality of Our Thinking.*

Preview:

1. Read the introduction, the summary and any study questions.
   For this effort this means reading the Abstract,

2. Read the headings, the captions, anything in boldface.
   There are several hadings, and one graphic that you can look over.

3. Read the first sentence of **EVERY** paragraph.
   That means you'll read about 77 sentences. About 1000 words, and despite the large numbers, if you read at an average pace, this effort will only take you about three and a half minutes.

4. Reflect on what you've previewed. How does what you've read relate to things you already know? What relevance does it have for you or for the subject you are studying? What questions come to mind?

   Much of what you read here, confirms what you just read in chapters 1 and 2. You can start to see that there are a wider group of people who subscribe to these ideas, not just the authors of this book. You can see, we hope, that since you will be living in the future, having some understanding of what's in store for you, will be helpful in anticipating what you need to do to be ready for the challenges ahead. It relates to what you are studying, because you are learning both how to use the PoweR Reading concept, and reinforcing information previously given to you.

Read

1. Read the whole chapter. Don't underline or make notes.

2. Underline or highlight the essential elements of what you've just read.
   What do you think are the essential elements of the first section, entitled, "The Nature of the Post-Industrial World Order"?

   _____

   _____

   _____

3. What do you believe are the overall key points in this article?

   _____

   _____

   _____

Review essential elements daily and you will be ready, almost effortlessly, for your test.

Two Week Study Log   Name: _____

Put a Check Mark Down For Each Day You Conscientiously Review Your Notes

SUBJECT	Monday	Tuesday	Wednesday	Thursday	Saturday	Sunday

Two Week Study Log
Name: _____
Put a Check Mark Down For Each Day You Conscientiously Review Your Notes

SUBJECT	Monday	Tuesday	Wednesday	Thursday	Saturday	Sunday

Information Central!

As an Information Age person, you need to know about the sources of your information. Each source will put their slant on the news content. This is neither good, nor bad. What you will need to learn is how to discern when you are getting facts, or the bias of the writer/author/editor.

Go to your library to complete this assignment. Be sure you get papers from the same date or week.

The Wall Street Journal (or the New York Times) Date: _____

Feature Story Title: _____

Is there a picture? _____   What is it like? _____
                yes/no   full color/black and white   photograph/drawing

The essential elements of this story, as presented by this paper are: _____

_____

_____

_____

The Christian Science Monitor (or the Chicago Tribune) Date: _____

Feature Story Title: _____

Is there a picture? _____   What is it like? _____
                yes/no   full color/black and white   photograph/drawing

The essential elements of this story, as presented by this paper are: _____

_____

_____

_____

Your college town's paper: _____ Date: _____

Feature Story Title: _____

Is there a picture? _____   What is it like? _____
                yes/no   full color/black and white   photograph/drawing

The essential elements of this story, as presented by this paper are: _____

_____

_____

_____

4
Organizational Skills

Organizational skills will be more important than ever in the 21st Century. Remember, change is constant. You don't want chaos to overtake your life. Remember, the pace is rapid. You don't want to be left behind. Remember, there will be oceans of information. You don't want to drown. A friend and colleague of ours has this theory that tiny gremlin-like creatures he calls entropees are constantly at work rearranging your things and misplacing your papers. The entropees seem able to accomplish their work, however, only in a poorly organized space. The key to coping in the Information Age is getting organized. It's also a HUGE boost to coping with college life.

It doesn't take a futurist to know that speed and efficiency are already requirements for most people. "Time is money," the saying goes. The majority of Americans are extremely busy. Whether they're in an office or a factory, a school or a hospital, in a store or traveling to make a sales call, they feel pressure to "take care of business." The amount of time Americans spend at leisure has steadily declined over the last 25 years. Why? Because they have more tasks to do, but no more time to do them in. Most intact families, are two pay check households. It takes two pay checks to make ends meet. With no full time homemaker, everybody's schedule is stretched. Many single parent families are also two paychecks: it takes two jobs by one person to keep the wolf from the door. That person's schedule is more severely stretched.

One of the ways businesses compete is by offering prompt service. "If you don't get your pizza within 15 minutes of placing your order, your lunch is free." "Your car will be ready by 5 PM, or we'll provide a loaner." "We've got to get these components to the plant by Friday or they'll get a new supplier." "Overnight isn't fast enough. Use Federal Express. Better yet, send a fax." E-mail is much faster than snail mail.

Juggling a busy schedule is no longer a bonus skill; it's a requirement. And knowing where to find the right document, computer disk, or address is equally important. Moreover, college is where it all begins. For many, it's the first time you're on your own. You have more freedom than you've ever had before. You also have more responsibilities. It's very easy for the freedom to choose to become the freedom to lose.

Let's take a look at your life as a collegian. If you live on campus, you don't have a parent to prod you to study, eat healthy meals, go to bed, and put up your clothes (freedom). You take care of the laundry, the shopping, and seeing that your room does not resemble the aftermath of a nuclear attack (responsibility). While you have fewer classroom hours (freedom), you have much more reading, essay writing, and home work (responsibility). Chances are good you also have to work part time to make ends meet (responsibility). If you're ambitious at all, you'll want to get involved in some campus activities, and that will take some more of your time. And you'd probably like to enjoy some semblance of a social or recreational life. If you live at home, you have to include the time to commute. You may also be a spouse, a parent, and a member of an extended family.

If you don't learn to manage your time and your things, it is very easy to degenerate from Taking Charge to Overtaken. Your grades will suffer.   Your health will suffer.   Your prospects will suffer. Get organized. Prioritize. Be efficient.

Seven Good Reasons To get Organized

1. You'll make better grades.

2. You'll do better work.

3. You'll get better job offers

4. Being organized is easier. The idea is to work smarter, not just harder.

5. It reduces stress. What good are a BMW and a yacht if you die of a heart attack at forty? Or get ulcers over final exams?

6. You'll have more time to party. Effective students accomplish a lot, but they still have time for fun. The only way you can get everything done and still play is by managing your time and resources effectively.

7. You're learning an important life skill, and you don't have to be Susan Spotless or Oscar Obsessed to do it. Most of us aren't naturally organized. All of us can learn how to make our lives run more smoothly.

Mastering Time

If you're a college student, you're a busy person, at least you are if you're serious about succeeding in the 21st century. We assume you're juggling lots of balls in the air. Do you know which weeks in the semester are going to be your busiest? How many tests you'll have to take and papers you'll have to write? Do you know approximately how many pages you'll have to read in all your classes over the entire semester? You should. You can. And you soon will.

Getting Started

The first step in time management is to set goals. The most important characteristic of high achievers is that they're goal directed - they know what they want. They've got clear goals, goals they can visualize. And they can see the steps that will take them to those goals. If you don't know where you're going, you're probably not going to get there.

You've got to get organized on paper. Otherwise your plans may turn into dreams and never come true. A plan isn't a plan if it it's not in writing. So says Peter Drucker, perhaps the world's leading authority on management. He's right. You've got to maintain daily, weekly, and semester schedules. It's a rare freshman who schedules everything on paper. It's a rarer professional out in the world of work who doesn't. Executives like Bill Gates have full-time personal secretaries who manage their time -- move them from meeting to meeting, make sure there are no scheduling conflicts, and resolve them when there are. Chances are, you don't have a personal secretary. Until you get one, YOU are your personal secretary, and you need to use a planner effectively. Your professors will hand out a syllabus or course outline early in the quarter. Use the different syllabi to make up your calendar for the entire quarter.

From this calendar several facts immediately become obvious. The student is responsible for covering twenty-eight hundred pages of textbook material. Additional reading will be required for the papers. If you assume the sixteenth week will be devoted to reviewing for finals, that figures out to be about 187 pages per week. About 27 pages a day if you count weekends. Thirty-seven, if you don't. The fifth, seventh, and eighth weeks are high demand weeks - when most of your papers and tests are scheduled. (Although the numbers will be different for a semester calendar, the principle is the same.)

If this were your calendar, it would be important for you to begin researching your papers that are due at the end of the quarter during the sixth week. You'd organize and do most of your writing during the sixth week. Otherwise, you'd be stuck with trying to dig up material on three

QUARTERLY SCHEDULE

Course and requirements	Week One	Week Two	Week Three	Week Four	Week Five	Week Six	Week Seven	Week Eight	Week Nine	Week Ten
Psychology 3 Tests 1Paper Final Exam 400pp Text				Test			Test	Paper		Final Exam
Math 5 Quizzes Midterm Final Exam Homework 200pp Text	Quiz	Quiz		Quiz	Mid-Term		Quiz	Quiz		Final Exam
	Home-Work	Home-Work	Home-Work	Home-Work	Home-Work	Home-Work	Home-Work	Home-Work	Home-Work	
History 2 Tests 1 Paper Final Exam400pp Text				Test			Test	Paper		Final Exam
Biology 3 Tests Final Exam 400pp Text			Test		Test		Test			Final Exam
Literature 1 Test 2 Papers Final Exam 400pp Text				Paper	Test			Paper		Final Exam

topics and pulling it together at the last minute. Remember, you're going to be busy with three tests and a quiz during the seventh week.

You can see why a term calendar is so important. But don't stop there. You've got to break up your quarter goals into smaller, achievable tasks. You then schedule these tasks into your weeks and days. We suggest starting off with a weekly schedule that you adjust from day to day as the situation demands.

The first step in constructing a weekly schedule is to write down everything that is fixed. Let's call the student who made up this schedule Sally Schein. She has done just that. She has signed up for sixteen hours of classes. She also works ten hours a week as an interviewer for a welfare agency so she can have some spending money. Assuming she sleeps eight hours a night and takes an hour for each meal, that uses up 105 of her 168 weekly hours. (Even though she is signed up for sixteen hours, she's in class eighteen. Biology adds up to six hours because of lab.) That leaves her just fifty-nine hours per week to get in everything else: laundry, exercise, dating, showers, errands, goofing off. Oh, yes, and studying. She's been advised to study two hours outside of class for each hour in class. So she figures she'll have to put in about thirty hours a week on the books. That leaves her about thirty hours for everything else.

It may seem far-fetched that you'd need to study thirty hours a week. We know that you probably studied less than ten hours a week while you were in high school. Many of you studied less than five hours in a typical week and may have done well academically. College is different than high school; it's harder. A competitive college is much harder. Fortunately, Sally's cousin attends the same state university where Sally is enrolled. This cousin had a disastrous first year because she didn't study enough. The cousin, in fact, got dropped and had to stay out of school for an entire year before she could be readmitted. The cousin's experience made a true believer of Sally. She is convinced that it takes time to do a good job as a student.

Sally finally ended up scheduling twenty-four hours to study each week. She thinks she can get by with that amount because she plans to be efficient. But she realizes she may have to adjust her plans. She has allotted herself about six hours a week to exercise. She knows she'll feel better if she does. She also plans to watch the nightly news most evenings after dinner and before she starts studying. Some nights she may go straight to the library and read the newspaper or *Newsweek* instead. On weeknights Sally plans to knock off studying by 10:30 or 11. She likes to wind down before going to bed by talking on the phone with her boyfriend, Chuck, or visiting with friends on the hall.

Sally is a psychology major. Early in the semester she decides to become involved in the Campus Crisis Center. She figures that will help her get a feel for what psychology is all about. It will mean giving up only four hours a week, and she's been told she can get a fair amount of studying done while she's waiting for the hotline to ring.

She has thought about joining a sorority, but she's not sure if she can afford the time and money. She'll go through rush next semester and decide. She has planned Friday and Saturday nights to be free for recreation and seeing Chuck. She has left a few other weekend hours unscheduled. She knows they'll be easy to fill up with rest and relaxation. She also knows she may have to use some of this flex-time for studying as the semester picks up.

As you can see, Sally's scheduled is a full one. If anything, we think it may be too full. It would be less stressful for her if she could cut back somewhere. For example, if she could manage it financially, it would probably make sense for her to drop her part-time work. She can get some career-related work experience through a co-op plan or on a summer internship. If Sally's finances require her to work while in school (which is quite common), she might consider taking a lighter academic load.

She also would be better off if she put in some more flex-time or catch-up time. Assignments and projects have a way of taking longer than you anticipate. Things come up that throw schedules off. Keeping an hour open each day is a good idea. There will almost always be a need for it.

It is probably apparent that this is the schedule of an eighteen-year-old freshman. As busy as she is, she probably doesn't have to contend with all the demands on a single parent. Or on those who have to work full time to go to college.

HINTS TO MAKE YOUR SCHEDULE WORK

1. *Put down all the fixed items*. Sally did this. She noted all her class time, sleep time, meal time, and work time. Then she added study and recreation and miscellaneous. Even had Sally been addicted to reruns of *The Simpsons*, if she watched regularly, she would have made a note of it.

2. *Prioritize every day.* Throughout your professional life there will be more things to do than you can do well. Successful people don't necessarily get the most things done, but they invariably get the most important things done.

3. *Schedule something fun everyday.* One of the reasons people don't follow their own plans is because they make out schedules that are unrealistically demanding. Sally has included several workouts that she looks forward to each week. She has arranged her time so

that she stops working every night at no later than 11:00. Then she can read or socialize. Weekends include even more social and fun time. A colleague of ours puts it this way: "All work and no play makes Jack a fool."

4. ***Work first. Then reward yourself with play.*** The typical student avoids work all day, then begins to buckle down about eight or nine o'clock. Or even later. During the day, tomorrow's paper or test was probably weighing on the student's mind, interfering with the television he was watching, spoiling the bull session he was involved in. He didn't really enjoy his play. Now he's faced with having to study past midnight. What he's done is punish himself for having played. Get the more difficult subjects out of the way first. Or the less interesting ones. Do them while you're fresh. Save your favorite subject for later, kind of as a reward.

5. ***Study between classes.*** As simple as this is, it puts you ahead of the pack. Instead of going to the student center after class, or your room, or the snack bar, go to the library. Once you're there, about all there is to do is study. A successful architect once told me that one of his most productive college semesters was one in which he busted his buns every weekday from eight to six. By working all day, he had time to goof off at night.

6. ***Don't schedule long blocks of study time.*** Research shows that you will learn more if you spread your study out over the course of the day. It's what psychologists term distributed practices in contrast to massed practices. This is because the last few hours of extended study time are less effective due to fatigue and boredom. Some psychologists say that the average student can stay focused for about a half hour. You'll probably study most effectively, then, if you study in several one to two hour blocks of time per day and break up each of these blocks with several short breaks. With practice, you can build up your endurance.

7. ***Reward yourself.*** Have a snack or call a friend after accomplishing something modest. Buy a CD after finishing up something big.

Planning for Life

We're not against good luck, but we think it usually comes to those who have their act sufficiently together to take advantage of the available opportunities. One of the best ways we can think of to make yourself luckier is to assume absolute and total responsibility for your own future. Whether you want wealth, challenging work in an exciting field, or the chance to make a contribution to society, it's up to you to get there.

We have laid out a four-year plan (see the Master Plan in Appendix I) to help you become an outstanding graduate. The Master Plan is neither sacred nor etched in stone. It is an example of the sort of comprehensive planning we're talking about. If you start managing your time and your life now, you will accomplish light years more than you ever thought possible.

Life-Planning Workshop

A Life-Planning Workshop is based on the premise that you are responsible for your own future in every area of your life. Your future doesn't just happen. You create it. Of course, it's true that you have personal and historical limitations. Shaquille O'Neill and Cindy Crawford were endowed with natural assets that most of us can only dream about. It makes a difference whether you were born during an economic boom or a depression, during peacetime or war. It also matters that you'll be launching your career(s) in the Information Age. And it's different being born into wealth and privilege than into poverty and oppression. Still, it's up to you to determine your future, regardless of the hand life has dealt you.

In a Life-Planning Workshop you might draw your own life line, from birth to death, and set the goals you want to accomplish before you die. You might fantasize a typical day in the kind of future you want for yourself. Or a special day. You might be asked to write a press release about yourself on your fortieth birthday. Or write your own obituary.

Attending a Life-Planning Workshop can be an interesting and stimulating way to make yourself a more effective, goal-directed person. Chances are that one of the student service agencies on your campus (see Chapter 10) offers such a workshop. If not, ask them to! Alternatively, check out web site **http://www.demon.co.uk/mindtool/lifeplan.html** and engage in an electronic Life-Planning adventure.

The High Cost of Chaos

Mary Elizabeth had problems. Her office looked like a family of chimpanzees had rung in the New Year there. One good sneeze would start a paper avalanche. She glanced sadly around the room, eyeing the uneven stacks of reports, the jumble of records, the half-open file drawer overflowing with folders. Somewhere in the midst of all that clutter was her desk. She was faced with the unenviable task of cleaning it out.

Her career problems with the prestigious firm of Dynamic Testing had begun innocently enough. She had misplaced several test items that went with the new licensing exam. She should have had her secretary enter them onto the computer, but she'd been terribly busy the day the new items came in. By the time she found them and incorporated them into the exam, she was only ten days late. But the test editor didn't like the format. He said it was out of sequence. Revising the exam put Mary Elizabeth further behind schedule. The printer attempted a rush job but didn't have the staff or equipment to speed things up. By the time the test distributor got the test, there was no hope of getting it to the testing sites on time. Sixteen centers nationwide were left with the costly task of rescheduling over thirty-five hundred people waiting to take their licensing exams.

Mary Elizabeth had always thought that her messiness was a sign of creativity. But now she realized it meant only that she was unemployed.

The Domino Theory

Hard to believe that so many people could be affected by one person's disorganization? Not really. In *The Organized Executive,* Stephanie Winston speculated that the Three Mile Island crisis could have been avoided if the manufacturers of the nuclear reactor had been more organized. The *New York Times,* on July 20, 1979, reported:

Officials of the Babcock & Wilcox Company conceded that they had failed to take proper heed of warnings last year. They said the warnings, contained in memorandums written by assistants, had been sent to the wrong people, and had been subordinated to more pressing matters.

In other words, as Ms. Winston puts it, "The memorandums fell through the cracks."

Confusion at the start of a project can snowball into disaster. Because a few people at Three Mile Island didn't have their act together, tens of thousands of people had to suffer through a nightmare.

Granted, a messy desk doesn't usually lead to nuclear meltdown, but if you want your career to soar, you've got to stay organized.

Nor do you have to wait till you graduate. Being an academic slob can cost you plenty long before you ever put on your cap and gown. Suppose you lose your notes for tomorrow's killer Organic Chemistry midterm. You search your room with a thoroughness and zeal that would make a secret agent proud. But no notes. You retrace your steps. Each classroom. The library. Still no notes. And Professor Shaft's tests always come from his

> **In *The Organized Executive*, Stephanie Winston speculated that the Three Mile Island crisis could have been avoided if the manufacturers of the nuclear reactor had been more organized.**

lectures. You call the one friend that's taking the same class. No answer. He might be in the study lounge. Or his girlfriend's apartment. Or the Chemistry Lab. Or. . . get the picture?

Most professionals have a well-organized office. It doesn't have to be spotless or impeccably neat in a fussy way. But professionals know they need enough order to enable them to take care of business. If you're serious about preparing for the 21st Century, you need to get organized too.

Getting Started

Find yourself a workspace. It's best to settle on one location and stick with it. Use it only for work. That way, every time you're there, you'll know it's time to get down to business. Your workspace should be as distraction-free as possible. It should have good lighting and a decent writing surface. It should feel good to you.

Many students find their rooms to be a wonderful distraction from study. After all, the phone the TV and the computer "call" you to them! In addition, friends often stop by and pull you away from your primary job: school. It is hard to develop a balance between healthy spontaneity and distraction that pulls you away from your studies and destroys your GPA. You need an organized workspace for sure. But remember that many, many students simply must study in a structured way, away from their comfy rooms and the many distractions in them. Your campus will have a variety of locations where you can adopt a corner for your study: use them!

Turning Your Room Into a Mini-office

Choose a desk or table that is approximately twenty-eight inches high and wide enough to give you room to spread out. An uncomfortable height causes strain, which is distracting and means you learn less. Get a comfortable desk chair. Use it exclusively for study. Select a lamp that doesn't waste desk space but still lights the desk. A lamp that attaches to the wall of side of the desk will leave more desktop workspace. Use lower wattage light bulbs. More watts don't make better light, just brighter light that may be harsher. Experiment. Find the best lighting for you.

Storage for books and supplies is important. You don't want to have to go on a hunting expedition every time you start to study for a different course. Bookcases, shelving, or, at the very least, bookends on the desktop can be used. An inexpensive desktop bookshelf can be made if you can't attach conventional shelves to the wall. Most lumber companies will cut wood for a minimum charge per cut.

The space under the shelf can be used to store smaller supplies. Having your things readily available saves time and avoids disruption. If possible, buy extra supplies and store them either in the top of the closet or under the bed. It's usually cheaper to buy in bulk. A little forethought can save you the hassle of no paper the night before your class essay is due.

Setting up a File System

Develop a file system, and use it. It will be easier to find what you need whenever you need it, not to mention eliminating tons of paper from your notebook. We also believe that virtually everyone in the Information Age will have to be more entrepreneurial in managing their careers. That means filing addresses of your contacts, information about job leads, and a portfolio of your work and accomplishments. Acquire winning habits now. Make your life easier.

OPTIONS FOR FILE STORAGE

File Cabinets: You can find inexpensive ones at office surplus stores, flea markets, used or discount furniture stores. A recent check of local discount stores shows they can be purchased for reasonable prices there as well. Opt for letter-size storage capacity, as opposed to legal-sized cabinets.

Heavy Corrugated Boxes: Find them at supermarkets, retail stores. Get one that will hold 8-1/2" by 11" folders without too much excess space. A box that has been coated in wax (used in transporting perishable food items) or one that held heavy items (small TV's, radios) is more durable. Cover with self adhesive decorative paper to make it more attractive.

Milk Crates: Called stacking or storage cubes when sold at stores. Most are moderately priced. Dairies sell milk crates for as little as $2. Provides easy access for files; some have ridges at top to allow for hanging file folders.

File Boxes: More expensive and stronger ones are metal. Less expensive ones are soft plastic. Hinges may work out of plastic with frequent use. Both come in letter-size and have hinged lids. You can find them at office supply, retail, or discount stores.

After you've gotten a file container, organize it. In categorizing, be as descriptive as possible without being too detailed. Instead of having a file on the library's hours and services, make a "College" file. If that is too broad, get more specific with "College, Services Available."

Suggested File Categories:

Current Course Work: tests, research notes, class notes, lab assignments, etc.
Past Course Work: tests, papers, projects. By subject.
School: tuition, services, campus maps, advisors, etc.
Medical: blood type, family physician, campus health insurance, diet, etc.
Housing: meal plans, utility bills, landlord, lease, etc.
Work: taxes, benefits, insurance, appraisal ratings, job descriptions, etc.
Extracurricular Activities: organizations, officers, bylaws, meeting times, activities planned, committee work, etc.
Job Search: potential employers, resumes, references and contacts, job search literature, etc.
Transportation: car repair bills, maintenance schedule, insurance, license tag receipts, bus schedules, etc.
Financial: checking and/or savings accounts, bank statements, tax records, etc.

Subdivide files that have lots of information on many different subjects. One way to do this is by using separate file folders for each subdivision; then organize them in an accordion on hanging file. Another way is to subdivide a standard file folder by using page indexes.

Equipment Needed:

File Container: See insert on Storage Options.

File Folders: Lettersize. One -third cuts have higher visibility because of staggered tabs.

Accordion Files: Also called expandable folders.

Hanging Files: Require special hardware to use.

Bold Pens or Markers: Create high visibility.

Labels: If you really want to get fancy, try color-coding individual categories for instant recognition.

Even with an organized filing system, you may find yourself swimming in a sea of cellulose. Naturally, you want easy access to important papers without having to sort through useless garbage. Here are some ideas to get you started.

1.   When it comes to paper, practice the OHIO system: Only Handle It Once.   Use it, file it, or trash it.

2.   When in doubt, throw it out.

3.   Keep a folder for each current course. Subdivide it into categories, such as TESTS, CLASS NOTES, RESEARCH PAPERS, HOMEWORK ASSIGNMENTS, and LAB WORK. Store these in front of your file box where they can be easily reached. File all relevant papers the day you get them. (Hint: As you file, review each page. This will reinforce what you learned that day.)

4.   Keep a folder for past courses that are related to your major or minor. When a class is no longer current, weed out useless or redundant material. Remove the dividers and staple the contents together.   Put all related material into one folder. For example, Abnormal

Psychology, Social Psychology, and The Psychology of the Terminally Gross and Disgusting could easily be stored in one folder labeled Psychology. File alphabetically.

5. If you have a glut of elective course material on the same subject, put it together. If it covers a wide variety of subjects, file several in one folder. Label it descriptively. For example, Electives: Fish Management, Temperate Zone Fruit Crops, The Movies as Narrative Art. If it isn't worth saving, donate it to a "Save the Trees" campaign.

SUMMARY

1. The speed and change that will characterize the 21st Century demand good organizational skills. This means YOU have got to get organized.
2. Set goals and determine the activities that will help you reach those goals.
3. Plan your time for the quarter or semester.
4. Establish weekly and daily schedules.
5. Prioritize every day.
6. Set up a work space.
7. Develop a file system.
8. Keep class material organized.

QUICK SCORING ORGANIZATION QUIZ

Points

1. <u>0</u> I have no address book.

   <u>1</u> I have an address book in my dorm or apartment

   <u>2</u> I have an address book in my purse or wallet.

   <u>3</u> I have the address and telephone number of my family physician in my address book.

2. <u>0</u> I have no appointment calendar.

   <u>1</u> I have an appointment calendar in my dorm or apartment.

   <u>2</u> I carry an appointment calendar with me.

   <u>3</u> My appointment calendar has important dates from my class syllabi marked.

3. <u>0</u> I have no place to keep important papers such as old tests, research papers, medical records . . .

   <u>1</u> I keep important papers together , but in no particular order.

   <u>2</u> I have an organized filing system.

   <u>3</u> I keep a separate folder for each current class that is subdivided by categories such as tests, research papers, class notes.

4. <u>0</u> I have no place where I regularly study.

   <u>1</u> I have a place of study which has adequate lighting, little to no noise, a comfortable writing surface, and easy access to office supplies such as pens, pencil sharpener, etc.

   <u>2</u> I have a place of study which is within easy access to my filing system.

   <u>3</u> My place of study has ALL of the following items: dictionary, thesaurus, and style manual.

5. <u>0</u> I don't know where the main library is

   <u>1</u> I know where the reference department in the main library is.

   <u>2</u> I know where the *Reader's Guide to Periodical Literature* is.

   <u>3</u> I have mastered the library's electronic filing system.

Scoring:

0	Points -	Evidence indicates you may not be alive and/or enrolled at an institution of higher learning. Time to get your act together.
1-5	Points -	You're not ready for the Information Age! Time to get started.
6-10	Points -	The smell of success is in the air. You are on your way to coping with the 21st Century.
11-15	Points -	The future is **now**, and you're ready for it.

Name: _John Knighton_

Quarter Schedule

Course & Requirements	Week One	Week Two	Week Three	Week Four	Week Five	Week Six	Week Seven	Week Eight	Week Nine	Week Ten

WEEKLY SCHEDULE

Time	Monday	Tuesday	Wednesday	Thursday	Friday	Saturday	Sunday
8 AM							
9 AM							
10 AM							
11 AM							
Noon							
1 PM							
2 PM							
3 PM							
4 PM							
5 PM							
6 PM							
7 PM							
8 PM							
9 PM							
10 PM							
11 PM							
Mid-night							

NAME: _____ Box: _____ PH: _____

How To Get Things Done

Ever notice that the best person to delegate a task to is a busy person? Busy people know that in order to get things done, they must approach the task in an organized manner. You are a busy person now that you are in college, so take a page, literally, out of the skills busy people use.

Look at the sample "to do" list below. Now look at your quarter schedule and determine what tasks you must complete in the coming week. Put down your own "to do" list below. Initially do not prioritize, just put down a list of things that must be done this coming week.

Sample "To Do" List		**Priority**	**My "To Do" List**
A2	Do Calculus Homework	_____	_____
A4	Work Out	_____	_____
B1	Write Home	_____	_____
B3	Apply for Financial Aid	_____	_____
C1	Write Résumé	_____	_____
A3	Read Chapter 3 in Psych Text	_____	_____
C2	Investigate Entrepreneur's Club	_____	_____
A1	Study for Chem Test	_____	_____
B2	Do Computer Science Program	_____	_____

Now go back and assign items a priority which you place out to the left. Items with an "A" MUST be done. These have the highest priority. Items with a "B" are important and you should try hard to get to them as soon as possible. You might work on one of your "B" items while you are waiting from something to print, or in-between classes. Items with a "C" designation, are items you identify as important, but which you may not get to immediately. They are, however, coming up, and you want to have it on your mind. So, for example, if you have a class cancelled due to instructor illness, you might use this unexpected time to walk over to Financial Aid and get an appointment, as well as, going by SGA to find out where and when the Entrepreneur's Club meets, getting both a "B" and "C" item accomplished.

It's not getting the most things done that is most important. It's getting the most important things done!

You have also identified some long-term goals. Each day when you make up your "to do" list, be sure to include that special, long-term goal somewhere on the list. You should see it *everyday* and have it at a level of consciousness whereby you can do even small, incremental things which advance you toward that big goal. So, if you dream of writing the great American novel, you might see a character you believe is unique and write a short description of that person down and save it in your "Novel" file for future reference.

5

Career Planning
Navigating the Unknown

Why are you in college? Probably lots of reasons. But most students have gone to college for the past 15 years for career-related reasons. Students say better jobs at better pay, more than anything else, is why they're in school.

A colleague who advises student athletes has a large poster prominently displayed in his office. It is a picture of a palatial, modern home with several expensive cars parked in the drive. The caption reads simply: REASONS FOR EDUCATION. This is probably putting it a bit crassly. We know that students have many motives for attending school, and we certainly applaud those who strive for enlightenment, self understanding, and personal development. Still, it's hard to focus on truth if you're worried about paying the bills. The cost of a college education continues to soar -- over $100,000 for a degree from an elite, private school. The state university that employs us estimates that an in-state student will have to spend about $35,000 for a bachelor's degree. That includes room and board and books. It's probably a conservative estimate, and Georgia Tech is regarded as one of the great bargains in all of higher education.

As we write this, politicians are proposing to scale back federally funded financial aid. There may well be fewer scholarships and grants to go around. Historically, the interest on any college loan you got was covered by the federal government until you graduated. That may change too. If it does the cost of college loans will go up still further. Nation-wide, students who got degrees in 1994 left the campus over $10,000 in debt. If you're going into hock up to your ears to get your degree, it's no wonder you'd like some assurance that some day you'll have your financial head above the water.

The bad news is there are no guarantees. It's a chaotic time to plan a career. The good news is there are a number of strategies which can help you succeed in the next Century.

If you buy the fact that knowledge is power in The Information Age, it's obvious that higher education will be strongly related to professional and material success. Increasingly, a college degree is regarded as a minimum requirement, a union card without which your choices are severely limited.

The other relevant Information Age principle is that the secure, life-time job is history. Very few of you who read this sentence will get a job out of college and stick with the same company for 30-40 years until you attend a retirement banquet and get your gold watch.

Let's take a look at some of the evidence for the death of the secure, life-time job. For many years, IBM was regarded as one of the best run corporations in the world. IBM was worth more than the GNP of most countries in the world. IBM was noted for its loyalty to its employees, a loyalty which was highly reciprocal. Many IBMers counted on and prospered through life-long employment with Big Blue, as the company was called by friend and competitor alike.

In 1995, IBM was in a state of turmoil. For several years, thousands of its employees each year had been laid off, pushed into early retirement, or demoralized by a state of chronic job insecurity, wondering: Am I the next to go? Of course, IBM is not the only corporation which is forging a different understanding with its employees. AT&T, General Motors, Delta, as well as many smaller companies are downsizing, right-sizing, and getting lean and mean. The March 3-9, 1996 *New York Times* ran an in-depth series of articles charting the depth of the carnage.

There is a contrarian point of view that has some merit. It goes like this. The quality of American education has fallen so drastically that high school and college degrees don't mean much any more. What ensures success is not the number of degrees you have, but the number of skills you have mastered. While certain professions such as medicine will always require a specialized degree which attests to expertise, there will be many endeavors which will not. There are, for example, many computer jobs which are filled by people who have learned the necessary skills on their own (Legions of self-taught hackers come to mind.) or via OTJ (On the Job) training.

Some people think that eventually the notion of a four-year college degree will go the way of the horse-and-buggy. People will continue to go to college, but in more flexible ways. A person might take a few general courses, and then specialize in a discipline that provides a set of marketable skills. Some will stick around for months, some for years, depending on their particular career goals.

The point to bear in mind here is that knowledge is the source of power. Whether you get it in or out of a formal setting, you're dead in the water without it.

According to Toffler, the principal reason for all the chaos is because we are in a state of transition from the Industrial Age to the Information Age. That's certainly a part of it.

Another reason is because of the globalization of the world economy. (There would, of course, be no global economy were there no Information Age.) General Motors competes with Toyota and Mercedes as well Ford and Chrysler. IBM competes with NEC and SUN as well as Texas Instruments. US Steel must do battle with steel manufacturers in Japan, Korea, and Brazil as well as with other American companies. That means American companies must cut out any and all fat. Sometimes, muscle and bone, are lost in the process.

Another factor is the outsourcing of many of our labor needs. It's cheaper to hire assembly line workers in Mexico than Michigan. It costs less to hire clerks to process insurance claims in Ireland than in Illinois. And if you don't aspire to a career as a clerk or instrument assembler, Motorola sends problems by satellite to India where engineers and computer scientists, often American educated, are paid a fraction of what their American counterparts earn.

> More important than missing out on the gold watch is lacking a viable pension plan. We will not elaborate on this issue now. After all, you're probably just a freshman. We will tell you that your first step after graduation should not be to purchase an expensive car; it should be to start a financial plan that you will invest in throughout your life.

Just note the titles of a number of recently published books: *Working Without a Net, The Jobless Society*, and *The Way of the Ronin*. (The ronin were samurai who had to adjust to free-lance status during the transition of feudal Japan to a modern state.) As competition, outsourcing of jobs, and automation tighten the screws on the job market, your problem will be how can you manage your career? More immediately, what can you start doing now, while you're in college? How do you shore up your future?

And if you're still skeptical about our argument, please read what Dr. Howard Figler has to say in the February 1995 Career Planning and Adult Development Network Newsletter.

A RETURN TO THE REAL AMERICA

For the past 50 years "regular employment" has been so much the norm that American free enterprise has gotten lost in the shuffle. That 50-year historical blip is over. In its place, people are learning to be more enterprising, to regard themselves as self-employed. Dan Lacey predicted the fading of steady jobs in *The Paycheck Disruption* and Cliff Hakim's new book, *We Are All Self-Employed*, tells us how to re-orient ourselves as career seekers. Waterman, Waterman, and Collard's 1994 article in the *Harvard Business Review* guides employers in understanding the big picture.

Free enterprise is making a comeback. Increasingly, present or former wage-earners are taking on the self-employment attitude by doing two things: (1) Giving stronger consideration to business ownership as a possible career, as either a primary or supplementary form of income, (2) Adopting an enterprise-oriented attitude even when they are employed by someone else. If you worked for someone, have the perspective that it's YOUR company, your money, and your reputation. You will see your job with a new pair of glasses.

It's teeth-grinding time in the US of A. With fewer steady jobs and more contingency workers, people wonder how they will make it. There's no escaping the answer -- those who embrace the free enterprise attitude will survive and prosper.

Entrepreneuring is woven into the fabric of this country, but we are oblivious to that because steady employment ruled during all of our working lifetimes. You can get some perspective on this by listening to what Abraham Lincoln had to say about career development:

The prudent, penniless beginner in the world labors for wages a while, saves a surplus with which to buy tools or land...; then labors on his own account for a while, and at length hires another new beginner to help him. This is the just and generous, and prosperous system, which opens the way to all, gives hope to all."

Lincoln's words remind us that self-employment and business ownership are the ways of our country. Employment is only a temporary condition; ownership is the long-term goal. According to Lincoln, it's moral, prudent, and it makes good sense to have control over your economic life.

John Hancock said that not only is ownership good for you, it's good for the nation:

"The more people who own little businesses of their own, the safer our country will. be... for the people who have stake in their country and their community are its best citizens."

Look at it this way -- even if you get a salary check each week, the company is only renting your skills, And who knows how long they will want you? As Bill Bridges has said, we are all temporary workers, but 80% of us are in denial.

The ground has been tilled for a new entrepreneurial era in America. Those who see themselves as self-marketers will prosper. Those who cling to the idea that job performance will sustain them will become victims of market forces. Let me give you an example. Neil "did his job" as a travel agent for several years until the agency lost its customer base and closed its doors. He had seen the service slipping badly. Tour bookings decreased as the staff lost its enthusiasm. Customer records were lost. Neil watched in dismay but said little, fearing that he would "rock the boat." "Not my job" became a prelude to disaster. Neil has since joined an agency where he speaks up regularly about business, and is building his capital to buy a stake in the ownership.

The Information Era makes it possible for many people to be self-employed without a large capital investment. Self-employment is an attitude. You have a set of skills and areas of knowledge. You put these to use where they will do the most good and yield the most gain. Your customers (which includes your employers) decide how your skills fit their needs, and money changes hands. In between your skills and their need is the fine art of selling. We all sell continually, we just don't call it that.

America was never meant to be a country where people indentured themselves to companies and called this "lifetime employment". Yes, you may do it temporarily, but you have greater freedom when you view yourself as being in charge.

Career counselors will spend a lot of their time helping people to grab hold of self-employment and free enterprise as concepts, because most are not ready for it. We have been parented by large organizations for a long time. Many will long for the good old days. But, of course, assisting people with their difficult career transitions is what we're here for -- to help clients adapt to the reemergence of American enterprise rather than hide from it.

Self-employed, consultant, independent contractor, small-business-person, or free lance: all are terms that will become increasingly common in the future. The main thing to bear in mind: **YOU'RE IN CHARGE!**

If you're in charge, several strategies follow:

1. Know thyself.
2. Know the world.
3. Learn to relate.
4. Get organized.
5. Learn to plan.

Know Thyself

Lots of people don't like their jobs. A lot of other people don't have jobs. Finding work that is personally fulfilling is one of the best ways we know of to make your life satisfying. Finding work that pays the bills in the volatile 21st Century is one of the best ways we know of to make your life secure. Since you're in charge of your career, it is vital that you know yourself well. This is true in at least two ways.

1. Choosing a field that fits. Since you'll be spending nearly half of your waking hours working, doesn't it make sense to spend these hours doing things you're good at and that interest you. Don't be an accountant who hates numbers. Don't be a nurse who dislikes people. Find a field that expresses you, challenges you, and permits you to grow.

2. Knowing how to market yourself. Since the secure, lifetime job with Mega Corp is a relic of a bygone era, you will have to persuade many different clients many different times to buy your services. If you don't know who you are and what you have to offer, you won't have many customers. Managing your career entrepreneurially is frustrating, anxious-making, and a threat to your security. Entrepreneurial career management is also invigorating, challenging, and the wave of the future.

Dr. Gene Griessman who wrote *The Achievement Factors* recommends that every college student should take a course in sales. We'll say more about this later, but you can't sell yourself for employment if you don't know who you are and what you have to offer. You can have a satisfying career, but it's not going to happen by accident. It takes a hard, honest look at yourself and an active search of the job world.

The Counseling Center/Student Development Center

OK, we're probably a little biased (We've both worked in college counseling centers.), but we think it's almost imperative for you to get career counseling. The stakes are too high for you not to. And the cost is too low to pass it up. Almost every university and college has an agency that provides free vocational guidance. Use it. If you want to get the most out of your counselor and, later on, out of your career; there are some other things you can do, too. First, here are the services you can expect from a typical college counseling center:

1. Individual counseling. A professional will help you appraise your interests, abilities, and work-related values. He or she can suggest sources of career information, including key individuals to contact.

2. Group counseling. Same as above, but with group support. You also have the opportunity to learn about different fields from the other members of the group.

3. Testing. No test can tell you what to do with your life, but the right tests can shed light on who you are. The more you know about who you are, the more likely you are to select career paths which suit you. There are vocational interest inventories, aptitude tests, and personality tests. Interest inventories such as the Strong Interest Inventory are quite reliable and valid. Basically, they tell you which occupational types you share key interests with. If you checked many of the same items that successfully employed accountants do, for example, accountancy is probably a good field for you to investigate. Aptitude tests measure abilities. You probably took The Scholastic Aptitude Test before coming to college. It was designed to measure general scholastic abilities. Because the abilities measured are so broad, they aren't terribly helpful in making career choices. What can be more useful are aptitude batteries which provide feedback on a variety of abilities. Two organizations are especially noted for giving ability batteries, The Highlands Program and the Johnson O'Connor Institute. Personality tests give you feedback about such variables as how friendly or aggressive or achievement-oriented you tend to be.

4.   Computer-based guidance. By interacting with a computer program you can learn the steps it takes to make a solid career decision. We're familiar with a program from Educational Testing Service (the nice people who brought you the SAT) called SIGI, which stands for System of Interactive Guidance and Information. (Actually, we have the new "industrial-strength" system which is called SIGI Plus.) In several hours at a computer you can find out what careers match your values and abilities, get information about those careers, find out what steps you should take to pursue a particular career, and actually make a simulated career choice that takes into account your possible job satisfaction and the likelihood you could succeed in a particular career. We think it's an excellent tool and recommend it often to our students.

5.   Occupational Information. Most centers have a library of career-related material. A good book to start with is the Occupational Outlook Handbook, put out by the U.S. Department of Labor. Then go on to other printed literature, video cassettes, filmstrips, and any data banks on computer file. The more you know about a field, the easier it is to determine if it really suits you.

Crystallizing a Vocational Identity

Maybe you're not actually enrolled in a college yet and don't have access to career counseling. Not to worry. There are many constructive steps you can take to help you identify career goals.

College Catalog as Career Counselor

Go through your school's catalog and read the statement of purpose of each major division. (Divisions are usually called Schools or Colleges, as in "School of Business" or "College of Engineering.") Now, go back and read the statement of purpose of each department in each division that interested you. Next, identify and list the required courses that go with each department that intrigued you. Look up the course descriptions. Eliminate the departments with courses that don't appeal to you. Investigate further the departments with requirements that you think would interest and challenge you. Check out suggested elective courses. Talk with a departmental representative. Question some seniors who major in the department. Go to the campus book store and thumb through some introductory and advanced textbooks. By now, you will have narrowed down your list of departments to a more manageable number.

But don't stop now! Do some more research. How marketable is a particular major? What careers does it prepare you for? Find out. Read up on it. Check with Placement or your campus Career Center. Would I be good at it? (I might be interested in astronomy, but unless I'm a whiz at mathematics, I'd never make it through all the physics.) Take an introductory course. See if it matches your interests and abilities.

Vocational Navel Gazing Made Easy

There are about a zillion variations of the following exercise. We have cut it down to the bare bones minimum.

Take four sheets of paper. Draw a horizontal line across the middle of three of them. On the top half of the first, list those classes that you have liked or excelled in. On the second page, list preferred hobbies and activities. On the third, jot down any jobs you have held. What tasks did you perform in each job? List them. Now, on the bottom half of each page list the interests, values, and abilities suggested by the classes, activities, and tasks.

Now, look at the bottom half of each page for patterns and commonalities. Distill those common traits into a vocational self on the fourth page. The major you declare and the career you choose should be as compatible as possible with your vocational self.

Know The World

How many of you would agree to marry someone sight unseen? OK, it's a dumb question. Mail-order brides and arranged marriages belong to another time and place. You certainly wouldn't rely exclusively on gossip or propaganda about another person before you took the big plunge. You'd want some objective information. And you'd definitely want to spend some time with this person first.

We believe that choosing a career is at least as important as choosing a mate. Yet we find an incredible number of people who are willing to settle for mail-order majors or arranged careers. No wonder there's so much job dissatisfaction out there. Know what you're getting into.

Most majors acquaint you with a field. They don't necessarily prepare you for a job. Employers hire people to fill particular jobs. The more knowledgeable you are about jobs that match your needs and skills, the more likely you are to find the right one for you. You will also more likely convince an employer to hire you.

Just about the best way to find out about career opportunities is to get some career-related work experience before you graduate. Reading about something is never as revealing as trying it on for size. Besides, you can discover things like how a particular company treats its employees or how the different divisions of a corporation work.

Obviously you've got to have some inkling of a career goal before you can look for career-related work. But what if you're really up in the air about your future? What should you do then? And is there any general information about today's job world that you should know?

If you're thoroughly confused, get counseling. Also, do the College Catalog and the Vocational Navel Gazing exercises described above. As important as it is to know your vocational self, though, it is equally important to know something about the job world.

The Job World

Find the Career Information Library on your campus. It's probably in the Counseling Center/Student Development Center or at the Placement Office/Career Services. If your college doesn't have a career library, you should be able to find plenty of information in the main library. Look over the Occupational Outlook Handbook. Check out any occupations that intrigue you. What sort of work is involved? What about pay and other benefits? What kind of training is required? Will you need additional degrees in order to advance? What does the future hold for the field? It's all in the Handbook, but don't stop there.

One of the best ways to find out about different kinds of work is through people who do the various jobs. Informational interviewing and networking are buzz words among professionals today and for good reason. You can learn about a career from professors and staff, from relatives and friends of the family, through your fraternity or sorority, at your church, mosque or temple, from alumni, and at your own job. All you need is the gumption to ask. And people like to talk about themselves, so most will be glad to discuss their work with you.

Conducting an Informational Interview

First, do your homework. Get an overview of the career you're investigating by reading up on it. It's presumptuous to expect a professional to teach you about the basics. Besides, if you know something about a field, you can ask much better questions. More intelligent questions not only get better information, they also make you look good. There is no advantage to seeming like someone who has spent more time watching *Wayne's World* than exploring the real one.

But if you come across as a serious, thoughtful person who is genuinely interested in success, the person you're interviewing will probably not hesitate to recommend you to others in the field. They can provide you with additional information and may be the start of your network of professional contacts. (How about that? You thought you were simply finding out about a career, and you're already building a network!)

Another reason you want to make a good impression is that this person might be able to hire you for an internship next summer. Or give you a strong lead to someone else who might hire you or give you your first job after you graduate.

The other bit of homework you need to do before the interview is on yourself. Your contact will be able to give you more relevant information if he knows who he's talking to. We recommend developing an oral resume. This is a short summary of your vocational interests, values, skills, and experiences. You give it early on in the interview, before you ask your questions.

Oral Resume of Janet Smith

Dr. Score, an industrial psychologist at Acme Enterprises, has just ushered Janet into his office. "So you think you might be interested in industrial psychology," he says. "What would you like to know?"

"A little bit of everything, but first I want to thank you for taking the time to talk with me. I'd also like to tell you a little about myself and how I got interested in the field, if it's all right with you. Dr. Schwartz said you could help me better if you knew a little about me."

Dr. Score smiles and nods for Janet to go on. She leans forward in her chair and begins. "I'm a freshman at State U., and I'm majoring in Psychology. I've always gotten along well with people--in school and band and church. But I've also been really curious about what makes people tick. I can remember watching *Awakenings* one night on TV and being fascinated. After that I thought I wanted to be a psychiatrist. I read about Freud and Jung. I tried to figure out what my dreams meant and what everybody's hang-ups were.

"Then, my senior year I took a psychology course and learned that there was more to psychology than just being a therapist. And that a psychiatrist was a medical doctor, which I knew I didn't want to be. Also, our class took a field trip to a state mental hospital, and that seemed like a really depressing place to work. I thought some of the research that social psychologists did was very interesting. For a while, I thought I might want to be a researcher, but I don't think I want to be in school that long."

"A lot of psychologists at the corporate level have PhDs," Dr. Score says. "And you pretty well have to have a master's to get started. If you want to be a clinical psychologist or teach in a university -- you'd best count on earning your doctorate. It is possible to succeed in industrial psychology, though, without a PhD.

"That's encouraging. "It's not that I don't like college. It's just that I'm not sure I could afford to go to graduate school for very many years. Dr. Schwartz is trying to start up a graduate co-op program, and that could help me finance a master's degree if that's what I wind up doing."

"I think that's an excellent idea, but go on with what you were saying."

Janet, who was nervous about imposing on Dr. Score, is starting to feel more comfortable. He seems genuinely interested in helping her. She settles back in the chair and continues.

"We all had to take career tests in high school. I had interests in common with psychologists and social workers, but I also scored fairly high in a lot of the business careers. I'm in Dr. Schwartz's Intro class, and he told me Industrial/Organizational Psych might be a way for me to combine my interests and get into a branch of psychology that has a lot of opportunities.

"I made good grades in high school, and I made three B's and an A my first quarter in college. I made just under 600 on both parts of my SAT. I'm pretty sure I'm going to make an A in Psych 301 this quarter. I don't consider myself a nerd, but I'm not afraid to work hard on my studies. I hope that gives you some idea about me. Can you tell me about your work here at Acme and how you got into organizational psychology?"

Listen attentively as your contact describes her field and what it's like to work in it. But do more than just listen. Obviously, it would be inappropriate to interrupt, but it's good form to interact. If some aspect of your contact's job particularly interests you, say so. Ask her for more details or how she feels about it. When you ask intelligent questions in a confident manner, you not only learn more, you are viewed as intelligent as well.

As you finish your interview, ask your contact if she can suggest other people who could give you useful information. Say your thank-you, and follow it up with a letter of thanks. Look over chapters 5, 6, 7, and 12 to get more ideas on interviewing and networking.

How, then, do you plan your career in the Information Age? You do so entrepreneurially. That means you're in charge, but you can't navigate without information about yourself and the job world. You must be aggressive, intellectually curious, proactive, and honest with yourself. You strive for self understanding. You keep your eyes peeled for information about the world outside yourself. Yes, you read "career information," but when you come to think about it, what isn't career information in the world of tomorrow. You need to read trade journals, watch the news, look at the business section in the newspaper, and keep up with science and technology.

THE JOB MARKET OF THE 21ST CENTURY

Students often ask us which careers have the most promise. The answer, of course, is that beyond the big brush strokes which the Information Age paints for all of us, no one knows for sure. The job market of the future depends on the interaction of the national and world economies, technological innovations, demographic changes, and a slew of other factors. Here are some educated guesses.

America Gets Middle-Aged

The huge clump of the population born between 1947 and 1964 and known as the Baby Boom will be moving into middle age. Middle-aged people care about financial security--where they're going to retire and whether they'll be eating lunchmeat or lobster. Insurance and financial services will be important to middle-aged Baby Boomers. There will be a big demand for people to market and sell such services. And most of these positions will be relatively unaffected by international competition.

America Gets Old

More people will live longer. In fact, the fastest growing segment of the American populace is people over 100 years of age. There will be a big need for health-related workers. At this time, it's anybody's guess just how health care services will be managed and delivered. Everybody's talking reform, but a consensus has not yet emerged on what changes will be made. Meanwhile, the costs associated with health care continue to rise, as do the numbers of people who do not have ready access to service.

Geriatric services of all sorts will be in demand. They will include housing, recreation, education, and entertainment.

America Gets Educated

More people will be more highly educated. In 1995, 45 percent of the work force became white-collar. Less well educated people will be more susceptible to unemployment as the economy fluctuates. But with more college grads, there will be plenty of competition for professional jobs. In recent years, humanities majors in particular have encountered employment problems. For this reason, fewer students are going into humanities.

In our opinion, this is unfortunate. Yes, familiarity with technology will be extremely important. But an extensive study by AT&T showed that the liberal arts may be the *best* undergraduate preparation for management. This is because the humanities and social sciences provide an excellent education in verbal skills. Managers must be able to communicate well--both on paper and orally. CBS, Inc., has donated $750,000 to establish a corporate council on the liberal arts. Frank Stanton, a former CBS president with a degree in English, directs research into how a liberal arts degree can help you in the business world. The trouble is that too many anthropology and literature majors fail to develop a career focus and have no career-related work experience. We're convinced even philosophy majors can get good jobs if they follow our Master Plan (see Appendix I).

Industrial Society Gives Way to the Information Era

Information will be American's number one product. Half of American's jobs have to do with information already. John Naisbitt in *Megatrends* predicts that the figure will be 70 percent within twenty years. By 1985, more people worked in universities than on farms. Many blue collar manufacturing jobs have been lost. In the future, crops will still be grown, and goods will continue to be manufactured. But it will take fewer workers to produce either. Expertise will be highly marketable. Since expertise has a brief half-life in an era of high technology, knowing how to learn will be one of the most valuable skills you can acquire.

High Tech Will Get Higher

Scientific and technological jobs will be on the rise. The demand for different types of engineers varies with the supply of energy and with political decisions about national defense, space exploration, and environmental protection. As we write this chapter, aerospace engineers are having their troubles because of economic problems in the airline industry and cutbacks in the national space program. The demand for electrical engineers, in particular, should keep on growing as should the need for mechanical engineers, systems analysts, and people who can work in the growing field of biotechnology. Scientists and engineers with management skills and training will be particularly hot properties.

Computer Literacy

Computer literacy will be virtually essential at work and at home -- which will increasingly be one and the same. Accountants will keep their books on computer files. Architects and illustrators will do much of their designing on computers. Managers will make many of their decisions with the aid of a computer spreadsheet. People in sales will show their wares on lap tops which play multimedia. Pretty much everybody will write with word processing, correspond with e-mail, and receive information via the Internet. Computers will grow cheaper, smaller, more powerful, and more user-friendly. Unless you're specializing in hardware or software, you won't need to know computer languages. But for the foreseeable future, your life will be a lot easier if you can type well using the touch system. You will have to be comfortable with a seemingly endless supply of new applications if you want to stay current. John Naisbitt compares computer illiteracy today with wandering around an enormous library in which all the books are randomly arranged. All that information, and no way to use it.

If you have the interest and the ability, careers in computers -- software or hardware -- will be promising. A growing specialty will be computer security.

Training and Education Will Be In Demand

Since we're entering a knowledge-based century, those who traffic in knowledge will be important. Most states are talking school reform. Teachers' salaries are on the rise. While doctors, lawyers, and bankers continue to earn much higher salaries than teachers, our guess is that teaching wages will continue to rise. For those who are able to deliver high-tech education, the future should be even brighter. Interactive, multi-media based learning modules will be in high demand. Georgia Tech has recently created a Master's degree program in multi-media design. *P.O.V.* magazine recently predicted that multi-media designer would be one of the most marketable careers of the future.

Can You Sell Doorknobs to Tent Dwellers?

The 1994-1995 *Occupational Outlook Handbook* predicts slower than average growth for manufacturer's representatives and people in wholesale sales. Retail sales opportunities will be greater, but retail usually pays less well and offers fewer benefits. Remember, however, EVERYONE must approach career planning entrepreneurially. That means you will probably have to market yourself and your services many times. Having the ability to form good working relationships with all kinds of customers and persuade them that you have what they need has always been an asset. In the next Century it will be a requirement.

Global Economy Requires Global Communication Skills

In 1985, we asked recruiters how important it was to know additional languages. "Not very," is what they told us. Now, companies often expect facility with more than English. Having command of an "exotic" language such as Chinese, Japanese, or Arabic can be even more attractive. A safe bet is certainly Spanish. Probably even more important than knowing other languages is familiarity with other cultures. We recently heard a management consultant tell an auditorium full of freshmen that virtually all of them would work outside of the continental United States within their lifetimes. Also, we were talking recently with an economics student back from a year's internship in Japan. The student was convinced that the biggest barrier to increasing our exports to Japan was the simple fact that American products did not have clear Japanese instructions on them. He added that it was typical for American corporate representatives to show up at a Japanese trade show without even a rudimentary

> **Having the ability to form good working relationships with all kinds of customers and persuade them that you have what they need has always been an asset. In the next Century it will be a requirement.**

knowledge of the Japanese language and culture. This puts American businessmen at a tremendous disadvantage with their Japanese counterparts, most of whom do speak English. Small wonder there's a trade imbalance.

The Rand Institute reported in 1994 that most colleges do NOT do a good job of preparing their graduates for the global economy. Language departments frequently focus on classical literature and devote no attention to the ability to read a foreign newspaper. Conversational skills often suffer at the expense of reading and writing. The absolute best way to study a language is to immerse yourself in it. Living in a language house will force you to speak that language. A language house is a residence hall in which the residents commit to speaking only that language -- say French -- within the hall.

Another excellent strategy is study abroad. The most effective study abroad programs have you studying, working, playing with students, colleagues, and families from the host country. The great thing about this approach is you are immersed in the culture as well as the language. But this means you need to know the language really well before you go. And this means you need to choose a language house early on in your college career.

We highly recommend the language house/study abroad sequence as the ideal way to prepare for the global economy. There are other, less challenging, methods that everyone can take advantage of. Most American colleges and universities have international students and faculty. Spend time with them. Get to know them. You probably can join the International Students Association through which you can rub elbows with a variety of cultures. Catch some foreign films. Attend some cultural events which showcase international talent. The bottom line is really cross-cultural sensitivity. Don't fail to meet the bottom line.

WHAT IF I'M STILL NOT SURE?

We're not surprised if you're a little uncertain. Life is filled with uncertainties. Some of you will be working twenty years from now in fields that haven't even been invented yet. If you want a 100 percent guarantee, you might consider inherited wealth. If you can't work that one out, and most of us can't, here are some other guidelines.

1.   *Money isn't everything.* Sure, it's important, and you'd be a fool to ignore your future financial security. But we're tired of talking to pre-meds who are more concerned with BMW's than Biochemistry. With engineering students who can't stand math and science, but figure they're going to ride the high-tech wave to megabucks. *Don't sentence yourself to a lifetime of work you're going to hate.*

A generation of psychological research on the workplace has found that people were most satisfied when they were doing what they really wanted to do. Research by Teresa Amabile of Brandeis suggests that they are most creative as well. After a certain level of income, salary and pats on the back have only a negligible impact on performance.

Besides, career choices are seldom limited to being a starving artist in Soho or a well-heeled financier on Wall Street. Why not be a creative director on Madison Avenue?

2.   *There is no magic timetable.* Not even our Four-Year Master Plan. We're convinced it's a good general guide, but divine revelation it isn't. You don't *have* to declare a major by your sophomore year. And there's no crime in changing majors. The main thing is *don't just sit on your hands when it comes to choosing a major and planning your career.* Do the exercises and follow the suggestions in this chapter. Don't wander passively through college.

3.   *There is no perfect career.* Nor does everyone "fall in love" with a career. True, some people are born doctors or lawyers or managers, but most aren't. Don't expect to hear angelic choirs every time you tackle a calculus problem just because you're majoring in physics.

There might be a dozen jobs out there that could meet your needs. Don't get tunnel vision and insist on one occupation and no other. What if you don't get into medical school? Or a good MBA program? Make sure you've got some decent alternatives in mind if everything doesn't go just as you planned it. Even the most successful people have their setbacks. You'll have many jobs throughout your professional life. And most of you will have more than one career.

Learn To Relate

We've already told you that the success stories in the 21st Century will have an entrepreneurial flair. Effective entrepreneurs know how to market themselves. No matter how competent you are, you still have to convince others to buy your services. That entails some self-assurance and some self-understanding -- not always in ready supply for a 20-something, much less for someone 18 or 19. The best thing we can tell you is that with practice you can get better, but that is only IF you practice. You get practice through involvement -- co-op jobs and internships (See Chapter 6.), campus organizations and activities (See Chapter 7.).

Another aspect of entrepreneurial career planning is leadership. Entrepreneurs are "in charge." If you're in charge of your career you must have a vision of where you're headed and what you want to accomplish. You must have enough desire to persevere in the face of obstacles and hardships. You need the ability to convince others that the pursuit of your goal is good for them as well. The prospect of being a leader may seem daunting, but leadership is comprised of a constellation of skills that you can develop. See Chapters 6, 7, and 16.

> The prospect of being a leader may seem daunting, but leadership is comprised of a constellation of skills that you can develop.

Get Organized

Organizational skills are useful for just about anybody who wants to accomplish anything. Systematic study produces better learning and higher grades than random chaos does. Attention to detail (which, we confess, is hardly our long suit) makes any job run more smoothly. In this section, however, we are specifically talking about organizing your career planning. Entrepreneurs set goals, develop strategies for reaching them, and then organize their efforts. Since we believe career planning in the 21st Century will have an entrepreneurial flavor, you must organize your career planning. If you're smart, you won't wait until you're a senior to start.

What to organize:

1. Contacts. Keep a file, Rolodex™, or electronic data base of people that can help you succeed. As a freshman, you'll probably want tutors, study buddies, professors, counselors, and advisors on this list. As you progress in college, you should add the names of career related contacts. We recommend anyone you've met at a career fair, people you've interviewed for career information, co-op counselors, and people who have supervised your work.

2. Resume. Maintain a resume on a computer disk. Keep it updated as you acquire new experiences and develop new skills.

3. Portfolio. Keep a folder that contains any awards, letters of recommendation, news clippings, and evaluations. Keep any outstanding work samples. This may seem formidable for a freshman, but as you continue your education, school work such as senior design projects and term papers can be included. If you've been an intern for a newspaper, you would naturally want to keep clippings of any articles you wrote. If you volunteered at a hospital, you'd keep the brochure describing the services your department offered.

4. Career Information. Keep a file of pertinent articles and reports on job trends and job search strategies.

Plan for the Future

Cultivate "the art of the long view," which happens to be the title of a book by futurist Peter Schwartz. Most of us don't have the time to do the exhaustive research that Schwartz and other futurists like Toffler, and Naisbitt conduct, but you can read what they have written. It makes sense to think about the future and how it will affect your life and impact your career. Read trade journals, *The Occupational Outlook Handbook*, and thoughtful news analyses and commentaries. In other words, expand your horizons beyond *Sports Illustrated, Glamour*, and your required textbooks.

SUMMARY

1. You're going to spend much of your adult life at work. Plan carefully how you're going to spend it.

2. Carefully assess your interests, abilities, and needs.

3. Thoroughly investigate relevant majors and careers. Stay abreast of current events and try to anticipate future trends.

4. Go to the source. Interview people who actually do the work you think you might like.

5. Get help planning your career from whatever professional resources are available on your campus.

6. Getting career-related work before you graduate is one of the best ways to test your career choice.

7. No one can predict precisely what the future job world will be like. Therefore, general skills such as the ability to communicate, computer literacy, and the capacity to learn new information are keys to future career success.

8. Organize your career planning effort.

Getting Connected to Campus

One of the principle reasons that students leave college during their freshman year, is because they are lonely. You are in charge of your destiny when it comes to this. For some of you it won't be a problem because you are so extraverted that you'd make friends while sitting in line to buy your auto tag. Some however, have a more difficult time making friends and putting themselves in new situations. One important thing to remember about establishing new relationshships here at college, is that everyone else is doing the same thing. You won't stand out; you'll just be one of the many.

Your Student Government Adminstration (SGA), located in the Student Services Building, ground floor has booklets with all the names and faculty contacts for the different student groups meeting on the GT campus. Go by and look at or ask for one of these booklets. Select two groups that you will be interested in for social reasons, and two for professional reasons.

Social Organizations

Name of Organization	Day and Time of Meeting	Location of Meetings

Professional Organizations

Name of Organization	Day and Time of Meeting	Location of Meetings

Select one of each to actually attend.

1. Your assignment is to meet two new people at each function.

Name of New Person	Meeting I Met Him/Her At

2. One way to get to know people is to share information about yourself and listen to them. What is something you learned about each of these people while talking to them.

3. If you did not like one of the meetings, choose a different group to attend next week. There are potential friends all over campus, and organizations that do everything from feeding the elderly to hanging with the local *Dr. Who* fans. You can opt to be a part of the Greeks, or you can join the organization that changes student life by being a part of the SGA. But, **you** are in charge. You get to decide what you will do, and if you will do it. It's worth it to try. Keep at it until you do find the group of people you enjoy hanging with.

Looking for Employment Information

There are lots of places to get employment information. There's everything from your college/university Career/Placement Office, to the want ads. You can retain a private employment agency, usually with a heafty fee attached, or use the local government employment service. Success rates from one to another are not significantly different. What we also know is that networking with friends and relatives is almost as effective as contacting a company directly.

Don't limit yourself to traditional means of searching alone. As children of the information age, you have the Information Superhighway at your disposal as well. There are a variety of gopher sites that have employment information. A superficial search located:

The North Carolina Office of State Personnel Job Listings

University of Michigan, North Texas, Texas, Wisconsin, Arkansis, and South Carolina

The Library of Congress

The American Physiological Association

Job Listings Around the Globe

Attorney Job Listings

Career Advice (The Princeton Review Gopher)

The Chronical of Higher Education

1.   Access your university/college gopher or World Wide Web (WWW) page to go look at some of these sites. The majority of jobs are for full-time positions. However, you can also use the power of the internet to find internships and get names of important contacts.

2.   At the University of Minnesota Gopher you can find the Occupational Outlook Handbook. This book is probably also available in hardcopy in your college/university library. Attempt to find it over the net. If you can't, or don't have access, go to the library and take a look at this book.. Look up three job titles you believe you might be interested in, or want to know more about.

Job Title	Projected Need	Minimum Requirements
_____	_____	_____
_____	_____	_____
_____	_____	_____

3.   Select one of the jobs and look into it in detail.

What is something about this job that you didn't know? _____

_____

How much interaction does it project this position will have with:

Data: _____   People: _____   Things: _____

4.   How can you envision yourself using the internet to help you search for future jobs?

_____

_____

_____

Choosing a Major

Classes I've Taken and Liked:	Classes I've Taken and am Sure I have no Future In:

The list above suggests the following general fields: _____

_____

_____

I've read over the course descriptions in the college catalog, AND the descriptions of classes for each of those majors. Knowing that, I've narrowed down my list to: _____

_____

_____

I will try to get informational interviews with a person in each of these fields: I have the following ideas for people I can interview: _____

_____

_____

I have appointments with the following people:

Name	**Date**	**Time**

Name	**Date**	**Time**

6
Practice Makes Perfect--The Importance of Work

You've been feeling rotten all day. The pain in your side has gotten progressively worse till you just can't stand it any longer. A friend drives you to the emergency room of the nearest hospital where your problem is diagnosed as acute appendicitis. You have to undergo an appendectomy immediately, and you can choose from three very bright physicians to perform the operation. One has read extensively about surgery in general and appendectomies in particular. He has never actually operated on anybody though. In fact, he has never even seen an appendectomy performed. The second doctor has read about such operations and he has seen them performed. The third has successfully performed an appendectomy several different times. Which doctor would you choose to open you up?

Most of us would choose the doctor who has the experience. Theory is great, but real-world practice counts for more on such an important task. Employers feel much the same way about paying someone to do a job for them. They want to know they'll get their money's worth. This is why students who graduate on a co-operative plan tend to get better jobs. Their career-related work experience makes them better qualified.

The Value of Work

We believe higher education is one of the most important investments you can make in preparing for the next century. Do not, however, make the mistake of avoiding the "real world" while you're in school. In particular, don't avoid the world of work. This has always been true, but real world experience will be more important than ever in the highly fluid world of work that lies ahead. We've said that the future belongs to the learners and the entrepreneurs. A successful entrepreneur is constantly upgrading skills, learning about the competition, guestimating about the future. That's the attitude you need in the classroom AND the workplace.

It's better to design circuits for McDonnell Douglas than to flip hamburgers for McDonald's. It's also better to manage for McDonald's than to push a broom at McDonnell Douglas. But any work is better than none at all. Working teaches you the importance of effort-- employers appreciate and reward hard workers. Do you have to work part-time to put yourself through school? A lot of students do. It can be stressful, but you learn how to be self-sufficient. You also learn how to budget your time--you have no choice if you want to keep your grades respectable. Working teaches you responsibility, how to get along with all kinds of people.

Work experience makes you more marketable. Employers like it when candidates have worked their way through school. We urge graduating seniors to highlight this fact on their resumes, even if they contributed only a portion of what their education cost them. But career-related work is even better. What you learn is more relevant to your future, a fact that won't be overlooked by prospective employers when you graduate.

> **Part-time and summer work that is career-related helps you to refine your goals.**

The right jobs while you're still in school will teach you about professional work. Co-ops and interns often work for corporations. They learn about a large company's different divisions. A nurse's aid might learn what it's like to work in a hospital or clinic. Even a file clerk can get a feel for how an office really operates. There will also be opportunities to make contacts--people who can write recommendations for you, give you leads for jobs, perhaps someday hire you for an important position.

One of the most valuable lessons you will learn is just where you fit into your chosen field. Or if you fit into it. Most college students change majors at least once. Better to find out as a rising sophomore than as a senior.

We emphasize the importance of career goals throughout this book. But that doesn't mean that all students settle on a career by the beginning of their second semester and, after that, it's smooth sailing. In fact, we believe choosing a career is a lifelong process. When you work summers in a law office, you get a first-hand feel for what the legal profession is like. This is a much more career-enhancing experience than what you got from watching the O.J. Simpson trial. Developing a career means continually trying on roles to see how suitable they are to your interests and abilities. Do I like doing this? Can I do it well? And is there a future in it?

Part-time and summer work that is career-related also helps you to refine your goals. Suppose you've known since high school that you wanted to work in a scientific/technical field. After some research you think that civil engineering might be for you. But which branch? Construction? Sewage disposal? Water treatment? Urban planning? Working in one or more of these areas can help you decide. And the sooner you get the experience, the sooner you'll know if it's right for you.

Career-related work enhances your academic experience. Sometimes it's difficult to see just how the theories in your textbooks can be put into practice. There can be a big gap between the ivory-tower atmosphere of school and the real-world problems encountered on the job. By working in your field of interest before you graduate, you can start to apply some of what you've learned in the classroom. And when you get back to school, many of your subjects become more relevant. You'll also have a better idea of what advanced electives to take.

Many college's and universities have a cooperative eduction plan. Georgia Tech's program has been in place since 1912. Over 3,000 students participate in the plan each year. Almost twice as many make the Dean's List as do students who aren't in co-op programs. Their work helps to make them better students.

One of the most valuable aspects of career-related work before you graduate is that you begin to develop the very skills and expertise that you will practice after you receive your degree. Do you want to make big bucks some day in sales? There's no better way to learn about selling than to start knocking on doors. Do you want to inspire a curiosity for learning in primary school children? Practice teaching will probably be your most useful experience. But don't wait until you're a senior to get a taste of it--find a job at a summer camp, a girls'club, or the YMCA. Do you want to be a plant manager? Try your hand on a production line for a while.

Many college students aspire to managerial positions someday. The sooner you get some supervisory experience, the better. A highly successful business consultant wryly related his son's first experience as a hotel management intern. The son had anticipated starting out behind the checkout counter. Instead, he was placed in charge of the cleanup crew in the main kitchen. He had to manage sixteen older, ethnically different, relatively uneducated men. It was a stressful internship for the student, but he learned a lot about people. He will have some very challenging questions to pose to his management profs when he returns to school. And he will be a much stronger job candidate after he graduates.

BE A STUDENT ENTREPRENEUR

We find that many college students want to own their own businesses someday. Well, you don't have to wait until you've save up $50,000 seed money. You can start while you're still in school. In fact there are students who establish flourishing enterprises even before they graduate.

Even if you don't plan on starting your own business in the future, starting a small one now can be an excellent way to develop new skills. The smallest undertaking can be a learning laboratory. In order to make a business go, you've got to come up with an idea and make that idea come to life. You've got to analyze the market, develop your products or services, market them, handle finances and accounting. If other people are involved, there are personnel questions to handle. And, of course, you've got to deal with your customers. Plus it's all *your* responsibility.

That sort of experience is music to an employer's ears. In many instances you can get academic credit for a business venture. And you can pick up some spare change, in some instances quite a lot of it. Mark McKee was the president of two companies by the end of his junior year at the University of Kansas. Pyramid Pizza earned $700,000 that year. Waddles Active Wear, which specializes in Hawaiian clothes, grossed $2 million. In 1986 Louis Kahn of Atlanta owned and operated a worldwide computer network, a computer mail-order catalog, a service for real-estate brokers, a small book publishing company, and an in-house ad agency. He was about to graduate from high school.

How do you get started? There is no one way. But students have made a go of all kinds of businesses--delivering munchies to dorm rooms, bumper stickers, caps with messages, flower shops--we could go on for the next ten pages.

Some years ago, Larry Adler started by doing magic shows at kids' birthday parties. Then he started selling baskets full of favors at the same parties. Then he began distributing the baskets to retail stores. He phoned around to find better favors for his baskets. He was so impressed with one item that he asked if he could represent the company that manufactured it. He was told they already had a sales rep in the area where he lived. Could he be their sub-rep? Well, what would it hurt? Go ahead and try. His first month he won a set of matched luggage for being a sales leader. No one else in sales had ever been a leader for that company during their first month. After that he represented a number of companies that marketed children's products. A reporter asked how he did it. Larry said he was successful because he knew what kids would buy. He probably did -- he was twelve years old when he was interviewed.

For the mortals among you, consider first taking a course in entrepreneurship. Many universities offer them now. Join the Entrepreneur's Club on your campus. Read *The Student Entrepreneur's Guide,* by Brett Kingstone, and popular magazines such as *Enterprise* or *INC.* Talk with other student entrepreneurs. Talk with your professors. But mainly, start thinking. Come up with a plan. And take action.

HOW TO GET A GOOD JOB WHILE YOU'RE STILL A STUDENT

It might seem like a tall order to find career-related employment when you're only eighteen or nineteen, but it can be done. Remember Larry Adler. Your school's co-operative plan or internship program is probably the path of least resistance, and we recommend both to you.

Co-op plans usually arrange ongoing, paid work alternating with school throughout a student's stay in college. By the time students are in their last semester of work, they usually make pretty good money. By that time they earn it, because they will have developed the skills that enable them to perform relatively sophisticated tasks.

Internships are more often one-time arrangements. Although many provide salaries, some offer only experience. If it's the right experience, it may still be invaluable. You know the old dilemma: you can't get a job without experience, but you can't get experience without a job. An internship may be your solution to the dilemma.

Internships also tend to draw less technically skilled students than do co-op plans. They provide an opportunity for someone to get a first exposure to a field, to try it on for size.

Even without the assistance of a formal program, you should be able to find some sort of job. In fact, landing a good job on your own is an impressive accomplishment and will be noted as such by future employers. Finding a job is a job in itself, and mastering the art of getting hired is a skill that you will use repeatedly throughout your life. When we wrote the book that preceded this one, we reported that college graduates would change jobs an average of eight times before they retired. In the Information Age, you may change CAREERS eight times.

Read Chapters 12-15, which discuss the different phases of the job search. Pay special attention to "Resumes While Still In School" in Chapter 14 and "Questions Asked of Co-ops" in Chapter 15. The sort of job you can get depends a lot on how many skills you have already developed. But suppose you haven't developed many as yet. You're full of potential, but without much actual experience or expertise.

Don't give up. It simply means that you're going to have to start at the bottom (better now than after graduation). Your first job may be as a gofer (go fer this, and then go fer that). But if you perform your menial duties enthusiastically and look for opportunities, you should be able gradually to assume some larger responsibilities. The idea is eventually to work yourself into a position that offers more challenge and fosters more professional growth.

In some cases you can earn academic credit along with your salary while you work. Sometimes you can get only one or the other. We recommend that you attempt to arrange some kind of credit. If there's no formal internship program on your campus, see what you can work out with your professors as an independent study. We heard of one student who got academic credit while working as cashier in a convenience store. She observed that different types of people used the store at different hours of the day. She recorded her observations systematically and eventually turned them into a sociology report.

WHAT TO LOOK FOR IN A FIRST JOB

There are three things to consider--experience, experience, and experience. Naturally money is nice too. If you're working your way through college it's a necessity, but you usually won't be paid well without experience. Conversely, if you are paid well, it's probably because you're performing some important tasks for your employer. In other words, you're getting good experience.

Joan Macal, while president of the Board of Directors of the National Society for Internships and Experiential Education, recommended the following guidelines for interns:

* Secure a written learning contract. What are your duties? What will you learn?

* Try to secure regular meetings with supervisors from both work and school.

* Request a written evaluation of your performance and learning.

LEARNING ABOUT LIFE: LEARNING FOR LIFE

The central theme of this book is that you are entering an era in which change is rapid and constant, and knowledge is power. Learning is not confined to the classroom. It's an ongoing, lifelong process. The world is your classroom, and you're in charge of learning as much as possible.

One of the hot new trends in the business community today is the "learning organization." Successful organizations hire eager learners, support their continuing education, and provide an atmosphere in which ideas are exchanged, skills are shared, and learning is pervasive. EDS, the software giant founded by Ross Perot is one such organization. Every EDS site has a bulletin board on which staffers post what they've been reading. Books and articles are exchanged. Ideas are discussed. An employee says that's one of the most exciting things about working for EDS. There is a culture of learning, and it's infectious. Since life-long learning is the only way to survive in the next Century, she figures working for EDS is better than unemployment insurance.

An executive recently informed a room full of MBA students that his corporation expects employees to chart their own professional development. The corporation will pay for just about any workshop or class, but it's up to the individual to find the right class, attend it, and get the most out of it. Many employees never get around to doing so. They will be the most vulnerable to downsizing.

While it's great to work for a learning organization, you must first become a learning individual. There is no job, no class, no activity from which you can't learn something. All you need is an inquisitive mind.

In conclusion, and at the risk of belaboring the point, get some career-related work experience. It is one of the very best ways you can invest in your own future.

S U M M A R Y

1. Employers value work experience, especially if it's career related.
2. Career-related experience teaches you about professional work.
3. Career-related experience helps you discover whether or not your chosen field suits you.
4. Career-related experience helps you to refine your professional goals.
5. Career-related work enhances your academic experience.
6. Career-related work enables you to develop the professional skills you will use after graduation.
7. Becoming a student entrepreneur is an excellent way to get experience.
8. Co-op plans and internships provide excellent opportunities for students to get their first career-related experience.

Learning Through Experience: The Real World on Campus

If all the world's your classroom, there will certainly be many learning opportunities scattered all over your campus. As you prepare for the rapid paced Information Age, it will pay you to capitalize on as many of these opportunities as possible. If knowledge is the coin of the realm and managing your career is an entrepreneurial adventure, then the time to dive in is now. No, you say.   I'm too shy, I'm too busy, I'm watching TV. Well consider the case of Robert Blair.

Robert is a senior business major with a 3.8 GPA. He is slumped in his desk chair, staring at the wall. He's depressed. You would be too if you'd just received you fifth flush letter. He can't believe it, all those A's and still nobody has shown much interest in hiring him. Meanwhile, Robert's roommate, Charles Neuberger, has already gotten two outright job offers. Charles has a few more Cs than Bs, and not very many As. How did he do it?

The answer is that Charles has developed people skills that you can't learn out of a book while Robert has avoided people by hiding behind books. Charles is a doer and a leader. He likes people, which is obvious every time he talks with a professor or administrator - his enthusiasm and self assurance are catching.

Robert is shy, which is certainly no crime, but it definitely is a handicap. His parents and others tried to encourage him to break out of his shell, but he resisted their advice to get involved in campus life. He told himself that fraternities weren't for serious students. Student government never really did anything important. Professional societies on campus were just playing grown-up. And whenever he felt lonely, he could always read more or play with his computer.

During interviews he was ill at ease, and there were questions about his participation in campus activities that he couldn't answer. If he had wanted a position in pure research, the gaps in his experience might not have counted so heavily against him. Although even then he might have run into some problems - most employers want their technical people to have good communication skills. Besides, Robert wanted to be an executive. He wanted his first position to be his beginning step on the road to management.

> **You will have to manage, lead, follow, persuade, sell, network, collaborate, delegate, and coach with countless people in hundreds of ways.**

In addition to short-changing himself in the area of people skills, Robert also appears to be operating on an out-of-date career planning model. His plan: make good grades, go to work for Mega Corp, become a manager, get promoted to the executive ranks, then retire in 30 years with a fat pension. The new job world, however, is vastly more fluid and dynamic. In fact, it's downright chaotic. For that reason, the people skills that make for successful entrepreneurs will be required of everyone. You will have to manage, lead, follow, persuade, sell, network, collaborate, delegate, and coach with countless people in hundreds of ways.

One of the best ways to cultivate the multi-dimensional talents the next Century will demand of you is through your involvement in organizations. A recent survey conducted by AT&T indicated that participation in extracurricular activities was an excellent predictor of managerial potential. So, come job-hunting time, expect to be asked about what you did outside the classroom. If you did nothing, how will you explain this fact? Did you join several organizations, but only to pad your resume? A good interviewer will find out whether you were really involved or not. Did you hold an office? What were your duties? On which committees did you serve? What did you accomplish?

Rather than looking at campus involvement as more fodder for your resume, we recommend that you look at extracurricular activities as opportunities for personal development. Do you want to be an executive someday? Then lead a group or head up some project. Do you want to have a network of professional contacts? Then a good place to begin is through a student professional association. Through the right group you can also learn about different kinds of people and get some exposure to new ideas.

We recommend that early on in your college career you identify one weakness or missing skill and try to develop it through some extra curricular activity.

And don't forget fun. You'll go nuts if you do nothing but chase success. What's the point of being successful if you never get any pleasure out of life? Besides, we are social animals. It is not likely you will ever have a better opportunity for developing close, possibly lifelong friends than while in college. One of the best ways to meet people is through clubs and activities.

TYPES OF ACTIVITIES
Student Government

Through student government you can develop a number of skills that you'll use throughout your professional life: leadership, communication, persuasion, administration, negotiation. You learn through experience (there's that word again!) how things get done in a organization.

Do you want to establish a student course critique on your campus? It will take time and energy. You'll have to rally student, faculty, and administrative support in order to get the idea accepted. Compromises will have to be made. And once the legislation is passed, there's the not-so-small matter of implementation. Who develops the surveys? Who decides on the final format? How are they administered and scored? Who writes up the critique? How is it distributed? And how is the whole project funded?

By involving yourself in a project of this magnitude, you can learn things you just don't usually learn in a classroom. And, yes, it does look good on your resume and sound good during an interview.

The Greeks

Which statements are true? Fraternities are elitist, anti-intellectual gangs of juvenile delinquents masquerading as college students. Members live *in* animal houses, *on* alcohol, and *for* sex. Fraternities exist to promote the personal, social and intellectual development of their members. Sororities are clubs for superficial, air-headed snobs. Sororities promote sisterhood, service, and individual growth.

The answer, of course, is none of the above. And all of the above. There are no perfectly good or bad fraternities or sororities. Some are, however, better that others on any given campus. If you decide to join a Greek social organization, here are some things to look out for when you choose:

Does the group go in for hazing? If it does in any more that the mildest way, it's not likely going to help you succeed while you're in school or after you leave it. Studies have shown that the fraternities who go in for the heaviest hazing tend to have the lowest morale and to harbor the most hostility between members. Succeeding in the next Century will be more competitive than ever. You want to be a part of a group that reduces stress, not adds to it.

Does the group maintain a balance between social/recreational and academic activities? Of course, you want to have some fun, but you're also dead serious about success. If you plan to succeed in the next Century, you won't want to risk your future by joining an outfit that can't think past the next keg party. Some tip-offs to the ones that might work against you: The organization is perennially on academic or social probation. During rush, the actives never question your grades or professional ambitions. They all have chosen easy majors and appear to have given no thought to their own careers or how they are going to survive in a knowledge-based society. Fraternities and sororities should be "learning organizations."

Another factor to consider is the kind of alumni associated with the group. It can be a definite advantage to have a built-in connection to alumni who are leaders in business, government, science, and the arts. But not all Greek letter organizations have produced a list of VIP graduates. Find out if yours has before you sign on the dotted line and learn the secret handshake.

The advantages of being in a social organization are, first of all, friendship and fun. No one needs to apologize for wanting to have a good time with good friends. Moreover, if (and this is a big if) the brothers or sisters in your organization are also serious about career success, you can help each other reach your goals during college and throughout your life. A "good old boy" network can be a big professional asset until the day you retire. Increasingly, this is true of "good old girl" networks as well. But a network of bozos will not get you very far. A network of ambitious, visionary brothers or sisters will.

Fraternities and sororities also expose you to the importance of teamwork. There has to be give and take for a Greek house to function effectively. By belonging to one, you learn when to pipe up and when to shut up, when to compromise and when to stick by your guns.

Most organizations offer the chance for you to lead. This is certainly true of the Greeks. Again, it's up to you to take advantage of this opportunity. Volunteer to head up the fund drive or to organize the spring picnic. And then do a good job. If you can do it right for the Phi Delta Sigmas, you may someday have the opportunity to do it right for IBM or for your own organization.

One of the strengths of fraternities and sororities is also a weakness: likes attract likes. It's comfortable to hang out with people like yourself, and we all need a home base where we can relax and be ourselves. The workscape of the 21st Century, however, will be populated by an increasingly diverse cast of players. If your contacts are limited to people who are replicas of yourself, you will not be preparing yourself for the global economy. Therefore, either join a social organization that does admit some diversity, or reach out beyond your own in other arenas of campus life.

Professional Associations

We think most students should join a student professional association related to their intended *careers*. Membership is probably not as valuable as career-related work, but it is a good supplement. The best source of knowledge about a career is from those who are successfully practicing it. Professional societies expose you to just such people.

You will also meet other students who share your goals. Pre-meds, pre-laws, and student entrepreneurs can support and encourage each other. It's a good place to form friendships since you have at least one thing in common.

If you take advantage of it, there should also be the opportunity to gain leadership experience. And it never hurts to list an office that you held on your resume.

One of the main advantages to joining a professional association is to extend your network of contacts (see Chapter 7). We know of one student who made it a point to see to the arrangements for everyone who spoke to his group. In some instances he picked them up at the airport and shuttled them back. This might seem like a nuisance, but it afforded him the chance to spend a lot of time alone with leaders in his field.

He could ask any question he wanted about his intended profession and get it answered in detail by an expert. He could try out new ideas and get them critiqued. Soon he began exchanging business cards and corresponding with these same people. By the time he graduated he had developed professional relationships with some very impressive folks.

Community Service

The Peace Corps recruits its volunteers differently than it used to. It now emphasizes the skills that can be developed on a tour, skills that will be highly marketable to employers when the volunteer's service is completed. Of course, working for the Peace Corps or Vista has always afforded opportunities for professional development. And so does working as a Candy Striper, tutoring underprivileged children, visiting geriatric residents, and organizing recreational activities for patients in a mental hospital.

Community service is another way to get experience. And experience is still the best way to learn about a field, develop professionally related skills, and fatten your resume. It also affords you a different kind of experience--the chance to learn about people who are very different from you.

College is supposed to teach you about the world; yet it can be very provincial in its own ivory-tower way. In most college settings you are denied contact with the very old, the poor, the sick, the unsuccessful. You are similarly shielded from these segments of the population in the business community. Community service, then, exposes you to more of the world and gives you the opportunity to make it a better one.

As we write this, President Clinton's national service corps--AmeriCorps--remains an option. Volunteers receive a modest stipend for performing community service and are awarded $4,725 towards their college education. You can get information at (202) 606-5000.

Groups Based on Age, Sex, or Race

From 1636, when Harvard University was founded, until the end of World War II in 1945, the vast majority of American college students were single white males between the ages of eighteen and twenty-two. Most came from well-to-do families. American higher education still has a ways to go before it serves all segments of our population equally, but students today are definitely a more varied lot.

There are now slightly more women than men on college campuses. More students are over the age of twenty-five, and a fair number are over forty. There are more African-Americans, Hispanics, and Native Americans. There are also immigrants from all over the world, as well as a significant number of international students who will return to their home country.

In the midst of all this diversity, it is very easy for any one student to feel lost and out of place. Assuming that your hearing is good imagine for a moment what it would be like to attend a college for the hearing impaired. Lectures would be signed instead of spoken. Not knowing sign language, you would feel lost in class and be a stranger in the residence halls.

While most of you won't face barriers that are this extreme, you may well face problems in adjusting that can interfere with your ability to learn. Even well-intentioned people tend to notice differences before similarities. You may be recognized more for the color of your skin, the sound of your accent, or the gray in your hair than for your intelligence and drive. As paradoxical as it sounds, probably the majority of you are one kind of minority or another.

Your chances for success in college improve when you're convinced you belong there. But it's hard to feel as if you fit in when you're a black student in a sea of white faces. Or a mother of children older than most of your classmates. How do you develop a social life? Who do you date if you're single? Who will understand your customs without your first having to explain them? Because of these factors some students feel more comfortable attending a college with a student body more like themselves. Some African-Americans seem to develop more rapidly on historically black campuses. Some women seem to prosper similarly by attending a women's college.

The majority of you will attend coeducational colleges that are racially mixed. Most of these schools have organizations in which membership is based upon ethnic background (African American Association), a common experience (a veterans' organization), gender (Society of Women Engineers), or age (a group for mid-life career changers). We believe it is important for you eventually to be comfortable with a variety of individuals and settings. But joining a group of students who share your cultural heritage may be an important first step in feeling at home on your campus. Groups whose focus is religious (Baptist Student Union), political (Libertarian), or issue-oriented (Save The Piranha) can also serve this function. Moreover, participation in such groups enables you to express yourself in ways unrelated to your career, and that's important too.

Student Athletics

We're talking about the *business* of intercollegiate athletics here, not intramural flag football between the dorms and the greeks. If you're in a revenue-producing sport at a Division I school, you've probably convinced yourself that you're going to be one of the elite group who makes it in the pros. You're probably very wrong. (Our apologies if you're the next Michael Jordan.) Most student athletes never make a nickel in professional sports. Most of those who do, last only a few years and don't make megabucks. Those are the hard, cold facts.

There are some advantages to playing intercollegiate sports, but first, let us tell you about the obstacles they pose to preparing for the 21st Century. The typical day of a student athlete begins at 6 A.M. with a strategy session, followed by mandatory breakfast at 7. There will probably be classes during most of the morning since the afternoon will be taken up with the sport. Weight training and organized practice can take five or six exhausting hours a day. Not much time or energy is left for studies, and there is virtually none for other extracurricular activities. It is against the NCAA regulations for a scholarship athlete to work for pay while enrolled in school, so career-related work experience is very difficult to come by. Most summers, athletes are enrolled in school and busy with weight training.

So, how does a student athlete refine his career choice? Develop marketable skills? Make professional contacts? Get a taste of working in his field? Keep her grades up? (Increasingly, there are scholarships available for women athletes.) The answer is that it's very difficult. You really have to be on your toes if you want to develop from a blue-chip recruit into a blue-chip graduate.

Here are some suggestions about how you can maximize your chances if you're a student athlete:

Time management is crucial. Get organized quickly, and stay organized. Take complete advantage of tutorial and advisory assistance provided for student athletes. But don't stop there. Get to know your professors. Find out from them how you can improve your performance. Attend your classes. Sit front and center. Participate. Try to develop marketable skills through your athletics. Be enthusiastic. Show up on time. Demonstrate good work habits during practice. Show that you're a leader.

Get to know influential alumni and athletic supporters. No, we're not talking about money under table. This is one of the best ways for you to make professional contacts. Let the alumnus or booster know that you're interested in his business, that you want to be successful off the field as well as on it. You won't be able to co-op, but you should be able to work out some kind of internship in your field for academic credit that will also give you some all-important experience. A series of part-time internships over the summers may be a possibility. You can keep your grades up, get exposure to your career, and keep the NCAA happy. Another option is to do a full-time internship after your athletic eligibility is over, but before you graduate. (It is not likely that a student athlete will graduate in just four years.)

And now for the advantages of playing a varsity sport. First, you'll be doing something you enjoy a great deal. In fact, don't even consider playing a college sport unless you love it. The sacrifices are too great. The pay is terrible. Sure, you get tuition, room and board, but you have to give up as many as fifty hours a week to your sport. It is probably much easier to work your way through school waiting tables or selling shoes than to do so on an athletic scholarship. Second, if you're in the right program, sports can build character, teach teamwork, develop leadership. We live in a competitive society. You can learn to compete. Third, there are opportunities for contacts if you take advantage of them.

Intercollegiate athletics, then, can be a plus. But if you're not careful, they can be a one-way street to a tainted degree or no degree at all. Two questions to ask of any athletic program: How many student athletes graduate? And how many student athletes are involved in successful careers after their playing days are over?

Groups For The Fun Of It

Yes, college is serious business, but it should also be a blast. We think it's a good idea to get involved in some activities not because you'll make contacts, not because you're developing some highly marketable skill, but simply because they're fun and you'll make some friends. Having a good time at least some of the time is not a luxury; it's a necessity for your physical and mental health. There are hundreds of groups which center around hobbies and recreational pursuits. They range from racquetball to rock climbing, from sky diving to scuba diving, from music to martial arts, from paint ball to pottery. So take your pick. Just for the fun of it.

S U M M A R Y

1.   Don't limit your education to the classroom.
2.   Use campus activities to your advantage.
3.   Develop people and other survival skills that will stand you in good stead in the next Century.
4.   Make contacts and close friends.
5.   Learn about your career.
6.   Enjoy yourself and have a good time.

8
It's Who You Know: Building Contacts

Don't travel alone as you head into the 21st Century. The Information Age requires knowledge. This means you will require contacts with useful information. The next Century requires an entrepreneurial approach to career management. This means you need to count on professional contacts for a variety of reasons: job leads, recommendations, collaboration, advice, support, and probably a dozen other things.

What student wouldn't love to get a glowing recommendation from a professor for a job or graduate fellowship? Or have some highly placed manager or entrepreneur make an unsolicited job offer. And wouldn't it be nice to have an expert in your field show you the ropes and help you on your way to a successful career?

OK, so you want important people on your side. Fine, but do you realize that it's up to you to make this happen? This chapter tells you how.

We advise students to start building their network of contacts the first day of their freshman year, or better yet, while they're still in high school. We often get resistance on this point along several lines.

Why would important people want to bother with me? Because it comes with the territory. Experts and people in power expect requests for information and assistance. Because most successful people want to help you succeed. This is especially true if they're convinced you're seriously committed to success. Because you make it worth their while. Life is give and take. If you help others, they'll usually help you. And if you're wondering what on earth you can do to help an older, established professional, we'll tell you later on in this chapter.

Isn't it insincere or maybe even downright manipulative to cultivate relationships for the sole purpose of advancing your career? Not at all. Most business relationships are just that -- relationships that exist for the mutual benefit of both parties. Naturally, it's nicer if friendship develops as well, but it's not necessary. One word of warning, however, don't settle for having only a network of contacts. You need friends as well -- people who accept you for who you are and not just what you can do for them.

Won't it detract from my success if I get help from others? Don't kid yourself. You can use a helping hand. We all can. This doesn't mean you get people to do for you what you can just as easily do for yourself.

But, as you'll see in Chapter 9, achievers take advantage of every resource in their environment. They actively seek out other people who can help them reach their goals. Don't waste ten years reinventing the wheel when you can buy tires at any service station in town.

But what if I'm shy? I have a hard enough time asking my roommate if I can borrow a computer disk. How am I going to ask some big shot to take time out of his or her busy schedule for me? Shyness can be a big obstacle to your success, so we urge you to take steps to overcome it. Use your campus resources (see Chapter 11): attend an assertiveness training workshop, take a speech class, get some counseling. In general, you can develop self-confidence by taking a series of small, gradually more difficult steps: next time ask your roommate for two computer disks.

Forward thinking students will develop a network of contacts:

1.   Experts who can provide information or assistance;
2   Successful professionals who can advise you on your career path;
3.   Persons in power who can open doors and give you job leads;
4.   Mentors who can do a little of all three plus provide general support as well.

Information and Assistance

One of the best ways to learn about a field or a particular profession is to talk with experts who are leaders in that area. We told you how to go about doing that in Chapter 3. We think it's a good idea to keep track of these folks by entering them in your address book. As your list grows over the years, you'll find that your wallet-sized book won't accommodate everybody. Or you won't be able to remember exactly what type of information this particular person can provide. At some point you'll want to organize your list of contacts better.

So you get a larger address book or index-card file box which you keep in your office. (Students can have offices too, even if they consist only of a well-organized desk in a dormitory room.) Now, in addition to addresses and phone numbers, you'll start to keep a little information about this person -- the dates when you talked and what you talked about, the person's position or title, and what organization the person is affiliated with. An alternative method of keeping this information is to maintain an electronic file.

Experts can be business leaders or professors. They may be other students. They can be friends of your family or members of your church or temple. You may need information about a prospective career, about a topic for a term paper, or the best place to stay at Ft. Lauderdale over spring break. The important thing is they have the information you need.

Helpful people can also provide assistance; how to solve a physics problem, a loan to tide you over for the last couple weeks of a school term, the key resource book you need to write your term paper. They can be a part of your overall support system.

Career Advice

We may be splitting hairs here, but we think advice is more complex and personal than mere information. Experienced professionals can do more than tell you the facts of their field. They can use their wisdom and experience to guide and advise you on your career journey. This doesn't mean you're obliged to follow every suggestion, but you should consider what a seasoned professional has to say. "Study Abroad: don't leave college without it." "Join Toastmasters. It'll pay off more than you can imagine." "Consider starting out in sales, especially if you DON'T plan a career in that area." As you can, see each of these pieces of advice are more than information. These veterans are sharing of themselves, basing their advice on their experience in the school of hard knocks.

Job Leads

As you will see in Chapter 13, contacts can tell you where the jobs are. This includes "permanent" positions with a company or the time-limited projects which we believe will be the norm in the 21st Century. Our research suggests that truly permanent jobs are going to be rare. Most career experts believe that contacts already are the best way to find a good job -- "permanent" or project. Of course, it is important that you build your network of contacts all along the way so that you can call on them when it's time to look for a job.

Opening Doors

Experts are frequently in positions of power, and it is a huge plus to have powerful people on your side. If it's nice to get a lead on a good job, it's even nicer when someone with clout will recommend you highly for that job. And it's nicer still when such a person actually hires you. Similarly, it's a great help when someone can pave the way for a loan to start up your small business. And it's best of all when that person himself will agree to be your financial backer.

Getting loans and full-time jobs probably seem remote to you at this point. There's a sense in which that's true. It is highly unlikely that you'll need a business loan any time soon. Nor will you likely apply for a full-time, professional level job for a while. You will still need help from people if you want to get the most out of college, which is to say that you need connections starting right now.

In part, you're laying the foundation for future success by reaching out to people as a freshman. As you near graduation you'll be asking professors for recommendations. Whom will you ask? If you haven't cultivated some good working relationships with teaching faculty, how will they be able to recommend you enthusiastically? Of course, you'll also want some professionals from your chosen field to say nice things about you. If you haven't connected with anyone during internships and co-op work, who will you have in your court?

It is far too common for students to wait until their senior year to start this process, but by then it's too late. You need to start building connections as a freshman. Plus, these connections will start paying off long before you get your diploma. Consider some of the following situations:

You're an officer on your hall council. You need to get a faculty member to speak at an evening program. Whom will you ask?

Your financial aid check was eaten by the computer, but the bursar's office will put a hold on your registration if you don't pay them. Who will intervene on your behalf?

You haven't managed your finances too well, and you need to get some part-time work on campus. Who will give you some leads?

You're applying for a job as a resident advisor. Who knows you well enough to write a strong recommendation?

Your sorority needs an advisor. It's your job to sign one up.

Contacts don't have to be big shots or geezers. It's helpful to have good working relationships with other students too. You should know someone in every course you take who will share lecture notes if you have to miss class. Getting dates, rushing a fraternity, getting tickets to a ball game or concert -- other students can help, but only if you know them. *This is particularly important if you're a commuter.* Moreover, other students can connect you with faculty and professionals who can help you solve a variety of problems.

> *In part, you're laying the foundation for future success by reaching out to people as a freshman.*

Mentors

If you can put all of these roles together and add some personal interest in your success, you've got a mentor. Highly successful people often point to a key teacher or leader who advised, guided, supported, and pushed them on their way. Plato had Socrates. Aristotle had Plato. Bill Curry, head football coach at Kentucky, was coached over the course of his playing carer by Bobby Dodd, Vince Lombarbi, and Don Shula. If you're not a sports fan, that's analogous to learning music from Mozart, writing from Shakespeare, or chemistry from Madam Curie.

One of the best ways to learn something is by watching an expert do it right. Psychologists call this vicarious learning, and it's something you want to get as much of as is possible. Just think what it would be like for a budding engineer to apprentice to a Leonardo da Vince, a novice manager to work for a Colin Powell, a beginning nurse to follow a Florence Nightingale on her rounds. Obviously, not everyone can study at the feet of a master, but just about everyone can find teachers and leaders who are farther along the road to success than they are themselves. It could be a professor or dean. It could be an employer. It might be the senior down the hall who's the top pre-med on campus or who's already a successful student entrepreneur.

But how do you get these people to help out little old you? We're glad you asked that. Listen up, because we're going to tell you.

Steps in Forming A Mentor Relationship

1. *Show them you're committed to success.* Before people take you on as a pro'tege', they want to know that you're a winner. You've got to convince them you're got the talent and drive to make spending time with you worth their while.

Representatives from student organizations often make requests of professors, civic leaders, and people in business. Will you teach our fraternity pledge class study skills? Can you give a talk on investment banking to our professional association? Could you conduct a resume workshop for our organization?

Even if they're not particularly critical, we have observed that professionals automatically form impressions of every student who makes the request and handles the arrangements. Does the student ask far enough ahead of time for the expert to clear his schedule? If not, the professional will assume the student doesn't know how to manage his time. He will also resent the implication that he, the professional, has so little to do that, of course, he can adjust his schedule at the last minute for the convenience of the student.

Has the student thought through her request carefully enough so that she can state it clearly? Notice the difference between: A.) Our group has a lot of liberal arts majors. Last year's seniors didn't do very well at finding good jobs. Could you talk to us about how we could improve our chances? and B.) We need someone to talk to us about getting good jobs.

An expert will have a much better chance of delivering a timely, relevant message to group A than to Group B. She will also be inclined to regard the representative of group A as brighter, more conscientious, and more mature.

Do the students follow through? Do they meet the speaker when she gets there? Do they have the overhead slide projector ready to go? Did they take the trouble to drum up a crowd? Do they send a letter of thanks? Is it well written?

Since so many students fail to observe minimal standards of professional courtesy, you have to behave truly abysmally to distinguish yourself as a real loser. For the same reason, it is easy to show yourself to be a winner. By simply being considerate of the professionals you deal with, you stand out.

Every college class you take provides you with an opportunity to demonstrate to a professor that you've got the "right stuff." Turning in quality work is an obvious first step, but don't stop there. Attend class and be punctual. Perhaps most important is that you participate in class. No, don't speak up just to hear yourself talk, but do contribute to the class discussion. If you don't understand something, ask for an explanation. An intelligent question usually gets a good answer. It also shows that you were intelligent for asking the question. Come prepared. If you've read yesterday's class notes and today's chapter, you're more prepared than most students. But your professors won't know this unless you speak up.

> **Every college class you take provides you with an opportunity to demonstrate to a professor that you've got the "right stuff."**

Many of you are attending large state universities and community colleges. Classes often have several hundred students in them. Graduating seniors sometimes can't identify a single professor who knows them well enough to write a decent recommendation. Don't get caught in that predicament. If you go to a big school, make it a point for at least one professor in your field to know you well and to think well of you.

You accomplish this by making an A and writing the best term paper or final exam the prof ever saw. At least that's what you try for. This should also be the class that you never miss and you're always prepared for. And no matter how shy you are, force yourself to participate in class discussions. You may not be someone with a 1300 SAT score and a 3.7 GPA. If you're working your way through school, you may not have much time for your studies. But surely you can concentrate doubly hard on at least one class.

Our university provides various ways for students to get to know professors. Every quarter hundreds of students "Take a Prof to Lunch" for just $5. Others participate in a "Faculty Friends" program. On the other hand, there are thousands who do neither. Nor do they stay after class to pursue a topic, show up at the various lecture series, or drop by a professor's office for advice.

When I (Bill) was in professional school, there was an especially engaging and eminent professor from whom I wanted to learn more. Some of my fellow students shared my interest in having more contact with this person. We asked him if he would have lunch with us so we could talk. He graciously consented. This grew into a tradition. Several times a year we would gather in my tiny efficiency apartment and pepper Dr. Harvey with questions. It was one of the most stimulating educational experiences I've ever had in my life. Some years later it was Dr. Harvey whom I asked to recommend me for my PhD program. In his letter of recommendation he introduced me to the admissions committee by noting that I had started the lunch and learn group.

The same principles apply on the job. Remember Chapter 6. Whether you're co-oping, interning, or working part-time -- show someone in power that you're blue-chip material. No, not by apple-polishing, brown-nosing, or toadying. As the saying goes, "You do it the old-fashioned way. You earn it." You earn it by showing up on time every day, working hard, and volunteering for extra work.

2. *Make it worth their while*. When you search for a mentor, you're looking for someone who will teach you, guide you, and help you. It's nice if someone volunteers for the job, but most people you'd want to learn from are busy, busy, busy. Usually they'll help you if you help them. Generally it's up to you to take the first step.

Volunteer to assist your prospective mentor with his work. Many professors do research and could use someone to tally scores or collate data. Out on the job, managers, project engineers, head nurses, etc., can generally use a helping hand. And so can presidents of sororities, professional societies, and student governments.

When you do volunteer to help, do your best. Do a bang-up job. Go the second mile. Demonstrate some loyalty.

3. *Expect the relationship to evolve gradually*. It usually takes a while for a mentor to warm up to you enough to take you under her wing. And after a solid relationship is established, it should continue to evolve. As you learn more and more from your mentor, you should gradually be accorded greater responsibility. The idea is to work toward becoming a colleague, not a lackey.

It sometimes happens that your prospective mentor doesn't want to take you on. No matter how hard you try, (s)he brushes you off . Try not to take it personally. Maybe (s)he's too busy, (s)he's already mentoring too many other aspiring students, or (s)he's just not a very helpful person.

At some point, your persistence becomes bullheadedness, and you're better off trying with someone else. Not everyone can have Bill Gates or Donald Trump for a mentor. Nor is the biggest big shot around necessarily your best prospect. Generally, a less prominent person has more time to give and a better disposition for doing so.

As you become more successful yourself, don't forget all the help you got along the way. We think one of the best ways to show your gratitude is by helping those who are just starting their own journey.

SUMMARY

1. It's to your advantage to have a network of contacts.
2. It's up to you to build the network.
3. Start your freshman year.
4. Establish relationships with successful people by showing them you're committed to success and by helping them.
5. Cultivate relationships with professors, professionals in your field, and other students.
6. You can find helpful people in many places, including: classes, professional organizations, campus activities, and at work.
7. Develop a filing system for keeping track of your contacts.
8. If possible, find a mentor who will help guide you on your road to success.

Networking Exercise

There is an urban myth around that you're within seven phone calls of contacting anyone in the world. Supposedly all you have to do is contact one particular someone, they call someone they know, and so forth. By the time seven people have been called, the last one in line should know the person you originally identified.

That's kind of how you go about searching for jobs, contacts, and favorable recommendations. You go out looking to see who knows who.

Fill out the tally list below. I personally know a particular person working in the following field(s) and could call upon them, <u>by name</u>, if needed:

Mark your answers in pencil.

✓ Investment Counselor	_____ Optical Engineer ✓
✓ Landscape Architect	_____ Nuclear Engineering ✓
✓ Accountant	✓ Chemist
_____ Real Estate Sales ✓	_____ Transportation Engineer ✓
✓ Contractor/Builder	✓ Tech Alum working for a major corp.
✓ Computer Scientist	✓ Statistician
_____ Urban Planner ?	✓ Physician
✓ Real Estate Developer	✓ Banker
✓ Mechanical Engineer	_____ Ceramic Engineer ✓
_____ Personnel Director ✓	✓ User-friendly tutor
✓ Law Officer	_____ Geologist ✓
✓ Lawyer	✓ Military Officer
_____ Architect ✓	_____ Systems Analyst
_____ Industrial Designer ✓	✓ Electrical Engineer
✓ Physicist ✓	✓ Advertiser
✓ Marketing Researcher	✓ Pilot
✓ Tech Alum who's an Entrepreneur *Randy Sah*	_____ Writer ✓
✓ Technical Sales	✓ Environmental Engineer
✓ Psychologist	_____ Foreign Service/
✓ Civil Engineer	Diplomatic Corps

When everyone in your group is finished, take out a pen and compare lists. Check off in **ink** the additional professional contacts possible if you use the resources available to you through your association with group members. Is there a difference between the number of people you knew and how many the group as a whole knew?

This is how it works. Now start building your list of associations.

But I Don't Know Who I Want To Be When I Grow Up!
and
How Do I Find a Mentor?
(Put a Check Beside Each of These Tasks You Do This Week)

A lot of students don't know what major to declare when first arriving. If that's true for you, you might want to try the following:

1. ☐ You probably have some ideas about what might be of interest. Call or go by the department(s) where you feel some attraction. Ask the secretary, or get "word" from another student to find out which professor(s) are the most likely to be willing to spend some time with a student.

2. ☐ Call this/these person(s) for an appointment.

3. ☐ Be punctual, and go **listen** to what they have to say about selecting a major, what experience you might want to collect in the near term, and what pre-requisites you may need to pursue a major in this area. If you have concerns, share them. If you're uncertain, share that.

4. ☐ Before you leave, thank this person for the time they spent with you. If you liked talking with them, ask if you might talk with them in the future if you have any other questions.

Always be nice to the secretaries. They don't have much power, but they do have influence. They don't have authority, but they are gate-keepers to those who do. Make friends with these very important and underappreciated members of the academic community. If you've been kind to them, they will remember it and reciprocate later when you might be in a "tight."

1. ☐ As you're taking classes this quarter, pay attention to the professors you have. Are there any that are outstanding in a positive way?

2. ☐ Go by and tell them you enjoy their class. (Anyone likes to hear this.) Tell them something specific, like, "I like the way you begin class everyday with a period for questions. That really get's my brain in gear and gets me thinking about some of issues of the day that are vital to our future."

3. ☐ Don't spend more than a few minutes with them unless you've been invited to. You don't want to be perceived as an annoyance.

4. ☐ Go back now and again, and ask where you can read more about something you discussed in class.

5. ☐ Visit this person about once a week, *briefly*. Bring them an interesting article you copied from the paper.

6. ☐ Do this with other professors and you will have a number of academic friends who will know you as more than your student ID number, and who will think of you when asked if they know of a student to be nominated for _____? They'll know you're the one!

133

Conducting an Informational Interview

1. A person I've selected to interview is: _____

    They work for: _____

    Their phone number is: _____ Their business address is: _____

    _____

    _____

2. Dress in appropriate business attire for your interview. Be respectful and use your best manners throughout. Arrive on time, and take a small notebook to take notes. Shake hands and introduce yourself with your oral resume.

3. Questions I might ask include:

    How did you get into this field?

    What level of education is presently necessary to excel in this area?

    What work environments do you work in, normally? (indoors/office, outside/on-site, indoors/laboratory)

    What does a "normal" work day look like for you?

    How many hours a week do you normally work?

    What salary range might an entry level person expect in this field?

    Is travel a necessary part of this work? If so, to where?

    What kinds of summer/co-op experiences should I seek to prepare me for work in this area? Might there be any opportunities for this with your firm?

    Who do you recommend I contact when I am ready to make application?

4. Thank your subject and leave when it seems appropriate. ALWAYS write a thank you note and mail to your subject within a week of your interview. _____
    (Date Sent)

5. I have placed the business card of this individual into my networking file with a short descriptor of when and under what circumstances I met him/her. _____ Yes _____ No

**Alumni: All the people who graduated from your institution.
Alumna: A female graduate of your institution.
Alumnus: A male graduate of your institution.**

The alumni of your institution may be willing to help students out in various ways. One way to help you get some idea of what your potential profession is about is to ask someone. Someone that may be willing to let you interview them, or spend a day on-the-job may be a member of your alumni. Go to your alumni association and ask if they have a formal mentor program? If not, do they have a list of local alumni who have identified themselves as being willing to speak with students? If neither of those, what about getting the names of a few alumni presently working in your area of interest so you may call them?

Alumni traditionally, are good sources for networking, job contacts and general information about your potential field of interest. If you can not meet with one, speak over the phone. Now is not too soon to begin your list of alumni contacts.

_____   _____
Phone Number of Your Alumni Assn.   Person you Contacted

_____   _____
Name of Person they Recommend you Call   Their Phone Number

_____
Date you Will Visit   Address

_____
Directions on How to Get There

_____

When you return from the interview, sit down immediately and write a summary of your visit. Who else did this person introduce you to? Did you remember to get their card? Write your benefactor a thank you note.

Write a three page essay on what you saw and learned by visiting this member of the alumni. What unexpected thing did you discover? Are your feelings about the job now different than before your visit? How helpful were the people at the Alumni Association? If you had it to do over again, what would you do differently? **Attach this sheet to the back of your essay.**

Planning for the Future

Where do you keep the business cards you collect? (You ARE collecting them aren't you?) Hopefully you keep them somewhere with short notes on the back side indicated what event or reason brought you together and the date.

When you get a card from a speaker at the Society of Women Engineers or when someone comes to make the keynote address for your Business Club Banquet, you should speak briefly with the person and get their card. You should also give them yours. That's right, yours. If you havent' got some yet, now's the time to get some made up. You already need them.

Your Name Goes Here in Bold P. O. Box Your College City, State, Zipcode PH: (XXX) 555-1234

Why on earth do you need business cards now? Are you planning to work after college? What about getting a summer job? Need a place to co-op? Maybe you need to interview someone for a class project? Part-time work while in school? These and other reasons mean you want to project the most business-like persona you possibly can. Be ready by having your cards made now and kept at-hand to exchange when the opportunity presents iteself.

It's a few months away, but what will you do with the upcoming summer? Now is not too soon to begin your job search. Open the yellow pages and identify the companies that work in your area of interest. Call them to ask for an informational interview? With who? Ask the person who answers the call who they think is the most considerate and kind person in helping others? Call three and then keep the appointments!

Name of Company	Person You Spoke With	Date of Interview
Name of Company	Person You Spoke With	Date of Interview
Name of Company	Person You Spoke With	Date of Interview

Go only to collect information, NOT to get a job. But, do ask if or how the company goes about identifying candidates for summer internships? Questions to ask:

- How did you get into this line of work?
- What is a typical work day like for you?
- Is an advanced degree required?
- What work experience should I seek now?

- What do you find most rewarding about it?
- What qualifications would I need to excel?
- What kinds of skills and experiences should I attempt to gather while in school?

Be **sure** to send your contact a thank you note (use their business card to get the correct address)!

Getting Connected to Campus

One of the principle reasons that students leave college during their freshman year, is because they are lonely. You are in charge of your destiny when it comes to this. For some of you it won't be a problem because you are so extraverted that you'd make friends while sitting in line to buy your auto tag. Some, however, have a more difficult time making friends and putting themselves in new situations. One important thing to remember about establishing new relationshships here at college, is that everyone else is doing the same thing. You won't stand out; you'll just be one of the many.

Your Student Government Adminstration (SGA), located in the Student Services Building, ground floor has booklets with all the names and faculty contacts for the different student groups meeting on the GT campus. Go by and look at or ask for one of these booklets. Select two groups that you will be interested in for social reasons, and two for professional reasons.

Social Organizations

_____	_____	_____
_____	_____	_____
Name of Organization	Day and Time of Meeting	Location of Meetings

Professional Organizations

_____	_____	_____
_____	_____	_____
Name of Organization	Day and Time of Meeting	Location of Meetings

Select one of each to actually attend.

1. Your assignment is to meet two new people at each function.

   Matt Rupert _____

   Eva Shen _____

        Name of New Person   Meeting I Met Him/Her At

2. One way to get to know people is to share information about yourself and listen to them. What is something you learned about each of these people while talking to them.

   _____

   _____

3. If you did not like one of the meetings, choose a different group to attend next week. There are potential friends all over campus, and organizations that do everything from feeding the elderly to hanging with the local _Dr. Who_ fans. You can opt to be a part of the Greeks, or you can join the organization that changes student life by being a part of the SGA. But, **you** are in charge. You get to decide what you will do, and if you will do it. It's worth it to try. Keep at it until you do find the group of people you enjoy hanging with.

9
What Makes
Achievers Tick?

Successful people are achievers, but what makes them go? Great **tomes** have been written on the psychology of achievement. We believe all this material can be boiled down to one short sentence: achievers are goal directed. Goal and Direction. Let's take a look at each.

GOALS

1. Achievers set goals. They aim for excellence: building a better "widget," writing an A term paper, instilling a love of learning in first-graders.

2. Achievers set *clear* goals. There is a difference between dreams and plans. Anyone can fantasize about fame and fortune, but a plan requires concrete, specific objectives to shoot for. The most effective people take the trouble to make their goals clear. Too many students say, "I'm going to get a lot of studying done this weekend," or "I want to make it big in the business world." The true achievers more likely say, "I'm going to study history for two hours Saturday morning and work math problems for two hours on

> **Anyone can fantasize about fame and fortune, but a plan requires concrete, specific objectives to shoot for.**

Sunday afternoon," or "I'm going to major in electrical engineering so I can eventually develop computer hardware." When you set clear goals, you can tell whether you're really making progress. If you are, success is a powerful motivator. If not, you can adjust your plans.

3. Achievers set *realistic* goals. Their goals demand talent and effort, but they are do-able. The most successful people don't generally take long shots. They don't depend on luck. Achievers like a challenge with some risk, but not the probability of failure.

One way psychologists have studied achievement is to watch subjects compete at a ring-toss game. If points are awarded based on distance from the target, players who throw from medium range almost always win the most points. They also reveal the highest drive for success on other measures. And, most importantly they tend to be the best students, the most effective salespeople, the most successful entrepreneurs.

Underachievers go after ridiculously easy goals or impossibly difficult ones. Achievers like a challenge, but they don't want to be overwhelmed. They aim for goals of moderate difficulty. Then, as soon as they reach them, they set their sights one notch higher.

4. Achievers set long-term, intermediate, and short-term goals. Successful entrepreneurs often have five-year plans, quarterly goals, and a weekly calendar. The best students operate similarly. The Four-Year Master Plan (Appendix 1) is an example of long-term and medium-range objectives. The section on time management in Chapter 3 covers all three types of goals.

DIRECTION

Direction implies action, movement, getting things done, making things happen. The director of a movie, more than anyone else, determines the quality of the film. A director is in charge.

Achievers are also in charge. They don't wait passively for success to come their way. They strive to reach their goals. Here's how:

1. Achievers think a lot about their goals and how to reach them. They daydream about them, juggling strategies and weighing alternatives. Since they think about how to reach their goals so much of the time, they come up with a lot of shortcuts, improvements, and better methods.

Just about everyone dreams of success. The true achievers go one step farther - they dream how to make it happen!

2. Achievers plan. They're more time conscious. They set objectives and deadlines on paper and keep score of how they're doing. This is why we urge you to use daily to-do lists and to map out your assignments for an entire semester.

3. Achievers prioritize. Working hard and getting lots of things done may not be enough if you neglect something important. It's getting the most important things done that makes you truly successful.

4. Achievers take it step by step. They implement the good plans they make. They break up large tasks into smaller ones, A year-long project can be divided into a series of shorter deadlines. A college education can be divided into four years, each year into semesters, each semester into weeks. A term paper can be similarly chopped up into manageable tasks.

5. Achievers overcome barriers. When they run into roadblocks, they keep trying till they find a way to get around them. Naturally, they can get discouraged too, but they bounce back from defeat rather than letting it keep them down. If personal shortcomings hold them back, they

find a way to compensate or they change. They never wait to be rescued. They actively seek out expert help whenever it's needed to get the job done.

One of our greatest satisfactions is watching college students develop. We've seen country bumpkins overcome their lack of sophistication. We've seen shy students join clubs so they can learn to conduct a meeting. We've known pre-meds who managed to eke out B's in calculus because they studied overtime and hired a tutor.

Successful people come in all shapes and sizes. One thing they have in common is that they don't easily take "no" for an answer. They're not quick to throw in the towel. They encounter their share of setbacks, but they keep on keeping on.

We recall one young woman from a rural background whose father had died when she was a child. Her mother discouraged her from applying to a competitive college. She filled out the forms by herself and also applied for financial aid. When she arrived on campus, she felt out of place, and she had to struggle to survive in class. Her boyfriend kept after her to transfer to the junior college in her hometown. Besides, who needed a college degree? She could always clerk in the local dime store. With some difficulty, she broke things off with her old boyfriend. She joined a study group, and that helped her with her grades. She got counseling to improve her self-confidence. She had to work part-time to make ends meet. At first, she waited tables, but eventually she did drafting for a small engineering company. She finally managed to graduate and began working full-time for the same firm.

It wasn't a very good job. Her attempts at finding a better one didn't lead to much, so she got help from her college's career planning center. She developed a better job search plan and improved her resume. She was discouraged to discover she was no longer eligible to set up interviews through the campus placement center. But she didn't give up. She began dropping by the placement office at noon and started having lunch with the corporate recruiters. Within a few months she had been invited to interview with several companies. She received several offers and accepted the one she felt was best for her.

We are proud to know this woman who was born into near poverty. Her family and friends advised her against pursuing her dreams. She made mistakes, and she encountered innumerable barriers to success. But she didn't give up.

Today, she is an engineer for a Fortune 500 corporation. She designs radar systems for supersonic aircraft.

IT'S ALL UP TO YOU

There is a ten-word phrase which contains the secret of your success. Just to make it more challenging, each of the ten words is a two-letter word. The fifth and tenth words rhyme. Can you create the phrase? The phrase appears at the end of this chapter.

If you want success you've got to believe it's up to you to go out and get it.

Who determines your destiny? You? Or is your future controlled by forces outside yourself? Your answer to these questions have a powerful influence on what you accomplish. If you believe you control your future, psychologists say you have an internal "locus of control." If you believe you're a passive victim to what fate brings, they say you possess an external "locus of control."

We believe the foundation of all achievement lies in believing that planning and effort can influence the future. So, are you the kind of person who lays plans to open a business in five years? Or do you figure, "Why bother? Something will go wrong. It always does." Can you pass up the Monday Night Movie in order to fine tune your resume? Or do you think, "It's not worth it. You've got to have connections to work for that company. Do you study harder after a bad grade? Or do you say, "It doesn't do any good to prepare for that teacher's tests anyway."

HOW TO GET MORE GO

Chances are, you believe you can strongly influence your own future. You probably are the kind of person who is motivated to achieve or you wouldn't have read this far. But suppose you're not. You might be reading this chapter because it's required for a course. And now you're convinced that you're very externally oriented and have very little in common with achievers. Well, don't despair. You can change.

Research psychologist George Burris taught underachieving college students some of the same principles we've outlined in this chapter. In just one semester he got results. Achievement motivation scores went up, and so did grades. Another psychologist, Richard DeCharms, worked with teachers of disadvantaged children. He emphasized that they work to develop an internal locus of control in their students. And the students' grades improved significantly.

DeCharms has developed an innovative way of thinking about power and achievement. He says people tend to be either Pawns or Origins. Pawns are passive, generally acted upon, and don't have much control over their future. Origins, on the other hand, actively determine what happens to them.

You can take the Pawn analogy one step further - individuals can be compared to the pieces in the game of chess. A pawn is the least powerful piece. Basically, a pawn can move straight ahead, one square at a time. It enjoys very little choice or power. When confronted with an obstacle, it can only wait until the obstacle is removed.

If however, a pawn is passed all the way to the end of the board, it can be exchanged for a queen. A queen can move vertically, horizontally, or diagonally. It can go forward or backward for as many squares as there are on the board. Talk about controlling your own destiny! The queen has the whole board to play with. The pawn has just one square.

Suppose a queen mistakenly thought she was a pawn. Her choices would be drastically limited. Conversely, if a pawn started acting like a queen, the sky would be the limit.

Why do some people become pawns and others become queens? Why do some students feel powerless to influence their futures, while others are convinced their efforts can make a difference?

Any kind of oppression undermines the development of motivation. Oppression can be blatant, like racism or poverty. It can be as subtle as overprotective parents. But it's too late to change where you grew up or how your parents raised you.

> **So what can you do if you want to achieve more? First, as simple as it sounds, you've got to believe that your own efforts make a difference.**

So what can you do if you want to achieve more? First, as simple as it sounds, you've got to believe that your own efforts make a difference.

If we haven't convinced you, please talk to a counselor. Virtually all counselors are committed to helping their clients become more independent, more in charge of their own lives.

Second, follow the suggestions in this book. We didn't pull them out of a hat. Our ideas come directly from the experts on achievement motivation, such as Harvard's David McClelland. Look at the Table of Contents. Every chapter has to do with planning, organizing, developing skills, using resources, and setting goals.

We can't make you follow our suggestions, but we urge you to try them. They work. Your performance will improve. You'll taste success. And success breeds success. We guarantee it. Here's a way to assess your own motive to achieve.

QUICK-SCORING ACHIEVEMENT MOTIVATION QUIZ

	Points		Score

1.
   0   I have no clear goals in life.

   1   I have a general idea of a career in which I want to succeed.

   2   I set daily objectives which advance me toward my long-term goals.

   3   I set daily, weekly, and quarterly goals which will advance me toward my long-term goals.

                                                           _____

2.
   0   I'm too proud to accept help, no matter how stuck or lost I get.

   1   I will accept help, but only when it's offered.

   2   I actively seek out expert help whenever I get stuck or lost.

   3   I am acquainted with most campus resources and regularly use them without becoming dependent upon them.

 _____

3.
   0   I tend to give up after the first setback.

   1   I eventually bounce back from a setback after a period of immobilization.

   2   I analyze my setbacks instead of kicking myself or blaming others.

   3   A setback inspires me to try again, using new methods if needed.

 _____

4.
   0   My fantasies about career success are limited to scenes from Lifestyles of the Rich and Famous.

   1   My fantasies about career success include practical details of my future world of work.

   2   My fantasies about career success include thinking about steps I can take on a daily basis.

   3   My fantasies about career success include long-range, intermediate, and daily plans to reach my goals.

 _____

5.
   0   Most of my goals are so high that I seldom reach them or so low that I reach them with very little effort.

   1   At least some of my goals are moderately difficult - high enough to challenge me but low enough not to overwhelm me with anxiety.

   2   Most of my goals are moderately difficult.

   3   Most of my goals are moderately difficult, and I increase their difficulty as I reach them.

 _____

TOTAL   _____

Scoring:

0 Points	If you don't crawl out from under the doormat and start moving, you will be overwhelmed in the 21st Century.
1-5 Points	You're taking the first steps toward success. Still a ways to go though.
6-10 Points	You're on the way, but watch out - success can be addictive.
11-15 Points	The stuff of champions. You're on your way to succeeding in the 21st Century.

THE SECRET OF YOUR SUCCESS:

IF IT IS TO BE, IT IS UP TO ME.

10
When the Going Gets Tough

Time for a check-up. Please complete the survey in Appendix 2. This survey is an instrument that we have developed right here at Georgia Tech. It was developed as a means to try and identify those students who exhibit habits and attitudes that contribute to a profile inconsistent with success. That is, we're trying to find out who is going to have some difficulty here. Now, we know that YOU aren't one of those students, but it's always good to be certain. Answer the questions as honestly as you can so that your score is a genuine reflection of you. It does no good to go to the hospital and have an x-ray taken of the leg that's killing you with pain, but which only shows what you WISH your bones looked like. The doctors would not be able to determine what the problem was and would not be able to help you. Same concept applies here. We take our mission seriously and want very much for students to succeed here. We know you have what it takes. We know that you aspire to great things. Let's work together to make sure you can get to that destination: graduation!

Now, what does your score mean? And why are we asking you to take a look at your own "hardiness quotient?" The answer to the second question is probably obvious to you. Reflect for a minute on the issues you'll be facing in the 21st Century: a rapid pace, constant change, information overload, dealing with people unlike yourself, uncharted career paths, and enormous societal problems. Everyone of these phenomena can be stressful, but change -- rapid, constant change -- is, we believe, the reality underlying all of these issues. You'll be expected to produce more in less time. You must constantly be learning new skills. You must acquire the facility of working comfortably with an incredibly diverse work force. Whatever job security you possess will come from your own resourcefulness and expertise. And you'll have to deal with international terrorism, urban violence, and global warming. The next Century is not for the faint of heart!

Since you don't have any other century available to you, you'd best gear up. Here's what we know about resilience and coping with change.

In the 1970's, Salvatore Maddi and Suzanne Kobasa studied executives undergoing stress. More specifically, they studied a group of managers and executives in a large corporation which was undergoing reorganization. Reorganization means many jobs will change, and more than a few will be lost. In companies that reorganize, morale goes down and anxiety goes up. Will I have to change jobs? Will I have to let good people go? Will I be out on the street myself?

During such a period, more people tend to get sick. They get more colds and cases of influenza. They get more migraines and back aches. And they have more ulcers and heart attacks. That's the bad news. The good news is that not everybody is equally vulnerable. Maddi and Kobasa found that some individuals were "psychologically hardy." These hardy individuals were sick less often and bounced back sooner after their illness. What makes them tick?

The hardy executives were different than their vulnerable colleagues in several important ways. They viewed change differently. They were more involved in their work. They felt a greater sense of control over their own lives. Everybody in the organization was subjected to stress, but the hardy executives looked at the stress in ways that somehow protected them from its **noxious** effects.

Specifically, the hardy executives regarded the change as a challenge. Their more vulnerable colleagues regarded it as a threat. The hardy executives were confronted daily with tough decisions to make, brush fires to put out, and troops to rally. They responded by committing themselves to the tasks at hand. They immersed themselves in their work, got more done, yet paradoxically, felt less drained.

If you've read this far, you're probably serious about preparing for the 21st Century. You want a secure future, and this book tells you how to do it. Just remember, career fulfillment is made up of may things. Money and prestige are only two of them. Don't make the mistake of majoring in Pre-Wealth! At least not to the exclusion of everything else.

Howard Hughes's billions didn't prevent him from being miserable. Phil Donahue's examination of life in a wealthy Texas suburb on network TV revealed a depressing emptiness behind the facade of expensive cars and designer clothes.

Occasionally, students ask us which branch of engineering offers the highest salaries. A few of these students want to choose their life's work on the basis of dollars alone. Actually, this doesn't even make good financial sense. The demand for graduates in different fields changes from year to year. Right now chemical engineering is hot. It may not be ten years from now. How ironic it would be to commit to a field you hate and have it dry up on you before you turn thirty.

Besides, extrinsic rewards less often foster creative results than intrinsic ones. Research by Brandeis University's Teresa Amabile indicates that being interested in your work may be the single most important factor in a creative outcome. And it is the creative results that bring in top dollar. So learn to live with the following paradox: working only for money often stifles creativity; yet creativity is usually rewarded monetarily. We think it's smart to consider the financial prospects a field offers, but not to the exclusion of everything else. Find work that you like. It will pay off in many ways.

> *Find work that you like. It will pay off in many ways.*

Focusing solely on the steps of your career ladder tends to produce tunnel vision. In today's rapidly changing world you need a broader view in order to be successful in your profession and in life.

You need the liberal arts, social sciences, and fine arts as well as business and technical knowledge. You need more then smarts - you need wisdom.

If it's unwise to equate success with income, it is equally unwise to make your self-worth equal to you success. To do so breeds fear of failure, and that undermines your willingness to take risks. If you can't respect yourself after a failure, you can expect anxiety, depression, and stress as your constant companions. Some students panic when they first see the Four-Year Master Plan (Appendix 1). How can they possibly get everything done? They feel overwhelmed.

Remember, there is no "must" in the Master Plan. You don't have to do any of it. If you manage to pull off half of it, you're probably well ahead of most other college students. The Master Plan is not an end in itself; it's only a set of guidelines. And when all is said and done they boil down to a few practical suggestions: Get organized. Whether you study five hours a week or twenty-five, use the most effective techniques. Clarify your goals. Get some work experience. Make some contacts. Use your campus resources. Learn how to find a job.

You can be competitive without becoming hooked on competition for its own sake. Some of you may prefer being a bigger fish in a smaller pond. Is an Ivy League degree really worth it if you have to wreck your family's finances to get it? Not everyone is necessarily happier at Microsoft than at Joe's Electronics. There are successful graduates who go into law, medicine, and engineering. Others join the Peace Corps, teach public school or enter social work. Still others practice their craft in an artist's studio or on a stage.

STRESS MANAGEMENT CHECKLIST

1. Manage you time and organize your things - two sure ways to reduce your headaches and save your stomach lining.

2. Don't spread yourself too thin. See number 3.

3. Learn to say "no." See number 2.

4. Cultivate friends as well as contacts.

5. Participate in at least one extracurricular activity because you enjoy it, not because it's going to pay off down the road.

6. Do something fun every day.

7. Exercise regularly. The busier you are, the more important this one is.

8. Eat sensibly.

9. Get enough sleep.

10. Learn to relax. We've included instructions at the end of this chapter for Deep Muscle Relaxation and Guided Imagery, but biofeedback, yoga, and mediation are also effective tension reducers for most people.

Read this checklist every day for a week.
Read it every week for a month.
Read it every month for a year.
Repeat as needed.

Recently we heard a psychologist refer to the very competitive university where he worked as a Type-A factory. Type-A individuals are goal directed, driven people who get a lot done, but find it difficult to relax. They are also heart attack prone.

Recent research by health psychologist Margaret Chesney, however, suggested that it is possible to be achievement oriented without the heart attack. The key is in your attitude. Anger and hostility seem to be much more injurious to your heart than ambition and hard work. The most deadly combination of all is the Type A who is unassertive and very angry. This person is too passive to get his/her own way very often, so s/he spends a lot of time feeling frustrated and mad. And because s/he lacks the ability to express him- or herself assertively, s/he has no constructive way of communicating pent-up feelings.

It would appear, then, that you can strive toward your goals if you're flexible about doing so. Frequent frustration and anger are the tip-offs that you're not keeping things in perspective. *If college life seems too hectic, see a counselor.*

In Conclusion, we offer two final bits of advice. Repeat them whenever the stress starts to mount:

DON'T SWEAT THE SMALL STUFF.

IT'S ALL SMALL STUFF!

Deep Muscle Relaxation Instructions

Find a quiet place and get into a comfortable position. Your bed or an easy chair is usually conducive to relaxing. Take your time when you practice DMR. Hurrying defeats the purpose. After you get more skilled at relaxing you can learn to speed the technique up. Most people get better results if they close their eyes while practicing this technique.

The entire exercise should take ten or more minutes, but with practice you can learn to relax in seconds.

1. Make tight fists out of both your hands. Study the tension in your hands. Now, let it go. Allow every muscle fibre in your hands to grow limp and calm. Notice that we say "allow." You can't really relax by trying harder.	2. Repeat this pattern with each muscle group in your body. Next, do your fore arms. 3. Upper arms. 4. Shoulders and neck. 5. Forehead. 6. Eyes. 7. Lips. 8. Jaw.	9. Chest. 10. Abdomen. 11. Upper legs. 12. Lower legs. 13. Feet.

Guided Imagery Instructions

Find a quiet, comfortable place and close your eyes. Imagine that you're resting securely on a beautiful, deserted beach. Beyond the white sand is azure water with gentle, rolling waves. Feel the warmth of the sun on your skin, the caress of the breeze in your hair, the grainy texture of the sand between your toes. Relax. Listen to the sound of the surf. Watch the rhythm of the waves as they rise and fall. Take in a deep breath of fresh air and relax deeply as you exhale. Notice a flock of gulls hovering above the waves. Study the slow, graceful movement of the wings of one of the birds. Watch the bird's wings gradually slow down. Yet it stays airborne, seemingly without effort. Become as relaxed as the bird.

Again the entire fantasy should take ten or more minutes. Following DMR with a relaxing mental scene often deepens the sense of calm, so experiment with combining the two methods. Practice is, of course, essential. Remember, relaxation isn't a luxury. It's a necessity. Money and position mean very little if you're not healthy.

Using Relaxation Techniques Situationally

Relax by using DMR or imagery. Once you're calm and tension free, you can prepare for any stressful task, such as a test or important interview. Simply imagine yourself handling the test effectively. Should you start to feel any tension or anxiety, redirect your attention to the beach scene (or whatever scene is most relaxing to you) until you regain your composure. Keep repeating until you can easily imagine yourself handling the task in question.

On the day of the test, be sure to show up at class on time. While the test is being passed out, quietly relax using the techniques you've mastered. Should you get flustered or find your mind racing during the test, simply pause and take a couple of minutes to relax.

SUMMARY

1. Plan a career that interests and challenges you. Money is an important consideration, but not the only one.
2. Don't equate external success with internal fulfillment.
3. Make the principles embodied in the Stress Management Checklist an integral part of your life.
4. The Master Plan is a set of guidelines, not the Ten Commandments.
5. It is not ambition that causes heart attacks, but unbridled ambition.
6. Learn Deep Muscle Relaxation and/or Guided Imagery.
7. Learn how to apply these relaxation techniques situationally.
8. If you feel you are under too much stress, get some help. See a counselor.

11
Your Secret Goldmine:
Campus Resources

A s you think about the many challenges that lie ahead it's easy to feel overwhelmed. How are you going to cope with everything? In particular, how are you going to cope with everything all by yourself? We have some good news for you. While it's true that your destiny is in your hands, you don't really have to prepare for 21st Century all by yourself.

Imagine that scattered around your campus are several large boxes with cash. Whenever your funds run low, you're free to drop by one of these handy mini-banks and help yourself. That's right, all you have to do is scoop up enough fives and tens to keep you in cheeseburgers and books for another month.

You'd expect these financial "free lunch" dispensers to get a lot of use, wouldn't you? Who could possibly be so dense as to miss out on such an opportunity? Yet agencies doling out thousands of dollars worth of services are often passed over by the majority of college students.

Ah, but that's different, you say. Money is money. Deans and counselors are somehow less appealing. Maybe so, but reflect for a moment on what money really is. You can't eat it or wear it. It doesn't even burn well enough to keep you warm. But you can trade it for food, clothing, and fuel. And also for books and tuition. Or for legal or medical advice. Or tutoring or psychotherapy. Or any of a dozen other services designed to help you succeed now and in the 21st Century. And as your 21st Century array of skills grows, any number of employers will pay you lots of money so that you can choose to buy whichever goods and services your heart desires.

As you gear up for the 21st Century, don't pass up free help. Take advantage of every opportunity and resource in your environment which will advance you toward your goals. Most high achievers do. Go back and review chapter 8 for detailed information on becoming an achiever. For now, trust us that this chapter is worth your while.

Most students are surprised when they learn about all the services that are available to them. We recommend that, at your earliest convenience, you carefully review your student handbook or the appropriate section of your college catalog. Then start using your campus resources. And if you school doesn't offer a service that you need, see if you can find it elsewhere. Remember, it's up to you to get whatever help you require to succeed. Nobody is going to rescue you.

PRIMARY RESOURCES

Library Services

The computer is transforming the way the modern library does its business. On-line databases have revolutionized traditional research techniques. Instead of wading through endless card files, going blind in front of the microfiche, and struggling through reference books the size of cinder blocks, you can do an instant information search by punching in a few keys words. Libraries can lease or purchase a database on just about any subject, including popular magazines, business and trade periodicals, scholarly abstracts, financial resources, conference proceedings, and high-tech journals. The databases may be available on compact disk or on the computer with the library's on-line catalog. Some libraries, such as the one at Northeast Missouri State University, link with others through an on-line cataloging system and provide access to almost unlimited information. The University of Georgia System, at the direction of Chancellor Stephen Portch, will soon have every on-line catalog at every institution available to every user throughout the system. But that is only the beginning. Through the Internet you can investigate library holdings at sites throughout the world.

> **Through the Internet you can investigate library holdings at sites throughout the world.**

The compact disc is another high-tech innovation that expedites data retrieval. Compact Disclosure is a compact disc system that provides most of the information contained in company annual reports. Many libraries offer instructional modules on videotape. And some provide assistance in writing term papers and offer seminars on research techniques. Increasingly, there are services and facilities for students with physical disabilities or language barriers.

Check with your library to see exactly what is available. Get to know a librarian or two. Don't enter the Information Age without one.

The College Catalog

Here is another storehouse of useful information. In fact, your college catalog is generally the actual legal contract that you have with your college or university. If you are ever uncertain about an exact rule or regulation, it is likely covered in your catalog. Keep your catalog from each year that you are in college. Why? Because over time, degree requirements change and rules are modified. Generally, you may graduate based on *any* catalog during the time you are enrolled continuously at a college. So, if you enroll in 1996 and in 1998 the requirements for the degree you've just spent two years working on change, you can opt to graduate under the 1996 catalog. This can be VERY important if the rest of "getting on with your life" is based on a specific graduation date, or if you find you might have to wait a year for a required course to be taught again!

Granted, the catalog is not exactly a page-turner, but you can save a lot of time and trouble if you use this resource regularly. Almost every day students ask us questions that they could easily answer themselves by checking their catalogs. One friend of ours is particularly keen on double-checking rules and regulations. She should be. She had to leave town just before her graduation. Several months later, she learned that she had not been granted a degree because she was short three courses. (There had been a miscommunication about her requirements.) But it was she, not her advisor, that had to pay the extra tuition to make up her work. Your school probably provides additional handbooks on student life and services as well. You should also take advantage of the information they contain.

Financial Aid

As long as the cost of a college education continues to rise, so will the need for financial aid. All the evidence points to the continuing escalation of costs. It costs to add necessary technical infrastructure (computers, software, networks) to your campus. For many years, colleges postponed necessary physical maintenance. Now, more than a few are saddled with buildings that are scarcely usable. Repairs are desperately needed. Asbestos must be removed. Facilities need to be added. Some of these costs will appear in tuition raises and housing fees.

There are three main types of aid--scholarships (or grants), loans, and student employment. They come from four different sources--colleges, the private sector, federal, and state governments. In general, most awards are based on need, but a fair number are based on merit (grades, athletics, musical talent, etc.). The trend recently has been to offer more loans and fewer scholarships.

It's possible to borrow a little over $17 thousand from the federal government for four years of undergraduate study. Currently the government subsidizes these loans by covering the interest which accrues while the student is in school. There is talk of eliminating this subsidy which would jack the cost up to nearly $21 thousand after four years.

Naturally, you'd rather avoid that much debt. So, don't sit on your hands. Try for scholarships. Apply early: Fall of your senior year in high school is best, but it's never too late. If you miss out one year, you can try for the following one. Talk with your financial aid office to find out what is offered by your school and how to apply for it. They maintain information on all federal and state programs and often have extensive files on funding from the private sector. By belonging to a particular religious, minority, special interest, or ethnic group, you may qualify for scholarships. But you'll never know what the criteria are unless you check them out.

When I (Joann) returned to college late in life, I made it a point to discuss my financial aid situation *prior* to beginning college. I came to know the financial aid director very well by stopping in and chatting now and again in a friendly way. About once or twice a quarter I'd stop by her office and just say, "Hello, how are you doing? Any new scholarship opportunities I need to know about?" Financial aid personnel are seldom visited unless there is a problem. They are more used to meeting hostile students than friends. If you make yourself their friend, you go a long way towards helping yourself. I financed a large portion of my undergraduate, and graduate education through merit-based scholarships, and some of them came from some pretty unusual sponsors. However, I was always happy to accept their financial support of my education. I recommend you always treat your financial aid personnel respectfully and in as friendly a way as possible. You need them on your side!

The Counseling Center

College life is hardly ever the four-year beer bust that the media portray. You might as well face the fact that college can be stressful. You could have a professor capable of sedating an insomniac. Your roommate might turn out to be Freddy Kruger. You're busier than you've ever been with less guidance than you've ever had. You're trying to break away from your parents, but you're still homesick. You have to make big-league decision about majors and careers, and you're competing against some pretty sharp cookies. Small wonder that, after drunk driving, suicide is the number-one killer of college students. Eating disorders are a problem for many coeds. Many women are coerced or forced into sexual experiences. This can precipitate a variety of psychological problems. Students of either gender may be confused about their sexual orientation. And many students needlessly suffer depression and anxiety, loneliness and guilt. We say needlessly because most colleges provide free psychological services for their students.

There still seems to be a stigma attached to getting counseling, but our impression is that there are two kinds of students -- those who can admit they need help and those who can't. This is not to say there are loads of emotional basket cases running around. Most students manage to get by. It's just that there's probably some kind of psychological service that can make life a lot easier for the vast majority of you. And the price is right because it's generally free. Once you graduate, therapy can easily run into thousands of dollars.

There is usually help for academic, vocational personal, and social problems. Services include individual and group counseling, testing and career information. Many universities provide couples' counseling whether you're married, living together, or just dating. Increasingly, computer-assisted instruction is available. (Two examples are SIGI for vocational decision making, put out by Educational Testing Services, and CASSI-GT, a study skills package put out by Georgia Tech.)

A staple of most counseling centers is outreach and psycho-education. Psycho-education is NOT education for psychos. It's psychological education for normal folks like you and us. Typical workshops and seminars include assertiveness, life-planning, dating skills, overcoming shyness, time-management, test anxiety reduction, study skills, career exploration, and self-esteem elevation. Some of these offerings provide great ways to develop marketable skills. Some make your life go a lot smoother. Others are simply stimulating and fun. If you haven't used the counseling center in some way before you graduate, you're probably cheating yourself.

New Student Orientation

College is different than high school. It is usually harder, bigger, and faster. You may be on your own for the first time. Or years may have passed since you last were a student, and you have less academic self-confidence than your professor has mercy. Aside from a few rules to keep, dormitories are marginally civilized, you can pretty much do what you want--including sleeping in, cutting classes, and never cracking a book--and no one will seem to care. If you flunk out, there will be another warm body to replace you. Isn't it obvious that you're better off knowing what to expect and how to cope with it?

In addition to handling college life, there is the matter of handling the particular college that you attend. Where are the buildings, the agencies, the administrators on your campus? And exactly what services are offered? What is expected of you?

Well, you can breathe a little easier because virtually all schools provide some kind of orientation for freshmen and transfer students. Most are voluntary programs, and we urge you to attend. Don't pass up free help. Even if there is a fee for the service, we believe it is cost effective to pay for it.

Orientation programs range in length from one day in the summer to several days immediately preceding the beginning of the term to a semester-long course for credit. Whether you consider yourself a strong student or a weak one, we recommend that you take the course if it's available. You'll get an in-depth treatment of how to succeed academically and usually some solid information about adjusting to the rigors of college life. The more brief orientation programs cover the school's academic structure and regulations, class schedules, campus services and facilities, residence hall life, commuter student issues, and social activities. You'll hear from assorted faculty and staff. You might get to sit in on a live or simulated class. Many schools provide parallel sessions for parents to address their particular concerns.

If your school doesn't offer an orientation program, contact the office of student services for more information.

Legal Services

Your landlord says that you owe $150 in back rent, and you say you don't. You don't want to part with the $150, but you don't have O. J.'s team of lawyers to argue your case. What are you going to do?

Most schools will offer some kind of legal assistance to their students. Generally, legal counselors are available to answer questions and handle simple legal matters - such as disputes over lease agreements. If you find yourself in more serious trouble, the counselors can refer you to an attorney in the community. If your college doesn't provide this service, discuss your concerns with the Dean of Students. You might also consider your community's legal aid service.

Military Organizations

The armed services offer some very generous scholarships. The military is also an avenue for developing leadership and other marketable skills. You are, of course, obligated to a certain number of years of service, so it is not a commitment to make lightly. Your choice of major has a strong bearing on which branch of the military will accept you. Engineers have a better chance with the Air Force. Liberal arts majors have the best chance with the Navy and Marine Corps, less with the Army, and least with the Air Force. For more information about ROTC programs, service academies, and tuition credit take a look at *How The Military Will Help You Pay for College,* by Don M. Berreton (Peterson's Guides: Princeton, NJ, 1985).

Resources For Entrepreneurs

As student interest in entrepreneurial activities has risen, so has official support by American universities. Most schools with business colleges offer coursework related to small business management or entrepreneurism. A few schools, such as Babson College, The University of Southern California, and Baylor University offer degree programs. If there's nothing official going on where you're enrolled, talk with some of the business faculty. Get them to arrange an internship or course credit for a business venture you want to start. At the very least, get all the free consultation you can from your professors.

Several organizations for entrepreneurs are affiliated with universities. They regularly hold conferences, produce newsletters, or sponsor seminars. Contact any of the following for information:

Caruth Institute for Owner-Managed Business
Southern Methodist University
Dallas, TX 75265-9990
214/692-3326;

International Council for Small Business (ICSB)
U.S. Affiliate Office: ICSB-US
Brooks Hall
University of Georgia
Athens, GA 30602
(Written requests only)

Journal of Small Business Management
Bureau of Business Research
West Virginia University
P.O. Box 6025
Morgantown, WV 26505-6025
304/2443-5837.

The Placement or Career Services Center

Placement or Career Services can be one of your strongest allies in getting a job. Their main function on campus is to serve as an employment agency. If your school is large, prestigious, or has many marketable majors, chances are that the center will attract recruiters - which means more opportunities for you. But don't make the mistake of counting on unknown administrators to devote countless hours finding you a cushy job that pays well. That's just not the way the world works. Take a careful look at Chapter 12 for a realistic look at what it takes to find a good job.

Many centers do not serve as a clearing house for employers to meet candidates. They will, however, offer workshops and consultation on job search, resume construction and interviewing skills. On some campuses they will help you plan your career from day one -- a service which is generally underused by students. Remember, the entrepreneurial management of your career will be essential for your success in the 21st Century. The time to get started is your freshman year.

Developmental/Remedial Studies

Some students get to State U. only to discover that they're not ready for college work. The reason is not important for our purposes. The solution is. If you believe you're in over your head, it is very easy to get down on yourself and feel ashamed and stupid. Or you can blame public education, your parents, or your high-school math teacher for your miserable state. Neither course of action will get you very far because neither course really involves any action.

Most campuses have some agency to help you find out if you're academically underdeveloped or disadvantaged. *Don't be too proud to use their services.* Here you'll find study skills programs, tutoring, preparatory classes, and lots of moral support. You might be a whiz in science and math, but a wimp in reading and writing. There's no law that says you can't take a differential equations class and remedial composition at the same time.

Campus Ministries

There is currently a revival of interest in religious issues among college students. If you want to be active in a church, temple, or mosque you'll probably find an organization to meet your needs. In many cases there are full-time clergy staffing an impressive facility and a variety of programs. In others there are volunteers who arrange meetings in dorm rooms. As the saying goes, "Seek and you shall find."

Health Clinic / Infirmary / Wellness Center

Most colleges have one of these facilities. Sooner or later, almost every college student needs one. They range from a single nurse in an office on some small campuses to a full-scale medical center with in-patient facilities at some large universities. Many will continue to administer a medical regimen for you that your private physician has prescribed. Some offer psychiatric care. Some have programs dealing with eating disorders, reproduction and contraception, sexually transmitted diseases, and substance abuse among others. You can often get over-the-counter medication at no cost, merely by requesting it. Read your catalog or student handbook to find out exactly what's available at the clinic on your campus.

Recreation and Physical Fitness

Most colleges have buildings and equipment that would make your high-school gym class look like a dungeon. You may find heated swimming pools, lighted tennis courts, indoor and outdoor tracks, squash, racquetball, and paddleball courts, courts for volleyball and basketball, fields for football, lacrosse, rugby and soccer. There may be Nautilus™ equipment, exercycles, trampolines, saunas, and whirlpools. Activities range from folk dancing, to martial arts, to white-water rafting, to intramural sports. Many colleges and universities have extensive intramural sports, where greeks, clubs, and the general student population can sign up for teams that play against one another within your college or university. You may be playing against a fraternity one night, and against the Habitat for Humanity team another. Find whatever you need to blow off steam and keep fit. College is a great time in your life to start a healthy life style.

Ombudsman

Several hundred colleges have an ombudsman. If you've got a grievance, this is the person to see. S/he can tell you what the appropriate channels are, who you should talk to, what your rights are, what should you say, and what forms you need to fill out. Unfair treatment by a professor, administrator, or agency is a typical problem that an ombudsman can help solve. If your school doesn't have one, your Dean of Students is probably your next best bet. Go in looking for help, not to ream somebody out. The simple request, "I need your help," is your best way to get the attention you need. And, while something may be causing you to be angry or upset, it is important that you let the person know how you are feeling or why, but not make him or her feel you are angry or upset with them. You are more likely to be successful if you can keep your emotions in "check" for such an encounter.

SPECIAL RESOURCES FOR SPECIAL NEEDS

Colleges today serve many more kinds of students than they have in the past. There are more women. More students come from ethnic and racial minorities. Many students are over the age of twenty-five. There are also commuters, married students, single parents, physically challenged and learning disabled students, and part-time students who are employed, to name a few. Whatever your unique situation, take advantage of your resources. Here are a few campus agencies that serve different types of students.

Resources For Nontraditional Students

You're older and may have a family. Many of you work, some of you, full-time. Most of you commute to your campus. You might be changing your career in mid-life, or you might be a displaced homemaker. You could be a veteran or a mother whose children are finally in school. You have different sets of needs and problems, but you all have one thing in common. You're different than the young adult just out of high school. You've seen more of life, you're more mature, you're concerned with different issues.

Your differences from "mainstream" students may leave you feeling out of place on campus. What could you have to talk about with students whose interests seem bounded by new-wave music and football weekends? In spite of impressive achievements many of you lack confidence in your scholastic abilities. It's understandable if you haven't taken a test in ten or twenty years. Your additional responsibilities often take time and energy away from studies. If you're a single parent of two who works twenty-five hours a week and takes three classes, you must juggle an incredible number of tasks every day.

We have devoted an entire chapter of this book to organizational skills. They are doubly important for nontraditional students. Budgeting your time effectively is an absolute must.

The other key to your success is to develop a support system. The difficulty in doing so is that organized campus resources have historically been designed for young adults who live on campus. The counseling center may close at 5:00 p.m. - which might be the earliest time you could use it. Happily, colleges are beginning to respond to the greater numbers of nontraditional students. More agencies, programs, and facilities are available during weekends and evening hours, and others are being designed for needs. If your school is dragging its feet in this area, inform the administration.

It is vital that you know just what is available. The trouble is, you may be so busy that you hardly have time to find out. In many cases there are special orientation sessions for returning students. If not, make every effort to attend the regular orientation, even if you have to take vacation or sick leave to do it. Does your college provide daycare? If not, is there a community day-care service with a sliding scale? Can a single parent live in married student housing? Is there a university ombudsman to help cut through red tape and listen to your grievances. Does the counseling center offer any program specifically suited to your situation?

Don't limit your support to administrators and counselors. It is a serious handicap not to know other students. How else will you get notes and assignments when you miss a class? Try to meet others who share concerns. You can work out car pools, baby sitting co-ops, and study groups. Often there are support groups for single parents, reentry homemakers, and the like.

YOU may need to organize a group if one doesn't already exist. Talk with your dean of students. Take out an ad in the school newspaper. If you want to be a success, you can't sit on your hands and wait to be rescued - you've got to take action.

If you're married, be very clear about the mutual expectations of you and your spouse. Will your spouse have to assume more financial or homemaking responsibilities? It's best to try and iron out such questions ahead of time. There are few burdens heavier than a resentful mate. Conversely, a truly supportive partner can make all the difference in the world.

Resources for the Physically or Learning Challenged

The Americans with Disability Act of 1990 defines disability with respect to an individual as:

1. A physical or mental impairment that substantially limits one or more of the major life activities of such an individual.
2. A record of such an impairment.
3. Being regarded as having such an impairment.

Examples of disabilities include: cerebral palsy, deafness/hard of hearing, blindness/visual impairments, mobility impairments, quadriplegia, attention deficit disorder, learning disabilities, cardiac disease, epilepsy, AIDS, brain injury, psychological disorders, muscular dystrophy, cancer, diabetes, and alcoholism. Students with a verifiable disability, visible or invisible, qualify for services in post secondary education.

Auxiliary aids and services include:

1. Qualified interpreters or other effective methods of making orally delivered materials available to individuals with hearing impairments.
2. Qualified readers, taped texts, or other effective methods of making visually delivered materials available to individuals with visual impairments.
3. Acquisition or modification of equipment or devices.
4. Other similar services and actions.

In other words, high tech products, specifically designed for the disabled, have made adjustment to college easier. Faculty and staff are learning to be supportive without being patronizing. All of these factors help validate your conviction that you can lead a full life in spite of being dyslexic or being confined to a wheelchair.

Colleges are becoming more sensitive to the impact of the environment on the physically disabled. Rampways, handrails, and elevators make the campus more manageable. In some institutions special transportation is available. On many campuses, such as the University of Nebraska at Lincoln, specially equipped dorm rooms are available. Other schools will provide attendants, some of them live-in, for little or no cost.

The latest equipment is mind-boggling. Typewriters that transpose into braille, readers that magnify or accept braille input, and Kurzweil reading machines are just a few of these wonders. The Kurzweil™ device can view any printed material, regardless of the language, and read it out loud. An assistive listening device (FM System) can be used to amplify an instructor's speech directly to a student with a hearing impairment. The instructor wears a small microphone and a transmitter. This allows reception of the lecture directly through the hearing aids or enhances the hearing of the student who does not wear hearing aids.

The College Guide For Students With Disabilities provides information about services and facilities on different campuses. If your school can't meet all your needs, there are a number of nonprofit groups that may take up the slack. For example, there is a national service organization that will record any educational book free of charge for anyone who cannot read standard printed material because of a disability (contact RECORDING FOR THE BLIND, The Anne T. Macdonald Center, 20 Roszel Road, Princeton, NJ 08540, 609/452-0606).

If you have a learning disability, you need encouragement and support. Because your disability isn't obvious, it may be difficult for others to understand your needs. Happily, many campuses provide specialists who work hard to give you, the LD student, a positive college experience. Generally speaking, you must be able to verify that you, in fact, have the learning or other disability.

Most established programs offer some of the following types of assistance: diagnostic testing and prescriptive planning, academic program advisement, psychological and career counseling, remedial programs, tutoring, and special course offerings. Other services and aids include typewriters, word processors, notetakers, alternative test arrangements, advocacy, and special housing.

There are approximately 380 four-year colleges and universities that will accept students with learning disabilities. More than 250 schools offer full-service programs. Ohio State serves over four hundred students. At this time DeSisto College in Florida is the only school in the nation that offers a complete curriculum for learning disabled students. For more information take a look at *Lovejoy's College Guide For The Learning Disabled,* by Charles Straughn II and Dr. Marvelle Colby.

Like other resources on your campus, it is up to you to reach out for the resources. Check with your dean of students or the office of the vice president for student services to find out what's available for you. If you don't ask for help, you won't get it. If you do, you probably will.

Resources For Racial And Ethnic Minorities

Our comments in the next several paragraphs are based on the experience of African American students attending predominantly white colleges. African-Americans are not the only group who have suffered from discrimination and oppression, however. Hispanics and Native Americans have also been treated unfairly at one time or another, as have members of just about every other racial, religious, or culturally different group you can think of. So this section applies to anyone who has suffered by virtue of his or her minority status.

With the end of legally segregated education in 1954, African-Americans have attended predominantly white colleges in increasing numbers. Their rate of graduation, unfortunately, has lagged behind their rate of admission. Scholars have identified several reasons for their lower rate of success.

First, there is the simple fact of being the minority and feeling out of place. For most of you, there is cultural shock. For many of you it is extreme. The fashions, musical tastes, and customs that you grew up with are suddenly rare or altogether absent. Everything seems a little strange. You're no longer sure what to say of how to act. All of this can bewilder you and shake your confidence.

For some of you, even the language is different. "Black English" may be the only way to communicate when you're back in the "hood." It may even be a legitimate subject of inquiry for linguists, but its use on a term paper will probably result in a lower grade.

Who do you socialize with? Who do you date? These are very important issues, particularly for young adults. If you're one of a handful of African Americans, your choices are very limited. It's common for African-Americans to feel lonely and isolated on a white campus.

For a number of African-Americans, there is a legacy of oppression to overcome. You are less likely to have college-educated parents. (This is, happily, changing.) Your high school may have lacked resources. And, when you look around the campus, you see precious few African-American faculty and administrators to symbolize the fact that you can make it.

Another factor is that racism has not been completely eliminated. While it is rarely blatantly oppressive, its presence in subtle forms can still be destructive. Faculty may have lower expectations of you. Other students may interpret your cultural differences in a negative light. The curriculum tends to be "white": Teacher and textbooks seldom mention African-American contributions to science, letters, politics or the arts.

So, in the face of all this, how can African Americans (or any other minority) succeed? You succeed first the same way anyone else does - by being goal-directed and hardworking and smart. The principles underlying the Master Plan apply to everyone. But because of the difficulties cited above, it is especially important that minorities make use of campus resources.

You should seek out any African-American faculty and staff on your campus. These are the ones who have made it. Here are role models and potential mentors. Similarly, as an incoming African American student, you should identify your brothers and sisters who are already here and succeeding. They can provide information and support and show you the ropes. Many schools have a special agency for African-Americans or minorities. It is important that you take advantage of this resource. Here you can learn more about your cultural heritage, form friendships, and find programs to meet you particular needs.

Finally, you must resist the awkwardness that being different from most of your peers can elicit and actively use all the campus resources that are available. The same applies to forming friendships and professional relationships with all members of your campus community. If you want to succeed in a salad-bowl society -- one that is made up of many different races and cultures, each retaining its own identity -- you must be able to relate effectively to all kinds of people.

Everyone who comes to college must adjust to a new culture. This is doubly true for international students and other minorities. It makes good sense for you to hang out with students who share your cultural heritage and to use them as family, support system, and home base. If you do this to the exclusion of the remainder of the campus community, however, your are severely limiting your opportunities, your network of contacts, and your possibilities for meaningful friendships. One thing we know about the future is that it will be characterized by diversity. You will be more successful to the extent your are comfortable with different kinds of people. You get comfortable by exposure: studying, working, governing, talking, debating, planning, and partying with people who are different from you.

> ### *Everyone* who comes to college must adjust to a new culture.

We have worked with a number of high achieving African-Americans. As their numbers grow, we hope they will give a new happier twist to the old lyric, "Why am I so black and blue?"

Resources For Women

In the 1970s women on campus were demanding their own services. In 1996, with more women succeeding in the professions and in managerial positions, the trend is to farm these services out to other campus agencies. Check with the Office of Student Services to find out exactly what is available.

A few universities, such as the University System in California, continue to provide women's centers for their female students. Most coeducational schools employ female counselors and gynecologists. Many colleges sponsor ongoing programs or short seminars designed for females.

Topics include discrimination in the workplace, the battered woman, the displaced homemaker, assertiveness/leadership training, date-rape, and career assistance for those interested in nontraditional fields.

Most schools offer some sort of self-defense training, whether through the physical education department or the Counseling Center. And most schools will provide nighttime escorts and/or shuttle services. On many urban campuses you would be well advised to use them.

If your school doesn't have what you need and you're interested in starting a program, there are several things you can do. Talk to someone in student government. Talk to someone in the office of student services. If funding is a problem, look into off-campus money. *Grants For Women And Girls* is an excellent reference book put out by the Foundation Center in New York City. It is the grants research tool most widely used by fundraisers for female programs.

SUMMARY

1.   Everybody needs to ask for help at times.
2.   Smart students never hesitate to seek help when they need it.
3.   Smart students are familiar with the resources available to them.
4.   College campuses are filled with sources of help in all areas of students' lives. Most services are free or available at minimal cost.
5.   Support services are especially important for nontraditional, physically or learning disabled, and minority students.
6.   Learning to recognize those times when you need help and knowing where to find it are two important steps in becoming a success in college and throughout life.

12
Career Planning 2
Charting Your Course

Once you finish your junior year, you'll be faced with some important decisions. Should you begin working full time after graduation or start on an advanced degree? Although there are twelve months before you graduate, you should start refining your goals now. Many organizations recruit new candidates heavily in the fall. Graduate and professional schools have February application deadlines. What's your next step?

CLARIFYING YOUR GOALS: THE NEVER-ENDING STORY

You have to know yourself and the job world before you can make sound career decisions. You've already chosen a major and a general career direction. Now it's time to get more specific. If you really want to be successful, checking your goals is an ongoing, lifelong process.

Graduate School

Will graduate school help you reach your goals? This is the first question you must answer before you seriously consider applying. If it's your next step because you don't know what else to do, chances are good you'll be in the same boat when you get your advanced degree. There are plenty of PhDs driving cabs and waiting tables.

For openers, read Appendix 5, "Should I get An Advanced Degree?" Then start asking people who should know. Counselors and placement workers can give you some advice. So can your professors. But don't fail to ask people in your chosen field. If you want to be a research engineer, the best person to ask about the marketability of an advanced degree is another research engineer or somebody who hires them.

In general, acquiring more knowledge as you prepare for the Information Age is not a bad bet. We believe, however, that knowledge and skill will count more than degrees. While you can't be a medical doctor without an MD, you don't necessarily have to have an MBA to be an entrepreneur or a manager or a consultant. You DO have to know what you're doing. Also, bear in mind that graduate programs are staffed by humans that have the same needs for work and job security that you do. Just because their program has become outdated, and no graduate of theirs has landed a job above parking lot attendant, doesn't mean they won't take your tuition. Make sure you are acquiring useful, up-to-date information and skills that are applicable to 21st Century problems. As we've already stated continuous, life-long learning will be the key to success in the future. Chances are, you will be stepping on and off one campus or another throughout your life. You'll also be learning on the InterNet, via video conferences, and off of computer disks and compact disks.

Some companies prefer to do their own training. They believe that they can better teach new employees how specifically to meet the needs of the company than can a graduate school. On the other hand more that a few corporations will help you get an advanced degree, provided you agree to continue working for them. They want a return investment. MBAs are very popular these days. We think you'll get the most out of your MBA after you've worked for a few years.

If you go to graduate school, it's important to find the program that's right for you. Factors to consider include cost, location, degree requirements, courses, and reputation. The reputation of a school is determined by the quality of the faculty, the library, and the research facilities. *The Gourman Report* rates the top schools in each field. Try to find a school whose philosophy is congenial with yours. A very good school might have a theoretical orientation, and if you want an applied and practical approach, you'll be out of luck. Probably one of the biggest factors relates to cost. How well can the graduate school support you financially? Graduate schools, in particular, usually award teaching and/or research assistantships to most of their students. In essence, you'll be working your way through school by teaching and researching in your field. A variation on this theme would be a graduate co-op program. You'd alternate between school and industry, with the industry paying you a salary. One of the advantages of this arrangement is the near certainty that you'll be getting education and experience that is relevant to the real world of work.

OK, suppose an advanced degree will help you reach your goals. In some cases it's a requirement - law, medicine, and college teaching come to mind. Can you get accepted, and will you be able to do the work?

Most graduate programs admit on the basis of grades and admissions tests such as the Graduate Record Exam, the Miller Analogies Test, and the Medical College Admission Test. Do some research at the library or counseling center. Find out what the requirements are. Pace's, Peterson's, and Barron's all publish reliable guides to graduate and professional programs. If your preliminary research is encouraging, you can find out more specific information from the catalog of the school in question. Your professors all went to grad school, so be sure and check with them. Should you decide to apply, you will need letters of recommendation from some of them. (Now, aren't you glad you started cultivating a working relationship with some of your profs several years ago?)

Your SAT scores are pretty good predictors of what you'll make on the GRE or the MCAT. If you don't do well on standardized tests, there are study guides and courses available to help you improve your scores.

Once you get into a graduate program, your chances are good that you'll complete it. Graduate education is very expensive, and schools don't like to flunk their students out. About 98 percent of all medical students get their M.D. The same strategies and tactics that produce success in college will help you get an advanced degree -- working hard in an organized way toward clear, realistic goals. Graduate work requires much more independent study. There are fewer tests and papers, but they are bigger and each one counts for more. Many degrees require theses or dissertations. In other words, you'll have to do original scholarship and write a book about it.

GOODBYE IVORY TOWER -- HELLO, REAL WORLD

Many of you will want to begin full-time employment shortly after your bachelor's degree. And you'll want to have a good job lined up and waiting for you long before you get your diploma. A lot of you will feel pressure to start paying off college loans rather than build up bigger debt. That means you'll be conducting a job search at the same time you're completing your senior year. To do this right you've got to know yourself. You can't market yourself if you don't know what you have to offer.

One way to assess your skills is to think of every job, school project, or extracurricular activity as being a series of lesser tasks (which, by the way, they are). If you further reduce the different tasks, you have a list of skills needed to do them.

For example, one student doing a social work internship participated in the development of a geriatric day-care center. Her tasks involved: assessing the needs of the target population; developing a suitable recreational program; scheduling activities; and coordinating transportation for participants. These tasks required the following skills to do the job: customer research, program development, and program administration. She was then able to use these skills in marketing herself to employers. If you're still stuck, try the exercise at the conclusion of this chapter.

Employers want to know what you can do for them, and they need to know quickly. Corporate recruiters scan hundreds of resumes and interview dozens of prospects every week. How can you show them what you've got, in language they understand?

THE STAR TECHNIQUE

Virtually all jobs consist of problems waiting to be solved. You need to show employers how you can solve their problems. If you have the right skills, you can do this. The STAR Technique is a method for identifying your skills and communicating them to those in a position to hire you.

Your skills--what you can actually DO for an employer--are potentially your strongest selling points. But don't just list them. Give examples to show how you are skilled at performing a particular task. Be descriptive and use action words. You can strengthen an example by including an outcome. If you quantify (e.g., 20% increase) the results, your example will have even more punch. Sometimes you can't readily quantify results; you have to imply them (e.g. familiarity with different computer languages implies proficiency in them.) If possible, include a positive outcome (e.g. successfully implemented new budgeting procedure). Remember, positive results create positive reactions.

Use the STAR (Situation-Action-Result) TECHNIQUE which is frequently used in personnel work, to communicate your skills with impact.

STAR TECHNIQUE

ST ....**SITUATION** .... WHAT WAS THE PROBLEM & SETTING?

A ....**ACTION** .... WHAT DID YOU DO?

R.............**RESULT(S)** .... WHAT WAS THE OUTCOME?

Achievements on Your Resume

Students sometimes confuse achievements with skills and abilities. You may have been an Eagle Scout, and that's great. But as a line on your resume it doesn't really mean a whole lot. Now tell an employer that: **Managed** a volunteer staff of 14 in the design and construction of a playground for handicapped children, finishing **on-time** and **within budget**. Now THAT is what an employer wants to see. They want to see those highlighted words that demonstrate specific skills.

Another example of how achievements are confused with skills and abilities is in honorific awards. Great! We're thrilled you were National Honor Society, maybe even an officer. But, tell me an achievement. You sell yourself when you use the STAR technique to develop something substantive: As vice-president of National Honor Society, **organized** a fund drive to raise money for the Leukemia Society; **exceeded** our goal by 14% resulting in special recognition from the Leukemia Society for surpassing our goal. What employer wouldn't like to hire someone who not only makes good grades, but has the skills and abilities to organize and exceed expectations! You get the idea. Now take all those achievements and transform them into skills and abilities using the STAR technique, so that you can **WOW** those potential employers!

Examples of skills using the STAR TECHNIQUE

- Organized Hall Council fundraiser and generated record income.
- Fluent in French. Conversant in Spanish and German.
- Wrote award winning series of articles on alcohol abuse for school paper.
- Developed new rush strategy resulting in largest pledge class in chapter history.
- Managed MR. TACO fast food restaurant with annual revenue of one million dollars, annual payroll of 1/4-million dollars.
- Implemented student-centered teaching to 5th-grade class that resulted in average increase in student achievement-test scores of 17%.
- Handled public relations for benefit concert in Student Center, resulting in first sellout in 7-year history of the event.

Employers have to deal with the real world of limited resources, fierce competition, and the bottom line. They're used to thinking in terms of practical problems, the action taken, and what the consequences are. A salesman takes on a slumping territory, talks to plant managers instead of office managers, and doubles orders in six months. A design engineer introduces computer-assisted design to a project and beats the deadline by two months. A manager introduces an incentive program for her staff, and absenteeism is halved, saving the company $500,000 annually.

Employers want results, preferably quantifiable results. More dollars earned. Fewer hours taken. A greater percent of the market. Better achievement-test scores from students.

You probably haven't made anybody megabucks yet, but the same principles apply at any age. A twelve-year-old gets more subscriptions on his paper route than any other carrier and wins a new bike. A high-school student organizes a lawn-care business and builds a clientele of twenty-five regular customers. A college freshman makes an A in Computer Science and learns C + and BASIC. A co-op student assists in developing a system of inventory control that gets the product to the customer three days faster that her company's leading competitor. A fraternity pledge trainer raises the pledges' grades by an average of four-tenths of a point, and for the first time in the organization's history an entire pledge class is initiated on time.

You can't just tell prospective employers that you have salesmanship, entrepreneurial know-how, computer skills, organizational ability, and leadership (which are the five skills implied in the paragraph above). You've got to show them. The STAR Technique enables you to do just that. We believe your skills should be the focus of your entire job-search campaign. You will highlight them on your resume, emphasize them during interviews, mention them in your correspondence.

Remember too, the chaotic career paths of the 21st Century will likely require multiple, ongoing, simultaneous job searches. Most of the success stories will be written by hardy entrepreneurially oriented people who have persuaded lots of others from their extensive network of contacts to purchase their services and products.

The ability to convey your marketable skills concisely, with impact, is itself an impressive skill. Think about it. You demonstrated analytical ability, communication skills, self-awareness, and organizational skills - a not-too-shabby list of selling points to have working for you every time you contact an employer.

Once you come up with your marketable skills via the STAR Technique, you've completed the most difficult phase of the job search. And since you have identified what you've got going for yourself, you'll also feel like a million dollars. We think that's a pretty good way to start any important endeavor.

If you get stuck, use the exercise following the summary to unstick you.

SUMMARY

1. Start making your post-graduation plans at the end of your junior year.
2. Clarifying your goals is an ongoing process.
3. Determine if graduate school will help you meet your goals.
4. Assess your marketable skills.
5. The STAR Technique is a powerful tool for analyzing your strengths and conveying them to others.

DEFINING SKILLS IN LIFE EXPERIENCES

WORK HISTORY

Job Titles   Main Duties

Work Responsibilities Most Liked   Why?

Work Responsibilities Least Liked   Why?

What skills and abilities did you utilize
in your preferred work responsibilities?

ORGANIZATIONAL WORK HISTORY

Position Titles   Main Duties

Work Responsibilities Most Liked   Why?

Work Responsibilities Least Liked   Why?

What skills and abilities did you utilize
in your preferred work responsibilities

COURSEWORK

Courses   Descriptions

Coursework Most Liked   Why?

Coursework Least Liked   Why?

What skills and abilities did you utilize
in your preferred coursework?

HOBBIES AND LEISURE PURSUITS

Activities   Description

Activities Most Liked   Why?

Activities Least Liked   Why?

What skills and abilities did you utilize
in your preferred activities?

Based on this exercise, list all the skills and abilities that you have defined. After your list has been compiled, circle the FIVE MOST IMPORTANT skills and abilities. This inventory will be a helpful tool in creating your job objectives for your resume.

13
It's A Jungle Out There: The Job Search

If you've been paying attention, you know that the job world of the 21st Century will be characterized by speed, change, technical sophistication, and competition. The workforce will be diverse. The perspective will be global. Companies will strive to be lean and mean in order to stay in business. They will be looking for flexible, resilient, highly skilled self-starters who communicate well and collaborate effectively. You hope they're looking for you. Our advice is not to wait for them to find you. Probably all of us have fantasies of being called out of the blue to fill an important position. Don't hold your breath. If you want a good job, it's up to you to find it.

As you try to identify open positions that would interest you, don't narrow your search prematurely. Where will you start your career? The same place where most people start -- at the bottom. It may even be worth your while to consider an internship after graduation. It's a way to get your foot in the door, get some experience, develop some skills, and make some contacts. Nor should you overlook part-time or project work -- particularly if the work is challenging and will enhance your credentials. The important thing is to get a start doing something that leads somewhere you want to go. While it's increasingly difficult to find clear-cut career ladders, any position that cultivates marketable skills is worth considering.

You wouldn't be reading this book if you didn't want to improve your chances for success. Each chapter outlines a different phase of an overall strategy for reaching your goals. By working harder and smarter than the average student, you are investing in your future. You are preparing to live and work in the 21st Century.

But there's one last hurdle--you've got to understand how the job search works. Not only must you be ready for the Information Age. You must know how to find the right Information Age job. And then you've got to convince someone that you can fill it.

GETTING STARTED

The Want Ads

It seems like a reasonable place to begin until you reflect on it. Companies will fill many vacant positions by promoting from within their own organization, by shifting employees laterally, or by locating a strong candidate through the "grapevine." Independent contractors with strong industry contacts will do a lot of project work that ends with the completion of the project. The jobs that remain find their way into the want ads. They are not usually the most desirable jobs.

On top of that, jobs are sometimes advertised after they are already filled. This is so the company will appear to comply with government guidelines for fair hiring practices. Richard Bolles reported in *What Color Is Your Parachute?* that about twenty-four out of one hundred job seekers get jobs through the want ads. We believe that your chances of success through want ads will be even smaller in the 21st Century. So it's one place to look, but don't confine yourself to the newspapers.

Our guess is that ads placed in trade journals are more likely to point to good jobs. If a company took the trouble to place the ad, they're probably serious. On the other hand, more time has elapsed, so the job may already be filled.

Employment Agencies

Bolles claims about twenty-four succeed using this route too. The bottom line on employment agencies is that they are paid a commission to get a job filled. They will work the hardest for applicants who have the greatest chance of being hired. It is not cost effective for them to do extensive counseling. They are turned off by the person who wanders in and says, "I have a degree in X. Find me a job." They want to work with people who have done some serious self-assessment and know what they have to offer.

If you use an employment agency, treat your first meeting like a screening interview because that's exactly what it is. They're deciding if you're worth their time. Take your resume. Practice the STAR technique. Use interviewing etiquette--proper dress, positive attitude, enthusiasm, etc. Know what you have to offer. Have a strong resume. Know how to interview before you start.

College Placement or Career Centers

There is no guarantee of a good job here either, but your success depends in large measure on the particular university and its placement center. One way employers have cut expenses in the last twenty years is by recruiting at fewer colleges. Obviously, if your college is not heavily recruited, it's up to you to find the right job. Even if more employers do come to your college, it's still important for you to launch a proactive job search. The Placement Center should be a part of that search, but you should not put all your eggs in that one basket.

Here are some hints to help you get the best results from your university placement or career service:

1. Sign up early. Don't wait until the last minute on any aspect of the job search.

2. Attend the orientation session(s). Comply fully with the established rules and procedures of the service. If you don't, you may hurt your chances for getting interviews with your preferred companies.

3. Get a list of which employers will be visiting your campus. Identify which of those companies you would like to work for. Establish a group of favorite companies and another group of acceptable alternatives.

4. Prepare your personal resume(s), data sheets, applications, etc. DON'T SKIMP. Do it right (see Chapter 14).

5. Take advantage of the seminars and workshops your placement center offers. Students typically want their college to find them jobs. Often, the career center is best at teaching YOU how to find and land a good job.

There is no standard way for a placement center to assign interviews. Some use a lottery. In some centers the companies are given access to student resumes and data sheets. The companies grant interviews only to those students whose records catch their eye. Many companies set GPA cut offs. They won't look at anybody under a 3.0, a 3.3, or even higher.

If at first you don't get an interview with an employer you're keen on, don't give up. Put your resume with a strong cover letter in the company's message slot while their representative is on campus. Tell them why you think you match their needs and request an interview. Another alternative is to show up personally at the placement center on a day when the company's recruiter will be there, but during a time when he or she won't actually be meeting with students--early in the morning, at lunch time, or near the end of the day. Ask for an impromptu interview. The worst that can happen is that your request will be declined. Another tactic is to wait for a no-show, and be ready to take their place. The chances aren't great that this will happen, but in the event it does, it really shows the recruiter just how interested you are in coming to work for them.

If your major is not highly recruited, check with your academic department. Your professors may have some job leads, and in some instances placement may be handled at the departmental level.

Join a professional association relevant to your professional goals. Sometimes they will have placement services for members. If you need information about such organizations, look in

The Encyclopedia Of Associations, which is found in most main libraries. Even more important than any formalized placement assistance, professional associations are excellent sources of contacts and information. Which brings us to our final method of finding a job.

Networking

Bolles says networking is *the* way to fly. He reports an 85 percent success rate. Rather better, wouldn't you say, than the one in 1,499 chance he reports for those who launch a blind resume campaign by mail. Having a good network was an advantage in the Industrial Age. It will be virtually a requirement in the Information Age.

If you've followed the Master Plan, you should have developed a network of professional contacts by now. If you feel deficient in this important area, review "Building Contacts."

Contacts can come from anywhere. Professors and employers are obvious choices, but also consider calling on family connections, friends who have already joined the work force, alumni from your hometown or from the town where you want to work. If you haven't already done so, join a professional association and start attending their meetings.

If it was smart to file your contacts as a freshman, it's absolutely essential that you be organized as a senior. We recommend a three-by-five card file system. On the front of each card put the name, address, phone number, and the person's position. (In many cases, you can simply tape the contact's business card to the three-by-five.) Also indicate your referral source as that will help you make the proper approach. On the back, put the dates when you meet and the nature of the conversation. The important thing is not to follow our system, but that you have a system that works for you -- whether it's electronic, loose-leaf, or on a Roladex™.

This is also a time when it is especially important to keep your calendar up to date. Immediately enter the time of every meeting you set--you don't want to miss any.

Bear in mind that when you're networking for jobs, you're not actually applying for work. You're trying to find out about your field. You're looking for leads. You're wanting feedback on your qualifications and credentials. Naturally, you wouldn't turn down a good job offer, but networking doesn't usually get you a job by tomorrow or even next week. But if you keep after it for several months, you should have a number of offers to consider. You'll also have contacts who can help you throughout your career.

APPROACHING THE CONTACT

If you write a letter, you can say clearly what needs to be said without distraction. The mail is slower, of course, than the phone, and your letter may be screened. The prospective contact may never lay eyes on it. In any event, you'll probably have to follow up your letter with a phone call to set up a meeting.

The main difficulty with phoning your contact is getting through. Part of a secretary's job is to protect her boss, so you may get put off. Here are some tips to help reach the contact:

When You Do Get Through

You must be ready. Know what you want. Know what you're going to say. This means thorough preparation before you make the call. We recommend having an outline of your intended comments at hand.

Introduce yourself by giving your name and referral source and stating the purpose of your

1. Phone after five. The secretary's having drinks at a fern bar, but the executive is probably still in the office. Maybe he or she will pick up the phone after the twelfth ring.
2. Make the secretary your ally. Get her first and last name, and refer to her by her last name. Give her some respect, and she might give you some.
3. Don't volunteer information that can be used to screen you out. Be diplomatic but persistent--"Professor Jones referred me to Ms. Jackson, and I really need to speak to her personally."
4. If the contact is on another line, say that you'll be glad to hold.
5. Generally speaking, it's better to say you'll call back than to leave your name and number. Somehow or other, busy people never seem to return unsolicited phone calls.

call. Don't say you're looking for a job. Instead, tell the contact that you will graduate in June, and you'd like to meet to talk about her area. Your experience and coursework have focused on XYZ, but you understand her area is rapidly expanding, and it's related to yours. Do your best to persuade the contact to meet you. Tell her you want to talk more about particular trends in her area. Identify the trends by name. If she's unwilling to meet with you, get as much information as you can on the telephone. If you keep trying, however, you will eventually find some qualified people who are willing to talk with you in person.

Meeting the Contact

Your purpose for meeting is to get information and advice. Review "Conducting an Informational Interview" in Chapter 5. One of the biggest mistakes you can make during such a meeting is to be vague and unfocused. So prepare thoroughly for the interview by researching the field or industry in question. Complete the self-assessment discussed in Chapter 9. Have a winning resume in hand (Chapter 14). Develop a new "industrial-strength" oral resume. Remember, you're not a freshman any more. (Well, actually, perhaps you are. Many freshmen and sophomores and juniors read over this material to prepare for part-time and co-op positions. You're concerns are important too.) You're one step away from being a successful graduate. Use the STAR Technique to highlight your key strengths.

Preparation is also one of the best antidotes to the jitters, so practice with a friend if you're still feeling nervous. Or talk to a tape recorder or a mirror. To really get a sense of presentation, you can have a friend impersonate the recruiter and have your "interview" videotaped. Study the tape to see how you can improve your presentation style (notice how often you say uh and ah; notice your posture, expression and voice tone). This is NOT too much trouble if you are lusting after that perfect job in the perfect location at the perfect salary and this person has the possibility of giving you the key contact to getting your foot in the door there!

When you finally meet the contact, remind her of your phone conversation and who suggested that you seek her counsel. Describe yourself to her via your oral resume. That will help her advise you according to your specific situation. It's also an opportunity for you to sell yourself. While you didn't come to her for a job, you certainly wouldn't turn the right offer down.

Making an effective oral resume is a skill that you can acquire with practice. It's not easy to give a thumbnail sketch of yourself that says something without its sounding like a canned speech. Try to strike a balance between being overly formal and speaking too conversationally. Try to relax, and remember: you're just one human being trying to tell another who you are so that the other's comments will be pertinent to your situation. You should also know that this is a commonly accepted business practice. It is unlikely that this is the first or last time your contact will hear such a presentation. You'll likely exchange pleasantries for a few minutes, but at some point it will be appropriate to tell your contact about yourself.

In Chapter 5, Janet Smith, freshman, conducted her first informational interview and made her first oral resume. Now, as a senior, she's networking for job leads. Notice that this time she is more focused in her remarks. The same is true of her questions.

Oral Resume of Janet Smith, Senior

"I really appreciate your taking the time to talk with me about current trends in Industrial/Organizational Psychology. Dr. Schwartz said you were doing some really interesting training work with people in sales and middle management. First, let me tell you a little about myself.

"I'm a Psych major, and I'll be graduating at the end of the summer. I should have around a 3.3 grade point average, but I've made all *A*s in my Psych classes except for one *B* in Physiological. I've done an internship at Acme Company under Dr. Score. Mostly I was involved in test construction. I wrote some of the items, helped with the item analysis, and interviewed most of the subjects.

"The thing was, I gradually realize that the interviewing portion of my job was giving me the most satisfaction. It's not that I didn't enjoy developing the tests themselves. It's just that I preferred having direct contact with people. One of the surveys we developed was designed specifically to assess the morale of people in sales. I could pretty well tell who was going to be successful based on the subjects' scores, but I wasn't supposed to say anything that would influence them. That part frustrated me. I really wanted to use the test results to help these people who were starting out in sales.

"I have done some training work already through my job as an area coordinator with the residence hall program. Before I could start out as a resident assistant, I had to learn basic communication skills and some crisis intervention techniques. This past fall I helped train the new crop of assistants. I consistently got very high ratings, both from the students and from the staff member from housing.

"So what I'm wondering is--How can I break into the training field? And is it possible to do this with only an undergraduate degree? What are my options, and what steps do I need to start taking!"

Basically, you're trying to find out through your questions how you can become more marketable. What specific skills should you try to strengthen? Do you need additional training or experience? While it's not appropriate to make a hard sell for yourself, do try to create interest in the mind of the contact whenever possible. For example, if she mentions the need for persuasive skills in her kind of position, recount a situation in which you were persuasive and ask her if that's the sort of ability she has in mind.

Ask her to react to your printed resume (see Chapter 14). What's missing? Is there any fluff that should be trimmed? And take this opportunity to expand your network. Could she suggest others in the field that you could talk with? Does she know of any leads for job openings.

Thank her graciously, and offer her a copy of your resume for her files. Then thank her again in a letter.

Before you start arranging meetings with the new contacts she gave you, do some more homework. Revise your resume according to her suggestions. Read up on areas of deficiency that she uncovered. Or get some more training. After each round of interviews, try to strengthen your suitability for the requirements of the position you're investigating. If you're persistent, you will gradually become a stronger candidate in possession of a winning resume. And at some point you will get interviews for some attractive positions.

SUMMARY

1. The job market of the 21st Century will be competitive and chaotic, so use every resource available to you.

2. The want ads and employment agencies are not generally highly effective avenues to good jobs.

3. The success rates of different college placement centers vary widely.

4. Follow your placement center's rules exactly to get maximum results.

5. Regardless of your placement center's success rate, you should be building a network of contacts which you will maintain throughout your life.

6. Start networking only after you've done your homework: self-assessment; a winning resume; preliminary research of field and position.

7. Attend some of the workshops and seminars that your college's career center offers.

14
The 21st Century Resume

If you're clear on your career goals and understand the job search process, writing a strong resume will be easy. Employers are looking for people who will solve their problems. All you have to do is show an employer that you're good at solving his kind of problem. Once you've convinced Dynamic Enterprises that you can meet their needs, you've created a match. You've also got a job offer on your hands.

The resume doesn't get you the job. The interview does that. But if your resume shows that you match the employer's needs, it will get you an interview. It is a graphic representation of who you are professionally. It's your personal ad.

Having a strong personal ad will be especially important in the volatile job market of the future. The world of work for individuals will be characterized by many jobs, multiple careers, murky career paths, self-employment, and working without a net. Chapter 12 argued that building and maintaining an extensive network of professional contacts will be an essential ongoing part of professional life. You will want many of these contacts to have your resume on file.

First Impressions

For employers, the resume is a screening device. Big corporations get hundreds of thousands of them every year. You can pay an employment agency a hundred dollars to come up with a work of art on thirty weight paper, but it's still junk mail to the guy who has to read a hundred of them a day. So you've got ten, maybe twenty seconds to show him that your resume is worth a second look.

It's got to look "marvelous." Which isn't all that hard to make happen. Use high quality eight an one-half by eleven inch paper--white, off-white, light gray, or beige. Maybe a designer or entertainer could go with something flashier, but most job seekers are best served by a conservative, professional look.

This is just one more instance where computer skills come in handy. If you don't know word processing as yet, now is the time. You simply must maintain a generic resume on a floppy disk. It will be ready for editing and updating for any opportunity. Don't run it off on a cheap dot-matrix printer. Use a laser jet or ink jet. Make multiple copies on a high quality copier, using the high quality paper we've already discussed.

NAME

Address	City	State	Zip	Phone

JOB OBJECTIVE: Most important piece of information on resume; used by employers as screening device or to signal job match; must grab attention and motivate employer to read further. Keep this concise and customized for each use.

EDUCATION: List in reverse chronological order, putting the most marketable facts -- school or degree -- first.

Mention any outstanding honors or achievements, such as high GPA, Dean's List .

Give examples of relevant coursework and school-related activities if a recent graduate.

SKILLS:
- Choose skills that are most relevant to job objective.
- Give short statements to support skills.
- Make support statements results-oriented.
- Position most marketable skills first.

EMPLOYMENT: Place strongest of the two sections, employment or education first.

List in reverse chronological order, putting the most marketable facts -- employer or job title -- first.

Give functional description of job if employment history is strong and supports job objective.

MISCELLANEOUS:
- Call this section anything applicable -- INTEREST ACTIVITIES, ACCOMPLISHMENTS, or ACHIEVEMENTS.
- Give only information that would interest an employer.
- Stay away from personal and chatty information.

REFERENCES: It is assumed you would provide references upon request. Leave this off your resume, unless you're desperately short of items.

REMEMBER: THERE ARE NO CONCRETE RULES IN RESUME PREPARATION. MODIFY THIS GUIDE, WHEN NECESSARY, TO MAKE THE MOST FAVORABLE IMPRESSION.

Appearance, as well as content, tells the employer a lot about you. Your resume reflects the kind of work you're capable of producing. It should show that you're well organized, that you can communicate clearly, and that you can make a strong visual presentation. The acid test: Does it look good enough for prospective employers to send out as their own work? If it doesn't, it's not good enough.

Use some of the tricks that commercial artists use. When they design ads, they play up important information in the white space, those areas free from text. In poorly constructed resumes we often see dates in those big chunks of white space known as the margin. Dates are not selling points. Instead, use information that is: job titles, degrees, skills, etc.

Stay away from long paragraphs. Your resume should not look like a page out of your American history text. Ads use a few key words, carefully chosen and strategically placed. You further focus attention by using bold print, larger type, bullets (•) or asterisks(*). Remember, you've got just ten seconds to get their attention.

The job objective is crucial because it informs the employer if there is a match. The job objective, unlike the rest of the resume, gets close attention on the first pass-through. Therefore, it comes immediately after your name and address at the top of the page. If you're offering what they're seeking, they'll read on.

THE JOB OBJECTIVE

The following is a component sheet useful in developing a job objective. Pick the ones you feel are applicable to your situation.

- Include the exact job title if you know it. Do not guess! The job objective is used as a screening device. If you apply for a job that does not exist, your resume will probably be eliminated before it is read thoroughly. Don't chance it.
- Make the objective meaningful. Everything else in the resume must support and reflect what is said in the objective.
- Be specific and to the point. Broad objectives are often misinterpreted to be vague and uncertain. Avoid the use of platitudes and cliches. They say nothing and cast doubt on the rest of the resume.
- Include the field you were trained in if this is a selling point. This is especially applicable to those in technical fields.
- Include the functional area of the company where you want to work. Examples of these company divisions are: research and development, production, technical services, information systems/processing, marketing and sales, and administration and finance.

- Include skills/qualifications that are relevant to the job you are seeking. This will help promote you as a strong job candidate. Ex: Seek a position in civil engineering as a Structural Engineer utilizing my skills in structures, computer programming and construction.
- Include the type of organization if it is important to you. Keep in mind that this may limit the number of opportunities open to you.
- Create different resumes for different job objectives.

Taking a Second Look

OK, she looked at your resume, and it looked good. Your career objective matches one of the positions she's filling. Now, she's willing to look more closely. And when she does, she must not see any misspelled words, typos, or grammatical errors. So proofread it carefully. Wait a day, and proof it again. Then let a friend take a look at it. Obviously, this means you don't start working on your resume at the last minute.

NAME AND ADDRESS

You want them to remember your name, so you put it at the top of the page. If possible, use a larger type size than you use on the rest of your resume. Check with your campus book store or copy center if you need help, or find a campus computer guru. Include your address and a phone number where you can be reached or a message can be left during working hours. You might want to consider buying or sharing an answering machine. Or you may be able to have messages left with a friend, neighbor, or relative. In some cases you can have messages taken at the departmental headquarters of you academic major.

Example

_____Mary Q. Student_____

Campus Box 007   Atlanta, GA 30332   (494)894-0000

_____

JOB OBJECTIVE

We've already mentioned that the job objective is the most important piece of information on the page. If employers don't see a potential match, they might not look further no matter how outstanding your record. Ideally, the job you're looking for is identical to the one they're trying to fill (see JOB OBJECTIVE COMPONENTS chart.)

Avoid platitudes and vagueness. All graduates want "A challenging position with opportunities for advancement." If this is your stated career objective, you've told an employer nothing.

Give any information that will tell the employer where you would fit best. For instance, identify where you want to work in the company (sales, finance, etc.); you may also want to indicate the key skills you have to offer (administrative, quantitative, etc.). Companies don't hire generic employees. They hire researchers, accountants, and personnel directors.

We also advise against listing plural job objectives unless they are closely related. You wouldn't, for instance, say you were looking for an "entry-level position in sales or research" because it makes you look as if you have no clear career goals. If you are looking at rather different positions with different companies, we strongly recommend a different resume highlighting the appropriate skills and experience for each position. This is why having a generic resume on a computer is invaluable. When it comes time to apply for a new job, it is easy to rearrange the material.

Use the actual job titles when you know them--catch the employer's attention right away by showing the possibility of a match. However, don't guess if you're not sure. Personnel may be doing the screening, and they might eliminate you if they don't see what they've been told to look for. If you don't know the exact title, use a standard area such as finance, sales, or research.

Everything else on the resume complements the job objective. The education, experience, and skills all show that you can do the job you're trying to get.

Example

Objective: Seek a position as an Advertising Sales
Representative.

Education

List your educational experience in reverse chronological order. If you went to a prestigious school, highlight that fact by using bold face letters or caps. Be sure to include a high GPA and any honors or awards. List the key courses relevant to the job you are seeking. Omit insignificant schooling such as the summer course you took at the junior college back home. Don't mention your high school unless you went to a truly outstanding one or had an especially distinguished record.

Example

EDUCATION:

St. Anselm's College	GPA: 2.9/4.0
B.A. Communications	6/95

Coursework: Marketing Advertising, Media Planning, Principles of Persuasion, Managerial Accounting & Control, Consumer Psychology, Communication Ethics & Law, Public Speaking, COBOL

Honors and Activities: Dean's List, earned 80% of college expenses, Young Business Leaders Club

SKILLS

As we mentioned in chapter 13, employers want to know what skills you have. You can embed them in your work history, but sometimes it's a good idea to have a separate skills section. There you can highlight the main skills required of the position you're seeking. By doing so you increase your chances of creating a match in the employer's mind.

Use the STAR Technique we discussed in chapter 11: situation, action, results. Positive results create positive reactions. And if you can quantify your results, you're talking in a language employers understand.

Example

Marketing	• Successfully participated in three-month long computer-based marketing game which simulated the soft drink industry.
Organizational Ability	• Actively involved in arranging campus international festival; responsibilities included: arranging media events, designing pamphlets and coordinating the various committees involved.

WORK EXPERIENCE

List in reverse chronological order. Play up your work if it's career-related or requires skills you want to emphasize. Whenever possible, use job descriptions that are results-oriented

Example

WORK HISTORY:	**MACY'S DEPARTMENT STORE** Sales Representative 9/93 - 6/95
Retail Sales	Created furniture displays and performed price markdowns which led to **10% increase in departmental sales** for 1995
Communication Skills	Reinforced and **interpreted company procedures** and policies to new company employees during training periods

Some students find it helpful to have two separate work sections - career-related, which is prominently displayed, and other work, which goes toward the bottom of the page. If you have paid for your own education or a good portion of it, say so. It indicates that you're hard working and self-sufficient. Even if work is not directly related to your job objective, you often learn skills that are relevant to it. For example getting customers for a summer lawn care business demonstrates salesmanship. The Chris Shore resume that follows, is an example of how a student who isn't very far into their college program, can "punch up" things so they look more appealing. Chris isn't a stellar student, but he's not a dope either. Chris' GPA is only a 2.9, but a recruiter might still be interested in him because he's got some great work experience. Since he didn't include his GPA the recruiter will have to meet him and talk to him in person, or over the phone to determine if he's a suitable candidate for the job they have in mind for him. Once Chris gets an interview, he can use his persuasiveness and "can do" attitude to influence the recruiter positively. If you look closely at the jobs that Chris has worked, he's really only been a grocery clerk. However, looking at his resume he's emphasized many of his skills and abilities acquired since arriving at college. You too can write a much different resume today, than you did right after graduation. Even if you've only been in school one quarter, you are now a freshman at college and you have a projected graduation date. Whatever professional and non-professional activities you choose to get involved with will enhance your resume with functional skills, once you identify them with the STAR technique and hone them down to the most crisp and effective wording you can. Be sure to ask others to critique your resume and make suggestions. A resume is a living thing that grows as you grow, and changes just as you evolve through your college and life experiences.

Michael Rod's resume is an example of a student with slightly more experience. He's been here a quarter and has taken some classes. He is using his knowledge and experience gained in the academic setting to sell himself to industry. Note how he puts all his college-related skills and abilities up front on his resume. He has a decent GPA, as well, and includes it for the interviewer's convenience. Hopefully these two resumes give you some ideas about how you can format your own to market yourself for co-op applications, part-time employment, or to apply for a grant, scholarship or fulfill the requirements of this course!

ADDITIONAL INFORMATION

An effective job candidate uses every inch of her resume to her advantage. She lists only information that would be a selling point. Most employers don't really need to know that you enjoy swimming and scuba diving. A marine biologist, however, might find it helpful to include these. An engineer cited her plumbing experience when she applied for a position that required wearing a hard hat. She wanted to show that being a woman didn't mean she was afraid to get her hands dirty. One candidate noted that hunting was one of his hobbies. He was applying for a position in a rural area where hunting was extremely popular. By mentioning his interest in guns,

<u>EXAMPLE OF A STUDENT RESUME</u>

CHRIS SHORE

Box 599 Holcomb, University of Arkansas, Fayetteville, AR 72701

JOB OBJECTIVE: Summer internship with a **daily newspaper.**

EDUCATION

- **UNIVERSITY OF ARKANSAS**
  Journalism Major
  Anticipated Graduation: December, 1999

- **FAYETTEVILLE HIGH SCHOOL**
  Graduated June, 1995

CAREER-RELATED EXPERIENCE

UNIVERSITY OF ARKANSAS PRESS   Sept. 1995 - Present

- Assistant, Promotion and Marketing
  In charge of **promotion** for *VINEGAR DAYS*, by Max Middlesex

- Intern
  Wrote Jacket copy and designed advertising layouts for national authors; collaborated on coordinating autographings; ACCOMPLISHMENT: Consistently high appraisals resulted in promotion to salaried position.

SKILLS

- **EDITING & PUBLISHING:** Currently being trained in **manuscript and newspaper editing** by University of Arkansas Press; editor of high-school newspaper; ACCOMPLISHMENT: Received **superior rating** from Arkansas High-School Press Association for editorial on possible teacher strike

- **INTERVIEWING: Feature editor** and **reporter** for high-school newspaper; ACCOMPLISHMENT: Received **superior rating** from Arkansas High-School Press Association for interview with city government leader

- **LEADERSHIP:** Participated in "CLOSE-UP" political awareness program for a week in Washington, DC; Student Body President, Alday Junior High School

- **PRODUCTION:** Experienced in all phases of publication production, including copy preparation, design, typesetting and keylining

ADDITIONAL WORK HISTORY

- Grocery Clerk   IGA   Summer 1995
- Sales Clerk   McGuire's Book Shop, Atlanta, GA   Summer 1994
- Grocery Clerk   IGA   Summer 1994

<u>**EXAMPLE OF A STUDENT RESUME**</u>

Michael Rod

Campus: Georgia Tech Box 57123   Home: 7110 Lovers Lane

Atlanta, GA   30332   Columbia, SC   29223
(404) 676-6923   (803)   788-1234
e-mail:

JOB OBJECTIVE   Electrical Engineering major seeking co-operative placement in research and development.

EDUCATION

GEORGIA INSTITUTE OF TECHNOLOGY   9/95 - present
Freshman   GPA: 3.4/4.0

Electrical
Engineering
- Vector Calculus
- Computer and Digital Design Fundamentals

RICHLAND NORTHEAST HIGH SCHOOL   1991-1995
                                        GPA: 4.4/4.0

Advanced
Curriculum
- Derivative and Integral Calculus
- Advanced Physics
- Advanced English and American History
- National Honor Society

Related
Activities
and Awards
- Junior Engineering Technical Society
- Engineering Explorers
- Richland Northeast Senior Achievement Award in Science

PEOPLE SKILLS

Developed strong leadership and communications skills through the following:

- Palmetto Boys State
- Member, Richland Northeast H.S. Band
- Student Government
- Church youth group

EMPLOYMENT

- Waiter, Quality Inn, May-September, 1994
- Busboy, Quality Inn, January-May, 1994
- Busboy, Collaro's Italian Restaurant, Summer 1993
- Assistant Plater, Davis & Rodgers Plating, Summer 1992

EXAMPLE OF A STUDENT RESUME

NICHOLAS BENNINGS

Campus: 37-G Addison Hall, Bates College, Lewiston, ME
Permanent: 1301 DALRYMPLE, Hartford, CT 06110, 203/299-4636

JOB OBJECTIVE: Seek internship or summer employment with a **metropolitan museum**.

EDUCATION:

BATES COLLEGE   GPA: 3.7/4.0
                                                     1994-Present

Anthropology Major
- Social Anthropology Course
- Cultural Anthropology Course
- Greek and Roman Art and Architecture Course
- Art of the Middle Ages Course
- Dean's List first semester
- Member, The Arts Society

MERRIMAC HIGH SCHOOL   GPA: 3.5/4.0

Advanced Curriculum
- Advanced English, and social sciences
- President, Art Club
- National Honor Society member

EXPERIENCE:

VANDERNESSEN MUSEUM OF FINE ARTS
                                                     Summer 1993
Volunteer:
- Worked with curator to set up museum exhibits
- Prepared art objects for shipment

FUN WORLD AMUSEMENT PARK   Summer 1992

Games Host
- Developed strong **communication** and **public-relations skills** through heavy customer contact

References furnished upon request.

he was able to show that he could be one of the boys even though he'd gone to school in the big city. If you can't find another place to include a selling point, stick it in here. Leave it off it's not relevant. Instead use skills developed through your service within your fraternity/sorority, by developing a statement using the STAR technique. If you are asked, then inform the interviewer where you developed the skill. Fraternity and sorority affiliations can be used to screen you OUT as well as in. Better not to take the chance, unless you are certain.

REFERENCES

Choose them carefully. If you've followed the suggestions in this book, you should have many to choose from. Ask them if they are comfortable writing a favorable recommendation for you. Make sure they have copies of your resume. It will help them to discuss you more knowledgeably when they are contacted by employers. Also, when they see the total package they might be able to come up with other job leads for you. We recommend not listing your references on the resume. It's better to use every precious inch of space to promote yourself.

WORDING AND PHRASING

You control the tone of your resume by the way you write it. There should be no negatives. We remember one student listing a course in which he made a **D**. In fact, that's about all we can remember.

Your resume should be crisp and have punch. Remember, it's your personal ad. Start sentences with verbs or action words, and you'll create the impression that you're a "doer," and not one who sits and waits. Delete pronouns and anything superfluous.

The whole idea is to boil your market ability down to its essence. Recruiters and interviewers, then, will find it easy to remember you. And why they should hire you. Not every recruiter has been trained by the Department of Human Resources. Frequently corporations send new, inexperienced employees to handle screening interviews at college placement centers. They don't necessarily know how to compare the credentials of the many different candidates. It is to your advantage to make their job easier. A sharp resume is a first step. Make it clear why you're the one their company is looking for.

ACTION WORDS FOR RESUME CONSTRUCTION

A resume will be the first impression an employer has you. Make it count! Set the tone by using both action and positive words. Starting sentences with verbs can make your message stronger. Be honest but don't diminish your abilities by using lackluster words.

The following is a list of action words to use in constructing your resume. Refer to it often.

actively	accelerated	accomplished
accurately	achieved	adapted
addressed	adjusted	administered
adopted	advised	analyzed
applied	appointed	appraised
approved	arbitrated	arranged
assembled	assessed	assisted
attentive	audited	authenticated
budgeted	built	calculated
capable	careful	cataloged
certified	chaired	changed
channeled	chiefly	chosen
clarified	coached	collaborated
commended	consistently	constructed
consulted	coordinated	contracted
counsel	created	credited (with)
debated	decided	delegated
delivered	demonstrated	designed
determined	detected	developed
devised	directed	diverted
drafted	drew up	earned
economically	edited	effective
elected	eliminated	enhanced
enthusiastic	erected	established
estimated	evaluated	examined
executive	exhibit	expanded
expedited	experienced	explained
expressed	facilitated	familiar
filed	finalist	finished
forecasted	founded	function

generated	graduated	funded
helped	hired	honored
illustrated	implemented	improved
increased	indexed	influenced
innovation	inspected	installed
instituted	instrumental	integrated
interpreted	interviewed	judged
knowledgeable	launched	lead
lectured	licensed	lobbied
logical	maintained	major
managed	manufactured	marked
maximum	measurable	mediation
merchandised	merit	methodically
minimal	moderated	modified
most	motivated	motorized
narrated	navigated	negotiated
obtained	organized	originated
overcame	participated	perceptive
performed	persuaded	pinpointed
planned	positive	prepared
presented	primary	principal
produced	proficient	programmed
progressed	projected	promoted
proposed	proved	provided
publicized	qualified	quoted
recommended	recorded	reduced (losses)
reinforced	renovated	reorganized
reported	represented	researched
resolved	responsible	responsibilities
restored	revamped	revenue
revised	reviewed	satisfactorily
saved	scheduled	schematic
selected	served	significantly
simplified	sold	solved
solution	specialized	spoke
stabilized	strategy	streamlined
structured	successfully	suggested
summarized	supervised	supplemented

supported	surveyed	systematized
taught	trained	upgrade
wrote		

TYPES OF RESUMES
Chronological

This is the most traditional type - which is its advantage. Employers are familiar with it. The disadvantage of the chronological resume is that it plays up your work history even if it's sketchy or unrelated to your job objective. If you've followed the Master Plan outlined in this book, you should already have a solid work history. If your professional history is weak, consider another type of resume. If you want to see an example of a rather ho-hum, but nevertheless, a chronological resume look at Martin Ferryweather's resume, which appears at the end of this chapter. The same information is rearranged and reworked in the next resume example to become a great example of another type of resume: a functional resume. A chronological resume can be made to look more attractive than what we've done here, and for some people a chronological resume is the right way to go. We wanted to illustrate how using white space, typing elements and organization can make a big difference in presentation. The ho-humness of the first resume is not related to the fact that it's chronological at all--the reason it's ho-hum has to do with the lack of white space and the fact that the information is in paragraph form (the reader has to work to get the information) and there are no enhancements through the use of typing elements.

Functional

Since work history is played down, you can emphasize the skills necessary to perform the job you're seeking. And since you're not following any prescribed order, you can position the most relevant skills, experience, for example, higher on the page. Its main disadvantage is that employers see fewer of this type, and that might bother some of them. Of course, it might also catch their eye. Look at the second resume of Martin Ferryweather. Note how typing elements and emphasis on skills have completely changed the appearance of Martin. The reader, likewise, does not have to work very hard to determine what he's been doing and where he's gotten his experience and what his experience is in. By investing some time and energy in to formatting and enhancing the appearance with typing elements and white space, Martin looks like a much more attractive candidate. Investing a little time to make your resume the best introduction possible, is well worth the time.

Hybrid

We believe there is nothing sacred about resume construction. Your ultimate goal is to create a message that effectively promotes you. We read the resume experts, and we considered the principles of advertising. We did some research of our own--asking recruiters and personnel directors how they appraised resumes. Our guidelines evolved from all these sources. But they're still only guidelines.

Different students may have unique situations that require novel resumes. What about the student who makes a dramatic shift in major or a dual degree program? Nontraditional students also present unique problems. How do you highlight your strengths if you're a middle-aged homemaker returning to the work force? (Returning to the *paid* work force would be more accurate.) Or suppose you're returning to school after a substantial work history. Students with this kind of background will have to use their creative talents to develop a resume that is a hybrid. It would emphasize "real-world" skills acquired while managing a household, or managing the complexity of a dual degree program. If you have had a substantial gap since your last job, you must come up with contemporary work experience to enhance your resume. Volunteer at a local charity to "brush up" on rusty skills and to build recent experience. Always be ready to explain any long interruptions in your work history. You don't want to explain that since you got laid off back in '91, you just thought you'd collect your unemployment until it ran out! Get into the "head" of the interviewer. Explain it as a shift in career focus, an opportunity to learn new skills by returning to school, or by discussing a depressed job market in your field; don't give more information than you must, and don't lie.

RESUMES WHILE IN SCHOOL

Most students look for jobs several times while they're in college. This can begin the second quarter of your freshman year if you're a co-op student. Part-time work, summer jobs, and internships also require some sophistication about the process of getting hired. (Chapter 5 explains the importance of work experience.)

Application Form

In most instances you'll have to fill out a standard application or data sheet when applying for a job. We strongly recommend that you supplement it with your own personal resume. Personnel forms are designed to compare all applicants on certain key categories--school, work, etc. It's harder to emphasize your strong points if you don't have top grades or an impressive work history. A personal resume gives you more flexibility. You can highlight whatever you choose. And including a quality personal resume makes you look more professional.

There are a few things that you can do to beef up the form that personnel sends you. Usually there will be a place for "Additional Information." Consider listing skills pertinent to the job in question here. (Once more the STAR Technique helps you to shine.) Try to use every bit of available space to convey pertinent information about you. On the back of some forms there is space for listing coursework and a small "Comments" section. Cite only the most relevant courses and/or those in which you made the best grades. If you write across the page, separating courses with commas, you'll have more room to cover skills and other pertinent information.

Job Objective

Be wary of being too specific when applying for summer jobs. Many employers don't want to hire someone for a narrowly focused area for two or three months. The exception to this rule is when the work is seasonal or consists of a time-limited project. When stating your job objective for part-time, long-term work, follow the same principles you would when applying for permanent, full-time positions.

If you're applying for a co-op position or an internship, identify the area where you want to work. You probably won't start on anything very high up the ladder. Expect some on-the-job training first.

Sample Job Objectives

Sophomore Nursing student seeking summer employment in a hospital.

Seeking summer employment in surveying.

Seeking part-time employment in retail sales.

Seeking part-time employment (10-20 hours/week) as electronics repairman.

Business major desires co-operative placement in marketing or sales.

Junior in Political Science and History seeks internship with government agency.

Other Information

Emphasize any high-school honors and achievements. Do the same for your collegiate record to date. Include data from high school that pertains to skills, work history, and activities.

COVER LETTERS THAT WORK

Cover letters should be strong enough to stand on their own and promote you even when separated from your other credentials. In other words, no "Dear Mr. Gronk, I'm interested in working for your organization. Enclosed, please find my resume. Sincerely . . ."

Use the cover letter to elaborate on any information that is briefly covered in the resume and is a selling point. Use key phrases taken from your resume. Advertising relies on repeated presentations, and you're advertising yourself. We all know "Just Do It," promotes NIKE because you've seen the commercial countless times.

Format

The opening paragraph needs to serve as a "hook." It should motivate employers to read further. Mentioning something interesting about the company (not just something found in the Yellow Pages) shows that you believe their company is worth spending time on. Like the resume, the cover letter needs to show how a candidate's skills meet the employer's needs. State specifically how you can help solve the employer's problems. Indicate why you're contacting the employer and how you found out about the job (magazine article, newspaper ad, professional contact, etc.).

You'll probably need to do some research in source such as the *Business Periodical Index, Reader's Guide, Moody's Index,* and *Dun's Career Guide.* Your placement center can help you find such information. You want to be able to say specifically why you're interested in the particular organization you're contacting.

Body of Letter

Present your case as a strong candidate. Briefly cite whichever of your academic achievements, skills, accomplishments, and work history is relevant. Give specific examples with details. Repeat some of the key phrases contained in your resume to reinforce your selling points. Tell them what your main selling points are. Mention enclosing a resume for their convenience.

Closing Paragraph

Ask for action. Be confident and assertive about doing so. You wouldn't apply for the job if you didn't think you were the right one to do it. State that you will contact them in ten days to two weeks. *And do it.*

Note how Nicholas Bennings's cover letter complements his resume. Either letter or resume can stand alone, but together they build an even stronger case for the candidate.

OPTICALLY SCANNABLE RESUMES

Many large and mid-sized companies are automating their hiring processes. The use of resume scanning software is increasing and changing the way resumes are written. Including "key words" for your profession may be critical to your resume being selected in a job search. The following rules should be followed when sending your resume to larger companies or companies that you know use optical scanners to review resumes. Electronic Resume Revolution by Joyce Lain Kennedy is an excellent reference on this subject.

- Use white or light beige standard 8.5 x 11" paper. Avoid colored or textured papers.
- Avoid graphics, shading, italic text, underlining, script, vertical lines, parentheses, brackets, leader dots.
- Use sans serif fonts, i.e., Helvetica, Futura, Universe, Optima, ITC Avante Garde Gothic   or very popular serif fonts, i.e., Times, New Century Schoolbook, Palatino, ITC Bookman, or Courier. Do not use decorative typefaces or fonts.
- Avoid graphics, shading, italic text, underlining, script, vertical lines, parentheses, brackets, leader dots.
- Use horizontal lines sparingly; always leave at least 1/4" of white space around them.
- Use industry jargon and abbreviations, i.e., CAD, ISO, Unix, MBO, TQM.
- Use general abbreviations sparingly. It's best to spell it out.
- A laser printer is best.
- Your name should be the first line of your resume. if a third party is forwarding your resume, their name or sticker should be at the bottom of your resume.
- When faxing your resume, set fax machine to "fine mode".
- Always send originals.

From the 1994-95 Career Guide, Georgia Institute of Technology

EXAMPLE OF A COVER LETTER

February 2, 1995

Museum of Natural Artifacts
    And History
1748 Lincoln Square
New York, NY 10025

The Coca-Cola Company
Post Office drawer 1734
Atlanta GA, 30301

Attn: Mr. Carson Donnelly, *Global Staffing*
      Director of Student Internship Program

Dear Mr. Donnelly:

I am interested in applying for a summer internship offered through the Museum of Natural Artifacts and History. American Historian magazine recently reported that the MNAH provided the "most extensive training--outside of a dig--to those students interested in archaeology and anthropology." Although you have twenty-five summer internships, it's obvious that you have to be selective in choosing participants. Here's why I can make a positive contribution.

First, I have prior experience working in a museum. While in high school I was a volunteer at the Vandernessen Museum of Fine Arts. There I helped the curator set up exhibits and prepare art objects for shipment. One project that I particularly enjoyed working on included over 250 Native American artifacts and featured a full-scale replica of a wigwam.

Second, my academic accomplishments include a GPA of 3.7 after one semester as an anthropology major at Bates College and membership in the National Honor Society.

Finally, I have strong communication and leadership skills. I have proven experience in leading groups, being a team member, and working with the public, all assets that are helpful in a museum environment.

I have enclosed a resume for your convenience. I am eager to discuss internship opportunities and will contact you in three weeks to arrange for an interview.

Sincerely,

Nicholas Bennings
37-G Addison Hall
Bates College
Lewiston, ME 04240

Rather than conclude with our usual chapter summary at the end, look at our Resume Checklist. Use it every time you make out your resume, and if you need some more ideas about how to format a resume, look at the examples that follow the checklist.

RESUME CHECKLIST

475-4228

You want your resume to be memorable to the employer--but for all the right reasons. An omission or mistake should not be noted as your resume's most outstanding feature. Use the chart on the following page to check for any oversights. Have it double-checked by a friend just to ensure you haven't missed anything.

676-2121

RESUME CHECKLIST

	DID YOU:	YES	NO
1.	Prominently display your name?	____	____
2.	Put in a complete address and zip code?	____	____
3.	List a daytime telephone number and area code?	____	____
4.	Specify your job objective?	____	____
5.	Position you strongest information first?	____	____
6.	Describe your education?	____	____
7.	Complete a work experience section?	____	____
8.	Detail your relevant skills?	____	____
9.	Include information on affiliations?	____	____
10.	Use both positive and action words?	____	____
11.	Check for accuracy of information-- names, dates, etc.?	____	____
12.	Verify technical terms and descriptions?	____	____
13.	Correct any poor grammar?	____	____
14.	Shorten or tighten sentences?	____	____
15.	Eliminate repetitiveness?	____	____
16.	Leave out anything important?	____	____

Martin E. Ferryweather

1423 33rd Street, NW
Vincent, Ohio   44646
216/833-5531   (home)
404/894-1111   (school)

EDUCATION: Attended the Georgia Institute of Technology from September 1991 to June 1995. Will graduate with a Bachelor of Science degree in Management in June. Took many finance and management classes.

Honors &
Activities: Lettered 4 years and started 2 years in a major college football program. Dean's List, 2 times. Elected team captain for various games at Georgia Tech. Served as coach for church league basketball team and junior high football and basketball teams. Active in Atlanta's Big Brothers program and in the Boy's Club of America.

WORK HISTORY:

Summer 1994   CLEANER'S HANGER COMPANY, Mendosa, Ohio, Assistant. Responsible for working with different groups in production and administration. Duties included: assisting in the repair and maintenance of production equipment and the facilities, filling purchase orders, assisting the managers behind the counter and making deliveries.

Winters
1992-94   HOLY INNOCENCE CHURCH, Atlanta, Georgia, Office Staff/Coach. Responsible for scheduling referees for games, keeping payroll records and answering questions concerning the church's basketball league.

SKILLS &
HOBBIES: Have programmed with Lotus, dBase III, BASIC and Volkswriter. Enjoy swimming, jogging and reading.

References Furnished Upon Request.

MARTIN E. FERRYWEATHER

1423 33rd St., NW/Vincent, Ohio   44646216/833-5531 (home)   404/894-1111 (school)

OBJECTIVE

To obtain a management position in the banking industry involving commercial loans and/or bonds and securities.

EDUCATION

GEORGIA INSTITUTE OF TECHNOLOGY   **June 1995**
  B.S. Management

> **Significant Coursework:**

- Commercial Bank Management
- Real Estate Investments
- Organizational Structure Design
- Economic Theory of the Firm

- Investments
- Accounting
- Finance
- Personnel Management

QUALIFICATIONS

Portfolio Management: Successfully assembled and managed stock portfolio for investments class project. Received an 800% increase in revenues at end of quarter.

Bank Management: Analyzed a bank's financial position and made effective recommendations to top management for class project. Bank's return on equity increased 6%.

Leadership: Provided leadership and guidance through various activities including Atlanta Big Brothers Program; coaching junior high football and basketball, and church league basketball; and Boys' Clubs of America.

Computer Skills: Competent in various languages, including: Lotus, dBase III, BASIC, and Volkswriter.

WORK HISTORY

Cleaner's Hanger Company, Mendosa, Ohio   Summer 1994
Filled purchase orders and maintained facilities.

Holy Innocence Church, Atlanta, Georgia   Winters 1992-96
Coordinated referee schedules and kept records of payrolls
for church basketball league.

ACCOMPLISHMENTS

- Provided 100% of college expenses and contributed to family support through athletic scholarship and summer employment.
- Lettered 4 years and started 2 years in major college football.
- Dean's List
- Elected team captain for various games at Georgia Tech

15
How To Be
A Silver-Tongued Devil:
Interviewing

We've said it before. We'll say it again. The job world of the 21st Century will be volatile, if not downright chaotic. You may have countless jobs and multiple careers. Your ability to communicate effectively to a variety of people in a myriad of situations will be extremely useful. Your ability to handle yourself effectively in an interview may be essential.

Dr. Gene Griessman, author of *The Achievement Factors* recommends that you take a course in sales, preferably from some organization off campus. He recommends sales training because that's almost certainly what you don't get from your classes. He recommends off campus because college and university professors tend to look down their noses at the field of sales, equating all sales people with the often stereotyped "used car *salesman*", a term used to characterize someone who has no ethics.

Some years ago, a savvy corporate recruiter began an address to a group of college seniors by asking how many of them were going into sales. Only a few of the several hundred in attendance raised their hands. The speaker smiled and corrected his audience. "Most of you are wrong. You're ALL going into sales. Every time you look for a job, you've got to sell yourself."

> ## Every time you look for a job, you've got to sell yourself.

We would add that you must also be a salesperson when you try to get your idea across at a meeting, win a debate or election, or convince your friends or colleagues to volunteer for your project. This is why selling has always been important.

If persuasive skills were valuable in the 20th Century, just think how much more important they will be in the 21st. That is why getting training in sales can be a tremendous asset to you. Dale Carnegie, Career Track, and Nightingale all offer workshops. There are also a number of videos you can rent which will help you learn the basics. Your Placement Center or your business school may have these available for check-out.

While all kinds of communication and persuasion are valuable skills, the job interview, itself, will continue to be extremely important. Bear in mind that most of the principles involved in interviewing for a job are transferrable to applying for ANY position: being selected for the

Freshman Leadership Society, becoming an officer in your fraternity/sorority, or getting an internship. The rest of this chapter will focus on this crucial skill. Happily, it is possible to summarize the essence of effective interviewing in one sentence:

Convince the employer that you match his needs.

This isn't always easy, but it should make things easier for you to focus on just one objective. Especially when it is the same objective behind your resume, your cover letter, all of your communication with employers.

Interviewing Game Plan:

Before the Interview
1. Conduct a thorough self-assessment (goals & skills).
2. Develop a good resume.
3. Research the company and industry.
4. Anticipate key questions and develop effective answers.
5. Have your interview wardrobe ready.

During the Interview
1. Be confident and relaxed.
2. Follow the interviewer's cues.
3. Show enthusiasm.
4. Emphasize your selling points.
5. Sell yourself as a match.
6. Ask intelligent questions.

After the Interview
1. Write notes about the interview.
2. Send a thank-you letter.

GETTING READY

A good coach never brings his team out on the field without first preparing the players for the game. They need to know who they're up against, what to expect, and how to score points. Otherwise, they might as well stay in the locker room.

It's the same with interviewing. The more you know about the company, the questions they'll ask, and how to sell yourself, the better your chances for getting an offer. There are four preparation steps.

1. Develop A Marketable Resume

By now you should have a winning resume. If you haven't, go back to Chapter 13 and pull one together. Make sure that your references have copies of your resume. It could be embarrassing for both of you if they have to "wing it" when employers call them. Besides, they might not remember all your shining qualities without a little prompting.

Keep your resume and calendar by the telephone. If an unexpected call from an employer turns into a telephone interview, you'll be at your best in discussing your qualifications--even if you're dripping wet. Also, you'll impress them with your time-management skills if you don't have to fumble at setting a time.

2. Anticipate Key Questions.

Randall Powell in *Career Planning Today* says that interviewers want the answer to four questions:

> *1. What are your qualifications?*
>
> *2. Do your qualifications match our needs?*
>
> *3. Why are you interested in our company?*
>
> *4. Are you the best person for the job?*

To get answers to these questions, they'll probe your background with other additional questions. Some may seem unrelated or vague. Some might make you sweat. But unless the interviewer is a rookie or a real sadist, her questions have a purpose. She's trying to find out if you're the right person for the job.

The questions can be open-ended: "Tell me about yourself." They can be very specific: "Explain why your grades are low." We've included a list of the most commonly asked questions.

QUESTIONS INTERVIEWERS ASK

Tell me about yourself.

Why do you feel qualified for this position?

What would you consider an ideal job?

What do you know about our company?

What are your short-term goals? Your long-term goals?

What are your strengths? Your weaknesses?

What have been your most satisfying and disappointing experiences?

Why did you major in _____?

Which courses did you like best?

Explain why your grades are low.

How did you finance your education?

Do you plan to continue your education?

What did you learn from your work experience? From school?

What managerial or leadership positions have you held?

Why did you leave your job(s)?

How long do you plan on being with us if we hire you?

Tell me about your extracurricular activities.

What was the last book you read?

Where would you like to work? (geographic area)

Are there any places you wouldn't want to work?

Are you willing to relocate?

How do you feel about putting in overtime?

As the competition for good jobs gets stiffer, recruiters are increasingly asking tough questions about how you've handled challenges:

Tell me about a difficult problem you've faced and how you handled it.

Tell me about your biggest challenge as a student (a sorority officer, an employee at a fast food restaurant, etc.) and how you handled it.

Tell me about a set-back you've faced and what you learned from it.

Have answers ready for these questions. And remember, when Ms. Manager says, "Tell me about yourself," she doesn't really want to know who you had a crush on in sixth grade or why you think hang gliding is totally awesome. She wants to know about your achievements, your career goals, and why you chose your major. The bottom line is always: Can you meet the needs of our company?

The STAR Technique (Situation-Action-Results) is a powerful way for you to show her that you can. See Chapter 11 if you need a quick refresher. Armed with a list of your skills in academic, extra-curricular, and work situations you can face even the toughest questions. The STAR Technique is especially helpful in fielding open-ended questions (Tell me about your extracurricular activities) and handling stress questions (Why should I hire you?). You can also use it to keep an unfocused interviewer on track.

Outline responses to difficult or complicated questions. When discussing your weaknesses make sure your response doesn't conclude with a statement that leaves a negative impression. Counter the negative by adding something positive:

My GPA is lower than I would like because I had to work twenty hours a week to put myself through school. I was still able to graduate in four years, and I feel I learned a lot on the job.

Or:

I wasn't sure of my major when I started school, and my grades reflected that. Once I settled on journalism, my GPA started to pick up.

Spend extra time preparing for "loaded" questions. You should never lie, but an employment interview is not the time to purge your soul of any doubts or ambivalence you might be feeling. A good reply to "How long do you plan on being with us if we hire you?" might be "I'm looking at this job as a career opportunity, not as a short-term position." You've shown your commitment to the company and indicated you view it as more than a stepping stone--both things the interviewer wants to hear:

Questions You'll Want To Ask

Your questions are important too. Remember, you're also evaluating them. Can they meet your needs? Besides, what you ask says something about you -- your enthusiasm, your maturity, your understanding of the problems facing your field. Never ask obvious questions, ones that could be answered by reading the company brochure. Also, steer away from questions about salary, vacation, and company benefits during an initial contact--that is, unless the interviewer brings them up.

Speaking of initial contact, bear in mind that screening interviews serve a different purpose than the round of interviews conducted on a plant trip. Your interview at the Placement Office will probably last about thirty minutes. The person who conducts it probably does not have the power to hire you. Your purpose is to stay in the running by not getting screened out. That is why you don't want to be pushy about salary and benefits. Those kinds of questions are more appropriately raised at the final stages of the interviews conducted on the actual work site.

Be sure to ask specific questions about the job as it relates to your background. For instance, ask about the hardware and software used if you're a computer programmer. Ask about laboratory equipment if you're a medical technician. A coach might want to know about the practice facilities and the equipment budget.

Suggested Questions to Ask

What can I expect the first month on the job? The first three months? The first six months?

Have you hired many graduates with a background similar to mine?

Is the job currently filled?

Why is the job open now?

What is a typical career path for this position?

What is your relocation policy?

How much travel is involved?

How can I become immediately productive in this job?

What opportunities are there for in-service training and professional development?

How would you characterize the managerial philosophy of the firm?

What have those who have previously filled this position liked best about it? Least?

3. Research the company thoroughly.

You can't make a strong case for being hired if you don't know anything about them. How does an employer know you'll be a help if you can't show you understand their needs? And just as important, how do you know they're the right company for you? After all, you'll be spending an average of two thousand hours a year for these people. That's a heavy commitment to rush into blindly, so find out what you can about a prospective employer.

We have focused heavily on the business world because the majority of graduates end up working there. We talk a lot about researching corporations. This is because there is greater access to information about corporate world. Yet many of you will work for schools, hospitals, governmental agencies, small businesses and so on. But the same principles apply in each case. The more you know about a prospective employer, the better off you are.

Categories To Consider When Researching A Company

1. *What the company does:* Sell a product or a service? How diversified is its line? A multinational corporation may have hundreds. A small private school, just one.

2. *The stability of the organization:* What is the outlook of the industry and the particular company? How big were sales last year? Is the company growing? Who are the competitors? What about the company's reputation? Are there plans for new products or divisions? Their idea is to avoid climbing aboard a sinking ship. Or better yet, to get in just before the company takes off.

3. *How the company operates:* What is its organizational structure? Are there many levels of employees or just a few? Is it publicly owned, a Mom and Pop store, or a governmental agency? How large? Where located? More than one location? What is management like? How old? How qualified? How did they get there? Are there training programs for employees? What is the typical path for someone with your career objective? How are the employees treated? What about salaries? Benefits? Is there a recognizable corporate philosophy?

Sources Of Information About A Company

As mentioned earlier, it is easier to research a corporation than the corner drugstore. Perhaps it would be more accurate to say that you have to rely on different sources to investigate a small organization. Generally speaking, you will have to rely on word of mouth. If you've followed the Master Plan, you will already know people in your field. You can develop other sources of information through networking. Touch as many bases as you can, and see what you can find out.

Here are some other tips when researching a smaller organization:

Check with professional associations. Is the prospective employer a member? In good standing? Chambers of Commerce, Better Business Bureaus, and Speakers' Bureaus can all provide a few basic facts. In a very small community, the office of the mayor or city manager may serve as a primary source of information. Local newspapers and periodicals are another important source. If you have the gumption to do it, visit a local bar, diner, or restaurant that serves employees or clientele. Strike up a conversation, and see what you can find out.

A nurse applying for a position at a hospital would want to take a look at the hospital's brochure, find out about the demographics of the clientele, and get information on employment practices from Nurses' Associations. Finally, our blue-chip nurse would likely visit with other nurses in the hospital cafeteria or snack bar and pump them for information.

Our university recently interviewed candidates for an important administrative position. All the candidates were highly qualified and had impressive resumes. We arranged for all of them to speak with a variety of students and staffers. One of them took an extra step by walking back to the campus on his own to eat in the student cafeteria, wander the grounds, and chat with whomever he bumped into. For his efforts, he learned a lot about us. We also learned something important about him and his interest in the job.

If you're unable to find much information about the particular company you're considering, be sure to research current trends in your field. Having such up-to-date knowledge will help you to ask the key questions to see how an organization measures up. You'll also come across much more impressively during the interview.

If you are researching a large corporation, ask for assistance at the library. Research librarians can provide you with a wealth of material on products, services, and key personnel. Some basic sources to investigate include:

Annual Reports: Every public business is required to publish an annual report. You can get a copy from the firm's public relations department or often from placement offices, career-planning centers, stock brokerage firms, public libraries, etc. It typically contains:

Statement from president

Current activities and future plans

Summary of sales and profits

Independently audited financial statements

Comparison of this year's earnings to last.

Employment Brochures: Organization which employ several hundred people usually publish employment (recruiting) brochures. These are available through campus placement offices and college libraries. Or you can directly contact the company's college relations or personnel department. These brochures are a good source of information on the corporate environment. Pictures and quotes give you clues about the company's management style.

Investment Reports: Many investment firms make an analysis of public business firms whose stock is available for purchase. These reports may include such information as sales volume, earnings, and current market demand for products. Sources for stock market reports include *Value Line Investment Surveys, Standard and Poor's Stock Reports,* and *Moody's.* You could also contact a brokerage house as a potential client and get information.

Product Information: To learn about the range of products that a particular company manufactures, consult the *Thomas Register,* an eighteen-volume annual publication. Volumes 1-10 are like the yellow pages: under each product category, all manufacturers are listed alphabetically and geographically. Volume 11-12 name all products made by each company. Volumes 13-18 contain sample pages from company catalogs. You can also get product information from trade magazine ads or from product brochures put out by the company.

Business Periodicals: These are good sources of information about corporate environment and current happenings. Features on top executives give you a feel for the management philosophy of a company. To find magazine articles look under the *Business Periodical Index* and *Reader's Guide to Periodical Literature.*   Other sources to consider would include: *Fortune, Forbes, Barron's, Financial World, Business Week,* etc.

4. Have interviewing clothes ready. First impressions may be superficial, but they matter. Don't get left at the starting gate because your suit is wrinkled. Have at least one conservative suit that flatters you and makes you feel comfortable. If you need to, ask a more sartorially sophisticated friend to help you pick one out. Or check out John T. Malloy's *Dress For Success* or Susan Bixler's *Professional Image.*

Dress the way successful people in the field you're entering dress. Neat, clean, and currently stylish is what you should aim for. Now is not the time to borrow Dad's leisure suit or Mom's pillbox hat. Be wary of overt outward expressions of ethnic origin or philosophical affiliation. If you opt to include a statement like this in your wardrobe, scope out the situation ahead of time, to be certain you are increasing your opportunity for selection, not eliminating them. You may also want to designate a couple of shirts or blouses as off-limits except for interviews. The same with a freshly shined pair or dress shoes and your favorite tie. And after each interview, look over your outfit and put it away for the next time. You don't want any surprise grease spots waiting for you.

DURING THE INTERVIEW

1. Be confident and relaxed.   (Step 1 for the actual interview, step 5 for the entire interview process.)

All employers want someone who is self-assured and able to perform under pressure. Try to look at each interview as an opportunity to do just that. And why shouldn't you be confident? You've worked hard to develop all your Information Age skills. And you've done your homework in preparation for the interview itself. Being prepared--it's one of the best ways to feel on top of any situation.

Arrive a few minutes early. You'll have the time to check your appearance, review your resume, and collect your thoughts. Take note of the surroundings. They can be very revealing -- especially if you had a hard time getting information about the organization. Look for company literature in the lobby. Talk with the receptionist. Observe the decor. Is it warm and inviting or cold and formal? All these things are clues to what this outfit is like.

If you're feeling more than the usual nervous energy, you can calm down by using one of the stress management techniques described in Chapter 9.

When you first meet Mr. Manager make eye contact and shake his hand when he offers it. Some male interviewers are unsure of protocol and may not extend a hand to a female candidate. We suggest that she offer him your hand as an ice-breaker.

2. Follow the interviewer's cues.

Wait until the interviewer indicates for you to take a seat. If she obviously stalls about asking -- a technique sometimes used in stress interviews -- announce to her that you'll sit and wait until she's ready to begin.

If you have the opportunity, take a look around the office before the interview starts in earnest. If the room has family pictures and other homey touches, you're probably dealing with a people person. An impersonal atmosphere tips you off that ideas are this interviewer's preference.

Each interviewer will have his or her own style. But basically there are three methods of interviewing:

Directed;

Non-directed; and

Stress.

Directed: When you deal with someone from personnel, chances are he'll ask specific questions based on an outline. There will probably be a set time limit, which doesn't allow for much wasted talk. These are directed interviews, and they're primarily used by trained interviewers for screening candidates.

Non-directed: The atmosphere is less formal. The questions are broader and more likely open-ended. The candidate is encouraged to talk freely. Inexperienced interviewers are more likely to be non-directed.

Stress: The interviewer uses techniques intended to increase tension --long lapses of silence, penetrating stares, and confrontational questions. The idea is to see how you handle the pressure. You obviously make points by staying calm and collected, but how do you manage this?

First, look at a tough interview as a challenge and an opportunity. You're better prepared than most candidates, so handling an unfriendly interview effectively will only make you look stronger than the others. Second, rehearse with friends, especially if you anticipate a stress interview. Make a game of it. See how impossible you can be with each other. The real interview will seem like a piece of cake in comparison. Third, read up on interviewing. Your public or school library almost always has many contemporary books available to coach you on how to approach this portion of your job search.

3. Show enthusiasm.

It's very discouraging to talk with an employer who seems bored out of his skull by your very presence. Well, interviewers can get discouraged too. They want you to be excited about their company. In fact, your chances of getting an offer are minimal if you don't look like you really want to work for them.

So give a firm handshake, maintain eye contact, lean forward, speak up. Listen closely to the interviewer. Reflect key points in your own words. Ask questions if you need clarification. If an interviewer is convinced that you really hear him, you've won half the battle already.

You've researched the company. Demonstrate this knowledge to the interviewer by asking intelligent questions: "I understand your agency is developing a program to combat adult illiteracy. Can you tell me about some of your plans?"

4. Emphasize your selling points.

One student recently came to Career Services for help after getting a flush letter. He reported that half his interview was wasted on small talk. The recruiter was about the same age as the candidate and shared a similar background. They seemed to hit it off because of their similarities. Unfortunately, this led to little more than a rap session. The interviewer probably concluded that the candidate was a nice guy but didn't have much to offer.

Go into each interview with a mental list of your selling points -- the skills and experiences that qualify you for this particular job. *Make sure you discuss each one before the end of the interview.* This is the single most important step in the entire interview. If you run into an inexperienced or unfocused interviewer, be tactfully assertive and take the lead yourself. Here are some suggestions:

That's interesting. Maybe we can talk about that more after the interview.

What you're saying reminds me of _____. Let me tell
     you what I did.

I've had a similar experience which really tested my _____
     skills. Let me tell you about it.

This is where your familiarity with the STAR Technique (Chapter 11) comes in handy. Use it well, and you can concisely tick off your selling points with real impact.

5. Sell yourself as a match.

Not only must you emphasize your selling points, but you must also establish a bridge between you skills and the company's needs. This means that you will highlight some of your qualifications more than others. Specifically, you should dwell on those of your selling points that are most crucial to the performance of the job you are applying for.

Obviously, use your own judgment here. If you're interviewing with a large corporation and hope to move up the corporate ladder, you will want to convince the interviewer that you possess management potential even if your first position has no managerial responsibilities.

6. Ask intelligent questions.

You took the trouble to prepare them. Don't pass up the chance to use them. With practice your confidence will grow, and you'll be able to pose thoughtful questions that occur to you during the course of the interview.

AFTER THE INTERVIEW
1. Make notes about the interview as soon as possible.

Write it down while it's still fresh. Otherwise you might forget something important, or get different companies mixed up. Key bits of data are:

1.   *Recruiter's name and title* (double-check the spelling);

2. *What you do next* -- submit additional information? Contact them by a certain date?

3. *What they do next* -- are there other stages to this company's selection process? Additional interviews? When will you hear from them?

4. *Impressions of the interview* -- good and bad points.

This helps you prepare for the next interview.

2. Write a thank-you note.

This is more than being polite -- it can close the deal. Use this letter to reiterate briefly why you match their needs. Did you forget to emphasize one of your strengths? Have you thought of any new reasons why you're the best qualified candidate for the position? Be sure to highlight that sort of information.

One co-op student used his thank-you letter to ask to be reconsidered. Another wrote: *I was so interested in the new project you mentioned that I had to find out more about it. I discovered that the laboratory equipment being used is similar to what I have been trained to use.*

The thank-you note can be just as powerful in the interviewing process as the cover letter. A strong one can reinforce the idea that you fit the employer's needs. A ho-hum one shows only that you follow business protocol.

SUMMARY

1. Your objective during the interview is to demonstrate that you match the employer's needs.

2. Prepare for the interview by:
   a. developing a good resume;
   b. anticipating key questions;
   c. researching the company thoroughly;
   d. having your interview wardrobe ready.

3. You interview well by:
   a. being confident and relaxed;
   b. showing enthusiasm;
   c. selling yourself as a match;
   d. following the cues of the interviewer;
   e. emphasizing your selling points;
   f. asking intelligent questions.

4. Follow up the interview by:
   a. making notes as soon as possible;
   b. sending a thank-you note.

16

Citizenship and Leadership

In Chapter One, we argued that the 21st Century will pose enormous challenges: environmental, civil, health-related, and economic to list but a few. In our view, these problems are interrelated to each other as well as to the other forces that will drive the Information Age. If knowledge is power, then it is vital to have an effective educational system. Otherwise, our society must cope with a growing underclass and the prospect of class conflict -- which in fact, is where we seem to be heading. Because technological change is accelerating, this problem will only snowball if it is not addressed.

Technology has drastically reduced the size of the world. Electronic communication travels at the speed of light. We watch wars on our televisions in real time. Third world viewers also watch commercials extolling the benefits of luxury automobiles, high tech cameras, and stylish sportswear. They are dissatisfied with any arrangement that leaves them on the outside looking in at this material bounty. This is one of the reasons communism lost its hold on its citizens. It's also why immigration is a very contentious issue in most of the developed world. If the have-nots can't get what they want where they are, they'll move to where they can.

With international travel increasing, immigrants eager to enter our country, and the global marketplace already a reality, infectious diseases are not easily contained by any border. Nor are religious, ethnic, or racial conflicts. Moreover, with an increasingly diverse citizenry, how are we to retain a viable national identity? What goals and values can we share that will unite us as a people? How can we create a civil society?

Because technology has made the world small, other people's problems are now our own. If urban youth are alienated and unemployed, their rage threatens us all. If the Mexican economy flounders, we get more illegal immigrants. If the Russian economy fails, we are faced with the prospect of a new regime that may be hostile toward the USA. Local pollution becomes international acid rain. Global warming affects the climate and shoreline of all nations.

John Donne wrote that "No man is an island." Ernest Hemingway reminded us that the bell tolls for each of us. So, why should you regard it as your obligation to make your school, your city, your country, and your world a better place? Because we sink or swim together. Citizenship is for the common good. Citizenship is also in your own interest.

Let us add that this is not an ideological position. It transcends liberal and conservative perspectives. Indeed this is one of the few principles upon which all our national leaders agree even though they may be divided as to just how to address the enormous challenges facing us. Conservative thinker William F. Buckley extolled the concept of voluntary national service in his recent book, *Gratitude: Reflections On What We Owe to Our Country*. President Clinton implemented a national service corps. So, whose job is it to be a better citizen? Yours and ours.

LEADERSHIP

In order to make a better world, we need better leaders. Citizenship requires leadership. So does professional success. If you can lead no one, your education is incomplete. True, you probably won't be President of the United States, a Four Star General, or a CEO of a major corporation. (But then, why not?) More likely, you will be a director, a teacher, or an entrepreneur. And you will almost certainly at some point chair a committee, propose an idea to neighbors or colleagues, or parent a child. Each and every one of these roles/activities requires you to lead. How do you do it, and can you learn the skills it takes?

For example, the basketball star David Robinson started out to get an education at the Naval Academy. HIS value and belief system did not permit him to "excuse" himself from duty, even when he grew head and shoulders above his Naval Academy classmates and exceeded the height for the Navy. HIS value and belief system meant that he did go and serve his obligatory two years of military service upon completion of the Academy, forfeiting a sizable sum in professional sports salary. HIS value and belief system means that now, while a star earning more than $36 **million** dollars, excluding product endorsements, he invests his personal time in talking to elementary school students; "adopting" 94 inner city fifth graders and assuring their tuition, if they will work toward and attend college; and by looking at all aspects of his own life, his personal relationships and his business relationships to constantly assure that he is behaving in an ethical and responsible manner. He is living his life in such a way that his value and belief system are congruent with his leadership, his achievement, and his conscience. He invests himself charitably not only with money, but with time, energy, and talent.

We believe there are at least seven characteristics that make for successful leadership: vision, commitment, respect, integrity, persuasion, life-long learning, and the willingness to take charge. Let's take a brief look at each.

VISION. Before you can lead someone to the promised land, you must be able to see it yourself -- even if you haven't been there yet. Indeed, the greatest leaders are able to create the future by vividly imagining it. John Kennedy envisioned a man on the moon. Stephen Jobs envisioned a world in which we all use personal computers. Mary Kay envisioned a network of small business women who were also saleswomen creating a business juggernaut. Why couldn't your vision be greater still?

While we encourage you to dream big, we also know that not every business prospers, nor is every dream realized. Nor is every vision about changing the world. Sometimes it's about changing a small part of it -- seeing the successful child in the troubled youth you mentor, seeing a team that wins by playing together, picturing a residence hall in which students are a community of learners.

A vision is related to the goals that together will make the vision a reality, but a vision isn't a goal or even a collection of goals. A vision is a portrait of a future you wish to create. Although it comes from your imagination, it is something you can describe vividly. It is something that you can see and so you can describe it to others. A vision can sustain you in tough times. It can compel others to work together in the service of that vision.

Where do visions come from? How do you become visionary? We believe you can become more visionary, but like everything else, you acquire vision only by paying your dues. First, you must understand yourself. You must know YOUR values, interests, abilities, and goals. You must create your mission before you can create one that others will buy into. Second, you must know the world around you. You can't create a new world (or even a small part of it) without first understanding the present one. Ignorant, uninformed people are not likely to develop very useful, much less compelling visions. If you're not making quantum leaps in knowledge acquisition from here on out, you'll be shortchanging yourself in the vision department as well as in the domain of leadership.

COMMITMENT. Ideas are cheap. Let us amend that. Ideas -- even good ones -- without the commitment and dedication to turn them into action are cheap. Many a lofty vision has died because the person who dreamed it did not invest the blood, sweat, and tears to make that vision a reality.

Commitment is also a necessity if you hope to enlist others in your cause. We're talking about YOUR commitment. If you won't stand up for your ideas, why should others? Generally, changing things for the better requires the help of others. This is true professionally. It's also true as you exercise your citizenship.

Think back on when someone wanted you to work for a cause. Did the captain ask you to sacrifice for the good of the team, but (s)he never passed the ball? Didn't make you very committed to the team, did it? Did the president of your organization ask you to work Saturday morning at the fund raiser, but (s)he slept in? Maybe next time you'll sleep in too. Leaders who aren't committed soon have no one to lead.

Commitment starts in the heart. It's feeling passionately about something. But commitment always boils down to action. It's standing up for your ideas. It's working long and hard without complaining to turn ideas into reality. So, how do you get committed? How do you kindle passion in your heart for something beyond yourself?

If nothing fires you up, we suspect you're avoiding life rather than living it. If you're a young adult just out of high school, you probably enjoy more freedom in your life than you've ever had or ever will have. You can spend your time playing computer games, watching TV, and taking naps. Or you can immerse yourself in academic and extracurricular life. You can join a professional society, start a small business, or work for Habitat for Humanity.

Sometimes, motivation fires you up to take action. But if nothing motivates you, we urge you to act anyway. Once you start doing, playing, and thinking, enthusiasm will follow. Who knows, you may just find yourself committed.

RESPECT. You can intimidate some people into following your lead, but people follow out of fear only so long as you have some power over them. The best leaders motivate people to want to follow them. How do you get people to want to? Having a compelling vision is certainly part of it, but others won't even consider your vision unless they're convinced you respect them. Think about some leader whom you would gladly follow through thick or thin. Chances are, you believe this person respects you.

You demonstrate respect by being considerate, by encouraging others, and by understanding them. While your first image of a leader might be some take-charge person giving an inspiring speech, you must learn to listen if you want others to listen to you. Good leaders are empathic: they can see things from the other person's perspective. The very best leaders understand others deeply, grasping what events mean to their followers and how they feel about those events.

INTEGRITY. There is inevitably an ethical component to leadership. Think of great leaders, and you think of honorable men and women. This doesn't mean our greatest leaders were saints, but they are remembered as having a firm moral center. It's not enough to have good ideas and charisma. You must have a coherent set of values. Your actions must match your words. If people don't know where you stand, they will not want to back you. If people doubt your word, why in the world would they want to follow you?

PERSUASION. OK, you've got a great idea -- an idea that's positively visionary. It's almost certain that you will need help to make your vision a reality. How do you get others to buy into your vision? Throughout this book we've emphasized the importance of communication skills. In order to lead you must communicate your vision to the people whom you want to help you. Not only must you paint a clear picture, you must persuade others to make a commitment to work with you towards the realization of your vision.

This is partly a "public speaking" issue. Can you stand up in front of a group and speak confidently and sincerely? Can you do this before a handful, a dozen, a roomful, a thousand? Speaking effectively before a group may intimidate or even terrify you, but it's a VERY useful skill. Among the activities that most executives claim to like is speaking before large groups.

This doesn't mean that you've got to be a declaimer of olympian proportions in order to be a leader. Some people are more persuasive one to one. If you saw the movie, *Malcolm X*, you may recall the lengthy conversations Malcolm had with the inmate instrumental in his conversion. The other inmate rarely raised his voice. Nor were his words flowery. But he spoke from the heart and convinced Malcolm to work for a much larger cause than himself.

If you're not sure of your persuasive abilities, work to improve them. Consider some of the following ways to improve in this important area:

Taking classes in public speaking

Attending assertiveness workshops

Participating in sales seminars and workshops

Volunteering to give a committee's report to the group-at-large

Joining organizations such as Toastmasters

Running for office in an organization

LIFE-LONG LEARNING. Throughout this book we've stressed the rapid pace of change that will characterize the 21st Century. In order for you to be successful, you must cope with this change through continuous learning, adaptation, and repeatedly reinventing yourself. This will be even more true for 21st Century leaders.

Leaders face almost constant new challenges. They must come up with new strategies and techniques for coping with a world undergoing revolutionary change. While leaders must be grounded in solid, enduring values they must keep abreast of technical, scientific, and cultural changes. How can any business compete if it uses outdated information technology? How can medicine advance apart from genetic research? How can marketing executives sell new products if they don't know the mood of the public?

Probably the most important characteristic you can possess is an insatiable curiosity -- a burning desire to learn. This desire must translate into action -- reading, experimentation, involvement, reflection. You would be short-sighted to confuse going to college with acquiring an education. You would be a fool to pass up the education that's available to you while you're here.

Moreover, right now is the time to cultivate the successful habits of the continuous, life-long learner.

TAKING CHARGE. Finally, leading means acting to improve things. You can't very well lead if you're not willing to make a decision, take a risk, and DO something to make things better. In a recent discussion on leadership a number of fraternity and sorority officers revealed to me (Bill) what they thought most held their organizations back. Too many of the members didn't want to get involved, didn't want to assume responsibility for improving things, didn't want to stick their necks out. They were waiting for the other members to fix things. The following story, created by the **prolific** Anonymous, neatly captures this problem.

"Four people named Everybody, Somebody, Anybody, and Nobody met to accomplish an important task. Everybody was sure Somebody would do it. Anybody could have done it but Nobody did it. Somebody got angry about that, because after all, wasn't it Everybody's job? Everybody thought that Anybody could do it, but Nobody realized that Everybody wouldn't do it. It ended up that Everybody blamed Somebody when Nobody did what Anybody could have done."

Leading might mean confronting members of your team who are shirking their responsibilities. It could mean suggesting a change to someone in a position of power. It could mean rallying people to address a problem. It could mean volunteering to serve on or chair a committee to address an organizational issue. It could mean something as simple picking up the trash yourself, registering to vote, speaking courteously to those whose station in life is lower thatn your own. It can also mean making small, but significant steps toward changing things in your own life, that move you closer to a special goal you have.

How do you get started? It's simple. Not easy, but simple. You take charge. What can you take charge of today?

COMMITMENT

Commitment involves passion, loyalty, and maybe more than anything else it means putting your time and money where your mouth is. Commitments can be civil, professional, academic, romantic, or religious along with many others. This exercise is an opportunity for you to identify your personal commitments and check how strongly you truly are committed to them. If your commitments are trivial or lack follow through, consider how you will change. List those persons, institutions, or ideals to which you are most strongly committed.

1. _____

2. _____

3. _____

4. _____

5. _____

Now place each of your commitments in one of the categories below, and see if you truly live your commitments. If your commitment doesn't match one of the categories, list your own ways which demonstrate the strength of that commitment.

I. Citizenship.
_____ 1. I'm registered to vote.
_____ 2. I vote in most elections.
_____ 3. I know who my congressman is.
_____ 4. I've worked in a political campaign.
_____ 5. I know the news well enough to be an informed voter.

II. Religious/Spiritual.
_____ 1. I attend church, synagog, mosque regularly.
_____ 2. I pray or meditate regularly.
_____ 3. I read and reflect on religious literature.
_____ 4. I contribute money in support of my beliefs.
_____ 5. I contribute time in support of my beliefs.

III. Philanthropic/Charitable.
_____ 1. I stay informed of the causes I'm committed to addressing.
_____ 2. I contribute money to the cause.
_____ 3. I contribute time and energy to the cause.
_____ 4. I'm a member of a group which serves the cause.
_____ 5. I avoid activities which harm the cause.

IV. Academic/Professional.
_____ 1. I attend almost all my classes.
_____ 2. I regularly do my homework.
_____ 3. I neither cheat, nor do I assist others to cheat.
_____ 4. I try to learn the material, not just get by.
_____ 5. I go beyond the assignments in order to learn more.

V. Other: _____

_____ 1. _____

RESPECT FOR OTHERS

There are many ways you can demonstrate your respect for others. We've listed three basics.

I. Empathy.
_____ 1. I can be silent when others need to speak.
_____ 2. I can hear the feelings and meanings behind the words.
_____ 3. I can ask questions that encourage self-revelation.
_____ 4. I avoid criticizing other persons.
_____ 5. I convey my interest by eye contact and body language.

II. Encouraging/Complimenting.
_____ 1. I compliment people when they succeed.
_____ 2. I congratulate people when they win an award.
_____ 3. I encourage people when they have setbacks.
_____ 4. I send notes or e-mail to encourage people.

III. Going the Extra Mile.
_____ 1. I keep track of people's birthdays.
_____ 2. I send birthday cards to friends & acquaintances.
_____ 3. I give gifts or stage a surprise when a colleague achieves something important.

PERSUASION

Place a check by the following items if they accurately describe you.

_____ 1. I ask questions in class.
_____ 2. I contribute to class discussions.
_____ 3. I offer my views during meetings.
_____ 4. If I disagree strongly during a meeting, I'll say so.
_____ 5. I can effectively report a committee's discussion back to the main group.
_____ 6. I can run a meeting effectively.
_____ 7. I know Robert's Rules of Order.
_____ 8. I can address a small group effectively.
_____ 9. I can hold a large group's attention when I speak.
_____ 10. I can make a strong case for my point of view.

If you're not satisfied with your persuasive skills, here are ten antidotes.

1. Prepare a meaningful question before class. Ask it during class.
2. Prepare a thoughtful observation before class. State it when appropriate during class.
3. Think about an issue likely to come up at your next meeting. Ask for the floor, and make your point.
4. Think about a perspective with which you're likely to disagree at the next meeting. Prepare a rejoinder. State your rejoinder at the next meeting.
5. Volunteer to speak for your committee.
6. Volunteer to run a committee meeting. Prepare an agenda, and stick to it.
7. Study Robert's Rules of Order.
8. Volunteer to speak before a small group on something that's important to you. Prepare thoroughly, and practice your speech.

9. Volunteer to speak before a large group on something that's important to you. Prepare thoroughly, and practice your speech.
10. Try to convince a friend or acquaintance to join you in some cause.

ADDITIONAL STEPS TO TAKE

1. Read books on assertiveness, sales, speech making.

2. Attend a campus workshop on assertiveness.

3. Take an elective course in speech.

4. View videotapes dealing with sales and persuasive speaking.

5. Attend an off-campus workshop in sales or speech making.

VISION

Identify something you'd like to accomplish that requires the help of others. It could be big -- World Peace -- or small -- on-site tutoring in your residence hall. It could be philanthropic -- house the homeless -- or personal/professional -- starting up your very own widget business. The main thing is to pick something you have some passion for. Probably it's a good idea to start out with something a tad smaller in scale than world peace, but don't be afraid of lofty aspirations. Dreams are important!

Another way to get started is to think of an organization of which you're a member -- a church, a club, a fraternity or sorority. Now, dream about this organization at its best. What would it be like, look like, sound like? What impact would it have on its members? The larger society?

Once you've settled on the object of your vision, allow your creativity to flesh it out. For example, think of the benefits of on-site tutoring: better grades and more successful students, but don't stop there. Imagine where and how the tutorial service would run. A vision has color and size. It is realized by reaching related goals, but it's more than those goals. It's the total reality of what you want to accomplish. You might paint a mental picture of successful juniors and seniors volunteering their time to tutor students on weekday evenings. You could describe their satisfaction at contributing to the development of their fellow students. You could describe the success of the students tutored and their gratitude and the impact of the program on campus community and culture.

Share your vision with a friend or classmate. Ask if the vision was engaging... inviting ... inspiring... compelling. What would it take to make it more compelling? Work on your vision until your ready to share it for real.

A good way to start is to mindmap your vision.

LIFE LONG LEARNING

Life long learning has been a key theme of this book. You won't fair well in the Information Age if you don't stay informed. This is doubly true of leaders. So, how do you currently stay informed? How do you intend to keep up in the future? Check the items that accurately describe you.

_____ 1. I frequently read a daily newspaper.

_____ 2. I can name at least four political columnists of varying ideological point of view.

_____ 3. I frequently read a weekly news magazine.

_____ 4. I often watch a national news show on television.

_____ 5. I often read one or more business periodicals (e.g., Wall Street Journal, Fortune, Business Week, etc.)

_____ 6. I follow the latest developments in science and technology.

_____ 7. I've been to a play within the past year.

_____ 8. I've seen a movie with subtitles within the past year.

_____ 9. I have read an unassigned work of literature within the past year.

_____ 10. I periodically read a professional or trade journal within my field of interest.

_____ 11. I attend meetings or conferences of a professional society.

_____ 12. I've learned some new computer skills within the past year.

_____ 13. I sometimes discuss my field of interest with others to find out more about it.

_____ 14. I have attended a serious concert/performance within the past year.

_____ 15. I occasionally watch television documentaries that cover history, science, or current affairs.

_____ 16. I have eaten the food of at least six different countries within the past year.

_____ 17. I have friends and acquaintances of a variety of ethnic and religious backgrounds.

_____ 18. I can readily identify most countries on a world globe.

_____ 19. I understand some basic features of most major cultural groups throughout the world.

_____ 20. I have read a serious nonfiction book which was not assigned within the past year.

_____ 21. I know the basic tenets of each of the world's major religions.

What other actions do you take to indicate your commitment to continuous learning?
What do your responses reveal about your commitment to continuous learning? What do you need to do differently in the future?

TAKING CHARGE

Most of us will never head up a major corporation or hold a major political office. Nonetheless, we can exert leadership in many ways -- by holding an office in a smaller organization, by speaking up at organizational meetings, by volunteering to handle a problem. Here are some ways you could stretch your leadership wings.

1.   Identify an issue about which you have strong unexpressed feelings in an organization to which you belong. Think about what you could say or do to strengthen the organization's stand on this issue. Craft a statement which you could make at a meeting. Imagine what it would be like to make the statement. What would the response of your fellow members be? Can you think of effective ways of responding to them? Pick an ally within the organization that you could share your views with. How does (s)he respond? Does (s)he have any suggestions for improvements. Are you accurately understanding the opposing point of view? Select a time when you will raise the issue and state your position. Go for it!

2.   Identify a concern or a problem which you have and a person in authority who could address your concern. Think of a **reasonable** course of action which the authority could take which would improve the situation. Make sure that the authority has the power to effect the change you recommend, that the action is cost-effective, that it will not cause undue damage elsewhere. Craft a recommendation you could make to the authority. Practice it with an ally. Make an appointment with the authority. When you meet, explain your concern, recommend your solution, and state your willingness to help implement the solution if that's feasible.

3.   Identify an office or position you would like to hold. It should be in an organization in whose goals you believe. Declare your intention to run for office. Or, if more appropriate, speak with current officers about your desire to assume a greater leadership role. If you run for office, secure the commitment of some friends who will help you. Get organized, plan a campaign, implement it. If the more likely route to power is through appointment, discuss your desire to serve on a particular committee or as a particular office holder. Explain why you think you can do the job. Ask for feedback and a commitment to be given the opportunity to lead.

4.   Read some books and articles on leadership and citizenship.

5.   Attend a Leadership Workshop.

6.   Sign up for an academic class in leadership.

INTEGRITY

Name an individual whom you judge to be high in integrity: _____

How long have you known this individual? _____

How long did it take before you recognized the person's integrity? _____

What characterizes this person that spells integrity? _____

_____

What actions does this person take that suggest integrity? _____

_____

Can you identify a situation in which this person's integrity was tested? _____

_____

How did (s)he handle the test? _____

_____

Name an individual whom you judge to lack integrity: _____

How long have you known this individual? _____

How long did it take before you recognized the person lacked integrity? _____

What characterizes this person that spells weak integrity? _____

_____

What actions does this person take that suggest weak integrity? _____

_____

Can you identify a situation in which this person's integrity was tested? _____

_____

How did (s)he handle the test? _____

_____

In what related ways are you like the person with high integrity?

In what related ways are you like the person with weak integrity?

How will you increase your personal integrity?

17

Succeeding in the 21st Century

You're a time traveller, heading into the turbulent 21st Century. In order to succeed you must be flexible enough to adapt to constant change. Your power will be based on your knowledge, but since knowledge is rapidly expanding, you must keep learning throughout your life. Continuous life-long learning means acquiring new information, but it's more than that. The knowledge-based Information Age requires some core intellectual skills that will be the basis of your success. You must know how to learn. You must be able to think analytically. You must be able to synthesize novel solutions out of disparate data to the complex challenges that will daily confront you. In the midst of all this change you must forge an identity based on enduring values that will guide you throughout your life.

Succeeding as a leader in the 21st Century also requires continuous life-long learning. You must create compelling visions and convey them powerfully to others. You are unlikely to envision anything compelling or persuasive if you're ignorant or naive. Nor will others follow you if you have not thought through a coherent set of values. You must also have the desire to "take charge," the willingness to assume responsibility for making things better.

In this book, we've also talked about being an achiever. Achievers are driven to attain clear, challenging goals in the face of obstacles by working harder and smarter and using expert help. Professional achievement in the 21st Century will more often require an entrepreneurial flair: You, not some large corporation, will have to take charge of your career. You will have to persuade others that you can help solve their problems.

Goals and vision, drive and persistence, communication and persuasion, learning and innovation, commitment and taking charge. Whether we're talking about success, leadership, or achievement in the 21st Century, the principles are remarkably similar. What it boils down to is that to flourish in the future you must master some very old skills -- planning, learning, thinking, and communicating -- but you must do so in a rapidly changing environment.

While learning must be a life-long enterprise, now is the time to acquire learning skills and cultivate the learning habit. You are surrounded by educational opportunities: professors, classes, libraries, computers, activities, organizations. You can capitalize on these opportunities by immersing yourself in them, or you can slide by with as little effort as possible. It's all up to you.

It's all up to you.

Why not roll up your sleeves and get started right now!

TAKING THE LONG VIEW

One of the marks of a well educated person is the ability to plan ahead. Planning will be difficult in the 21st Century because of the complexity, extent, and pace of change. Nonetheless, we believe effective planning will be one of the key differences between the successes and the failures in the years ahead. At this point, projecting yourself into the future will be a daunting task. Do you have enough information to make truly educated guesses? In fact, you probably don't. If nothing else, we hope this exercise will promote the ongoing information gathering that will make your projections useful to you.

Pick a field or career direction that interests you (e.g., architecture, electrical engineering, or defense analyst). Try to forecast what the field will be like in 20-25 years when you're in the peak of your career. Take into consideration the influences on this career from the following factors: demographics, politics, scientific and technological changes, cultural changes, and the environment.

Politics

Science & Technology

Demographics

Culture

The Environment

What the field of _____ will be like in 2020 AD:

PLANNING FOR SUCCESS

In light of what you've read in this text and covered in class, devise a plan to take you through college so that you'll be poised for success upon graduation. (Remember, a plan isn't a plan unless it's on paper.) Identify specific steps you will take and skills you will master year by year while you're in school. Upon completion of this plan, look at the Master Plan in appendix I. What did you include that we omitted? What did you omit that we included? Compare your plan with the plans of some of your peers. Note any differences and use them to improve your plan.

Once you're satisfied with your plan, start setting some deadlines for yourself in your personal planner. You may also want to post your Personal Plan somewhere in your room and/or include it in your planner-calendar. That way you'll be reminded of your top priority goals every time you make out your to-do list.

FRESHMAN YEAR

SOPHOMORE YEAR

JUNIOR YEAR

SENIOR YEAR

THE MASTER PLAN

The citizen of the 21st Century will think globally and plan strategically. You can start preparing right now by mapping out your strategy for getting the most out of college. Here is our Master Plan for using college as a springboard to success in the Information Age. Use it as a rough guide for creating your own plan.

FRESHMAN YEAR

Your first mission is to immerse yourself in the academic enterprise. Get organized. Become a serious student. Acquire basic computer skills. Begin to identify majors and careers of interest. Learn to manage stress. Start networking.

Develop Organizational Skills
Establish weekly schedule.
Identify semester deadlines.
Use To-Do list; prioritize & monitor daily.
Master use of a planner.
Develop a file system for school work and personal information.
Organize an effective work space.

Develop Learning Skills
Learn how to use the library.
Review material regularly.
Learn effective reading, writing and notetaking techniques.
Get to know your professors.
Learn where to access "Word."

Master Computer Skills
Locate computer clusters.
Know e-mail.
Master a word processing program.
Explore the Internet.
Learn mathematics software if needed.

Finding Direction
Do a thorough self-assessment.
Determine compatibility of majors to you interests and abilities.
Explore various career fields.
Investigate coursework required for different majors.
Get career counseling as needed.
Get advisement.
Explore co-op & internships.
Create resume disk.

Stress Management Skills
Develop an exercise program.
Maintain a healthy diet and good sleeping habits.
Learn to relax & keep perspective.

Going Global
Learn a language.
Investigate "language house" living arrangements.
Read about international events.
Attend events sponsored by International Students Association

Getting Involved
Join a campus organization.

Start Networking
Connect with professors.
Connect with alumni.
Connect with people in field of interest.

SOPHOMORE YEAR

You use your organizational, learning, computer, and stress management skills throughout your collegiate career. You declare a major and begin to consider electives. You join a professional organization and contribute to it. You develop job search skills and secure career related employment.

Declare Major
Plan a schedule for taking required course work.
Get to know your advisor.
Look for electives that are compatible with your interests and complement your major.

Join Professional Association
Join student chapter affiliated with your major.
Attend local meetings regularly.
Be as active as your schedule allows.
Develop contacts by attending national meetings, conferences and/or seminars when convenient.

Expand Network of Contacts
Maintain current network.
Develop new contacts.
Use a Rolodex™ or other filing system.

Enhance Computer Skills
Learn spread sheet software.
Learn graphics/presentation software.

Going Global
Live in a language house

Secure Career-Related Employment
Begin co-op or part-time career related job.
Seek work assignments that will help develop skills in areas you are lacking.
Develop contacts for mentoring and future employment.
Learn all you can about this field and your fit within it.

Develop Leadership Skills
Volunteer for projects.
Develop public speaking skills.
Develop ability to manage projects.
Learn how to run a meeting.
Take a Leadership class

Develop Job Search Skills
Reevaluate your marketable skills.
Learn the STAR Technique.
Write a strong resume that stresses your skills.
Attend job search workshops when available.
Learn basics of interviewing for information.

JUNIOR YEAR

You assume more active and responsible positions in your extra-curricular activities. You cultivate contacts on and off campus. You learn more about your fields of interest. You find out about graduate and professional schools.

Evaluate Chosen Field
Keep up with your field through contacts and trade journals.
Talk to your professors and employers.
Visit your library, counseling center and placement office.
Check out job qualifications necessary in your field.
Continue co-op/internship.

Research Graduate or Professional Schools of Your Choice
Determine the benefits of an advanced degree in your field.
Identify strong graduate programs.
Apply for graduate or professional school entrance exams.

Continue Leadership Development
Enhance skills in communications and management.
Attend Leadership workshops & seminars.
Run for office or assume responsibility for a project.
Develop contacts for mentoring and possible job leads.

Going Global
Select a Study Abroad program.

Keep Up With Computing
Learn key software applications.

SENIOR YEAR

You're almost there! Apply for graduate programs and take entrance exams if you plan to get an advanced degree. Gear up for the job search by writing your resume and preparing for interviews.

Take Graduate or Professional School Entrance Exams
Prepare for exams thoroughly.
Check campus resources for available preparatory programs.
Check bookstores and library for preparatory books.
Arrive at test site early and well rested.
Be prepared for 3-4 hour test session.

Arrange for Interviews through Campus Placement Office
Attend programs explaining procedures of placement office.
Follow all procedures carefully.
Maintain contact with Placement Office staff.

Write a Winning Resume
Develop a clear job objective.
Detail skills or experience using the STAR Technique.
Tailor your resume to the company or graduate school you are interviewing.
Highlight key words and phrases that are your biggest selling points.

Get References
Decide who can give you the strongest references.
Talk to references about possible job leads.
Inform your references about your strongest selling points.
Supply references with copy of your resume.

Apply to Graduate Schools.

or

Look for Permanent Employment
Tap network of contacts.
Look for opportunities to develop new skills in learning organizations.
Develop strategy for expressing match of company's or graduate school's needs to your interests and abilities.

Master the Interviewing Process
Research typical questions you might be asked.
Prepare effective questions to ask the interviewer.
Role play upcoming interviews with friends. Ask for feedback.
Send thank-you notes to each interviewer.

Take Plant Trips or Visit Grad Schools
Investigate what happens during the plant trip or in the graduate school selection process.
Send any requested additional information.

Evaluate Offers
Determine what your needs are versus what the company or graduate school has to offer.
Seek guidance, if necessary.
Choose the best offer.

College Adjustment Inventory (CAI)

Directions: **At the top of the computer bubble sheet, please fill in your name, your instructors's name, and your student identification number (usually your Social Security Number). <u>Be sure to darken the nine bubbles corresponding to your student identification number</u>. For each item please darken the corresponding bubble on the computer sheet that best describes you. There are NO right or wrong answers, so please be honest. Please answer ALL items and fill in all computer bubbles CAREFULLY and COMPLETELY. Thank you!**

1	2	3	4	5	6
Strongly Disagree	Moderately Disagree	Slightly Disagree	Slightly Agree	Moderately Agree	Strongly Agree

1) **I generally do all the homework that is assigned.**

2) **I feel overwhelmed with all the challenges I have to cope with.**

3) **I try to avoid the classes that have the heaviest workload.**

4) **I have investigated careers which interest me and have a good understanding of the daily activities of the people who work in those careers.**

5) **After tuition and essentials, I have very little money to spend.**

6) **I'll work as hard as I have to to make good grades.**

7) **I love getting immersed in a big project.**

8) **I <u>rarely</u> feel tense or nervous.**

9) **I can focus quite well on the material I study.**

10) **I can picture myself making a significant contribution in my career.**

11) **My parents know what they want me to be, but I'm not sure.**

12) **I'm usually upbeat and optimistic.**

1	2	3	4	5	6
Strongly Disagree	Moderately Disagree	Slightly Disagree	Slightly Agree	Moderately Agree	Strongly Agree

13) I do **NOT** have any significant financial concerns.

14) I intend to be recognized as a leader in my field someday.

15) Darken bubble number three on this item.

16) I set high standards for myself.

17) I'm wondering who I can talk to about finding a part time job.

18) I do **NOT** need to improve my study habits.

19) I do **NOT** have a plan for reaching my academic aspirations.

20) I have no regular study schedule.

21) I worry that my parents can't afford to send me to college.

22) I don't mind all the hard work at this place because I know its going to help me succeed.

23) I take good class notes, and I study them before a test.

24) I don't have to excel. I'm comfortable in the middle of the pack.

25) I have investigated my academic major and have a good understanding of the classes I'll take and the schoolwork I'll do while I'm in college.

26) I am **NOT** sure if I will be successful at school.

27) I need to talk to someone about getting a loan so I can get through college.

28) Whether I like a class or not, I study as hard as I need to.

29) I need help in getting financial aid.

30) Darken bubble number three on this item.

31) I have no clue what I want to do after college.

32) I proofread my work and correct any errors.

33) I don't know if my efforts are going to make any difference.

1	2	3	4	5	6
Strongly Disagree	Moderately Disagree	Slightly Disagree	Slightly Agree	Moderately Agree	Strongly Agree

34) **My philosophy is: "Work first; play later."**

35) **Schoolwork isn't that big of a deal to me. Actually, I'm not especially serious about studying.**

36) **I am NOT certain I can achieve my ambitions in life.**

37) **I'm often worried about money.**

38) **If I have a hard time solving a problem, I will keep trying for quite a while.**

39) **So long as I get my degree, I'm not going to worry about my GPA.**

40) **I often have to turn in my homework past the due date.**

41) **I don't like working on difficult problems.**

42) **I wait until just before the test to read my textbooks.**

43) **Sometimes I don't turn in my assignments.**

44) **I intend to be in the top 25 percent of my class when I graduate.**

45) **Darken bubble number three on this item.**

46) **My financial resources will see me through college.**

47) **My going to college was really my family's idea.**

48) **Grades aren't so important. I just want to graduate.**

49) **I'm worried that my job will interfere with my school work.**

50) **When I have troubles, they don't keep me down for very long.**

51) **After a while, frequent change in my schedule bugs me.**

52) **I'm confident I've picked the right major.**

53) **I know what my goals are in life, and I'm confident I'll reach them.**

54) **I am unsure about what I want to do with my life.**

1	2	3	4	5	6
Strongly Disagree	Moderately Disagree	Slightly Disagree	Slightly Agree	Moderately Agree	Strongly Agree

55)   **Surprises really throw me off.**

56)   **I tend to get involved in too many projects and activities.**

57)   **I'm in college because I didn't know what else to do.**

58)   **I love college life -- both scholastic and social activities.**

59)   **I don't have any money problems that will interfere with college.**

60)   **I'm sure this is the right college for me.**

61)   **I am uncertain about what subjects I like.**

62)   **I know I must budget my money carefully.**

63)   **I expect I will need to work at a paid job ___ hours a week.**

   1) 0 hrs.   2) 5 hrs.   3) 10 hrs.   4) 15 hrs.   5) 20 hrs.   6) 20+ hrs.

(Questionnaire continues on the next page.)

64) **I am:**

    1) NOT a mother/father.
    2) A mother/father.

65) **I am:**

    1) Female   2) Male

66) **How do you identify yourself:**

    1) American Indian or Alaskan Native
    2) Asian or Pacific Islander
    3) Black (not Hispanic)
    4) Hispanic
    5) White (not Hispanic)
    6) Other

67) **I am a:**

    1) Freshman   2) Sophomore   3) Junior   4) Senior   5) Fifth year senior or higher.

68) **English is:**

    1) My first language.   2) **NOT** my first language.

69) **I am:**

    1) Single   2) Married

70) **My mother has the following education:**

    1) Less than a GED or High School diploma
    2) GED or High School diploma.
    3) Some College, no degree.
    4) Bachelor's Degree.
    5) Master's Degree.
    6) Professional or Doctoral Degree.

71) **My father has the following education:**

    1) Less than a GED or High School diploma
    2) GED or High School diploma.
    3) Some College, no degree.
    4) Bachelor's Degree.
    5) Master's Degree.
    6) Professional or Doctoral Degree.

Thank you for completing this questionnaire.

Appendix 3

Personality

Many of the programs that use this book, use some personality testing to help you arrive at greater insight into self, and insight into your relationships with others. We can not begin to adequately cover the wide variety of testing that is available. We will address, however, one of the most popular personality constructs.

One of the most popular theories about personality was developed in the early 1900's by a Swiss psychoanalyst named Carl Jung (1875-1961). A contemporary, and for a time, the friend of Sigmund Freud, Jung spent a lot of time developing a theory of personality. He said, that it is "...one's psychological type which from the outset determines and limits a person's judgement." The concept is designed to "...deal with the relationship of the individual to the world, to people and things."

Over time, this theory of psychological type has been studied extensively. Isabel Myers, in conjunction with her mother, Katharine C. Briggs developed a system for teasing out an individual's type preference. They drew on Jungian theory and more than two decades of watching and testing individuals to come up with their first inventory in the early 1940s. Today, the instrument has a test bank of over a million individuals, and it is likely that millions have taken some form of the instrument. It is popular and is used in a wide range of contexts.

The Myers Briggs Type Inventory™ (MBTI) is not the only personality instrument based on Jungian theory, and so you may receive some variation of it. In fact, you can find a version of the Kiersey on the Internet at **http://sunsite.unc.edu/jem/faq-mbti.html#attending.** Where we work, we prefer the Keirsey Temperament Sorter for economical reasons, but the theory behind the instrument is the same.

So What is This Theory?

In this view of personality there are four continua. You answer questions in such a way on whichever inventory you take, that you are likely to divulge a tendency for how you make decisions. For instance, if you are the kind of person who is energized by being with people, you will tend to make a decision about being with others, based on that fact. You refresh yourself and recharge yourself by being in the company of others. Individuals who show a tendency for extroversion are about 75 percent of the population. You are MORE likely to want to be with other people than your opposite on the continuum, the introvert.

Now please hear this LOUD AND CLEAR! Introversion is not a social handicap! Introverts merely make decisions based on a tendency for being with one or two people, and they refresh and recharge themselves through withdrawal. They DO want to be with people. And, shyness is NOT the same thing as introversion, although some introverts are also shy. Introverts refresh themselves through reflection and time alone. They are competent and capable people and can move into social situations by choice. Their *tendency* is to be reflective alone, or in the company of just a few people.

Because introverts tend to feel more comfortable alone or with one or two people, they often have a few very close friends. The extrovert, on the other hand, has many people they call friends. They often have hundreds of friends. But, when you get to the core of what they are describing, they are often talking about acquaintances. There are introverts who have friends by the score and extroverts who have only a half-dozen friends. But the trend is that introverts have fewer, closer friends; extroverts have many and somewhat more superficial friendships.

I (Joann) am an extreme introvert, yet I can and often do teach classes and do workshops and public speaking. When I am done, I feel drained, and in fact have felt so tired by being with really large groups that I have had to rest and be alone for a few minutes before going on to other duties. My colleague, Bill, is an extrovert and comes back from workshops and public speaking energized and wants to tell me all about it.

Introversion and extraversion are neither good nor bad. They just are what they are. In fact, it's one of the personality characteristics that may actually be present at birth! Right from the start, when researchers approach newborn infants, some show curiosity and are engaged by the stimulation of someone talking to, or playing with them (extroverts), while others withdraw and show less interest in being involved with someone (introverts). It is always important to remember when interpreting your personality type information, that <u>THERE IS NO WRONG WAY TO BE</u>. In fact, a world where everyone was just exactly like you (the perfect type, of course) would be boring, and there wouldn't be much creativity or variety. *We need every one of the types for there to be balance and variety.*

To review the first continuum:

Introversion<- - - - - - - - - - - - - - - - - - - <- - - - - -> **Extraversion**

Energized by Reflection,	Energized by being with
being alone or in the	others. Specializes in
company of just one or two.	Spontaniety and mingling

You probably fall somewhere between the two polar opposites. In fact, even introverts have some degree of extroversion in them. And extroverts have some moments when they want to be reflective and alone (Sounds amazingly like introversion, doesn't it?). Young people in particular, often find they fall right at the very middle in one or more continuum (Yes, that means there are more continua coming!). What does that mean? Well it can mean a couple of things. One is that you likely are still in the developmental part of your life called "Late Adolescence." You are still forming as a person. In fact, your freshman year at college, you will undergo some of the most profound changes in your life! You are still developing your values, beliefs and your persona (that part of yourself that you let the world see). It could be that you fall right in the middle because you're still working on the concept of who you are and figuring that out. Separating who you are as a person, from who you were as a child of your parents, is one of the biggest jobs you will accomplish while in college. You may need to work on self development more before your preferred type becomes more evident.

Older people (perhaps some non-traditional students and perhaps your parents) sometimes find that as they get older they begin to develop the sides of their personality that they did not tend to use as much. This is called differentiation. Being open to different possibilities and seeing the value of other ways is a part of the maturation process. This is why older people are often thought to have "wisdom" -- because they are open to many more ways of collecting information and making decisions than just their preferred modes.

Especially with the shorter versions of these instruments, you may not have had the opportunity to answer enough questions to give the most accurate portrayal of yourself. And, in this kind of instrument, YOU are the best judge of your type. No one else can tell you if you are or are not something. If you score very closely or with equal scores on a continuum, you may want to read the descriptions of both types and decide for yourself which you most strongly identify with. Don't let others influence your decision, because in this case, YOU are the best expert on how you feel, make decisions on what your own preferences are.

The next continuum is iNtuitive versus Sensate. Since the "I" has already been used for introversion, we move to the "N" in intuitive to identify this preference. Intuitive individuals are very forward thinking. That is, they live much of their lives in the future. They spend a large portion of their time thinking about what they are going to do. As a consequence they often become like Johnny Appleseed, planting seeds (starting projects) for trees (s)he will not be around to enjoy. The intuitive who moves on, then often leaves a project for a sensate type (their opposite type on this continuum) to finish.

Another characteristic of this preference is that intuitive people have the equivalent of emotional radar. What do I mean by that? Well, just as a radar at an airport rotates around in a circle "looking" for weather or planes, a person with a preference for intuitive decision-making, is able to look at others and through subtle cues, they can often discern what that other person is feeling. For example, both my daughter and I are intuitives, but we don't share any of the other personality preferences. So, we can sit across from one another and I can discern that "She seems to be upset." Likewise she is intuitive and can look at me and discern in some subtle way that "Mom looks anxious." However, because we don't share any of the other preferences, we must actually ask one another what's going on to know how the other arrived at that state!

Intuitives are made of the stuff of creativity. The great scientists are intuitive because they need the intuitive's creativity to be innovators. Much of what we value as artistic talent or innovative thinking comes from individuals with a strong preference for the intuitive. Being able to bend an existing concept a little to come up with something totally unique or previously unheard of, is the realm of the intuitive.

Sensate people make decisions based on information obtained through their five senses. So sensate individuals often want to touch or taste things before making a decision. Their world and subsequent perceptions of it are filtered through the five senses. They also are very practical individuals who make decisions based on experience (history) and the present reality. They have acute powers of observation and an incredible memory for details. If you are going to need precise directions on how to go somewhere, you want your directions from this person! Working with facts and looking at relationships of one thing to another would likely appeal to someone with a strong sensate preference. And, when talking to a person with a strong sensate preference, giving examples to illustrate your concept will make the learning process easier for them.

So, knowing what you know about the intuitive and the sensate, you can listen for clues to help you determine what preference another person has. The sensate buyer wants to know facts and figures about car performance. Speak to them in their realm, and you're more likely to make the sale. The intuitive buyer will want to know what options are available, and what the value of the vehicle is likely to be in five years. In a job interview, the sensate asks, "What have you done in the past that makes you believe you can handle this job?" The interviewer with an intuitive preference, wants to know, "Where do you believe you'll be in five years?" Since three-fourths of the population is sensate, you're statistically more likely to be conversing or relating to someone who makes decisions based on that preference.

To review this continuum:

Intuitive<- -> **Sensate**

Lives in the future.	Values history.
Emotional "radar."	Data driven.
Creative thinker.	Practical and pragmatic.

The third continuum is thinking versus feeling. Individuals who make decisions based on a tendency for thinking, do so using impersonal, objective judgement. Individuals who make decisions based on personal impact are characterized as feeling types. Remember, as with the other continua, the people who tend toward a preference for objectivity (thinking types), also have the capacity to feel. And, those who make decisions based on personal impact, feeling types, also have the capacity to think. Just because a person has a strong tendency for making decisions out of the personal mode, feeling, does not imply they can not think. Neither does it imply that the individual who has a strong preference for making decisions based on objective criteria (thinking) lacks feelings.

Thinking types think more linearly and can show step-by-step processes by which they arrive at a decision. So, if you need tutoring in mathematics, you'll want to get a strong thinking type to help demonstrate the systematic process by which you derive a mathematical answer. Feeling types often don't know precisely how they arrive at the answer to a mathematical problem, but it's correct at the same rate as the thinker! There is no advantage to any one type over the other.

Individuals with a preference for making decisions based on thinking, often retain information in incredible detail. A thinking type will remember the color of a vase on the mantle piece, and how many forks are in the place setting. A feeling type takes in information in a more global way and therefore is more impressionistic, remembering vaguely there might have been a fireplace and I think the table was pretty. One misunderstanding that often comes up between thinking types and feeling types has to do with the concept of feelings. Strong feeling types show their feelings in a more overt way by facial flushes or blanching, sweaty palms and a more rapid heart rate. These physiological changes are not as overt on a thinking type, and so a strong feeling type sometimes believes, based on what they see, that the thinker is not feeling. Nothing could be further from the truth! However, this phenomenon contributes to a misunderstanding between types because the thinker appears so much calmer when the feeling person is easily perceived to be affected by emotion.

To further confound the issue, this is the only continuum that demonstrates an influence by gender. Since about sixty percent of men are thinkers and sixty percent of females are feeling types, you can see some potential for conflict right off. This is why a man often decides he wants a particular car based on reviews by *Road and Track Magazine*, but his wife or girlfriend is more impressed by the color. Other examples of how this conflict is played out between genders could be a scenario where a man (thinking type) asks directions from a woman (feeling type). Remember feeling types get global impressions. So, she explains how you go down this road for a while.

"How far?", he asks. "Oh, I don't know, maybe three or four or five miles," she replies. "Well, is it three or five?" he asks. "Oh, I just go until I see a little white house on the left, and then I know my turn is coming up," she says. While our male traveler wants the information in tenths of a mile, he's speaking to someone who doesn't likely remember street names, and may use telephone poles as reference points. Conceptualizing directionality by North/South/East or West to the woman, is often as useful as explaining Quantum Mechanics to a shoemaker. Remember that both types are valuable and have insights in ways that we need to make our world the interesting and intriguing place that it is. There is no "good" or "bad" here, and both types do get to their destinations.

Is this difference between the sexes socialized or is it biologically based? We don't know yet. Women are certainly socialized to be more nurturing and to care more about feelings (both of self and others). Men who demonstrate strong feelings can be characterized in this society as more eccentric (the passionate artist) or more effeminate. A tendency for feeling also feeds passion, however! When women demonstrate a tendency for logic and intellectualism, it has, in the past, often been discouraged. Perhaps this accounts for some of the lower numbers of women entering the fields of science and math? Research will have to continue before we know more about this. And, remember too, the examples above are based on stereotypes of extremes. There are certainly thinking women out there (Me!) and there are certainly feeling men. Extreme examples just happen to make better illustrations.

In the mean time, to review:

Thinking<- -> **Feeling**

Objective Decision	Personalized Decisions
Intellectualizing	Emotional
Less overt expression of feelings	Overt expression of feelings

The last continuum is judging versus perceiving. Now, remember, this theory came from a fellow who wrote about this in German. And, there are some things that just don't translate well. This is one of them. Judging has nothing what-so-ever to do with being judgmental and perceiving has nothing what-so-ever to do with your perceptive ability. This has to do with a preference for having your options left open, or a tendency for closure. What is that? Well, people who want their options left open often delay decision making. If you are leaving things perpetually open for opportunity, you may find yourself doing many things at the last minute, or making many spontaneous decisions. Those who have a preference for closure, want to know what time they should be there and what they should be wearing, and will ask so they can put the time in their appointment book.

Judging types often have appointment books and are often more conscientious about time. They are peeved when perceiving types, who live on a time schedule all their own, do not follow through on an obligation. Is a perceiving type going to stop by? Yeah, probably some time. The judging type wants to know, "When?" "Oh, sometime." "But, what day?" "When I feel like it." Do you see the potential for difficulty? If the appointment is forced, the perceiving type may still not follow through, internally interpreting it only as a nuisance or perhaps disregarding it altogether.

Administrators who are judging types attempt to follow through on deadlines. Perceiving types see deadlines as mere "alarm clocks" that have human chimes which walk in your office and let you know when something is due by asking, "Is that report ready yet?"

Judging types often like order and will go to great lengths to arrange their environment in very particular ways. This is not an absolute, but it is a trend. Similarly, perceiving types often do not have preferences for the structure of their environment. So, if you walk into a perceiving type's room, there may be some mild order in that the clothes may be all in one corner, and the books are stacked on the desk, but order and tidiness are not words that immediately come to mind. If you put a strong judging type in the same dorm room or small apartment with a strong perceiving type, and shake vigorously, you have the makings for a spectacular argument! One (can you guess which one?) will attempt to convert the other (which one?) to a reformed neatnick. The other just hears that occasional "alarm" go off that says it's time to start thinking about laundry...or perhaps just buy some Lysol™ to spray the place down, and s/he'll shut up. Is the judging type really going to make a change in the way the perceiving person approaches life? No. Can negotiation for ground rules occur? Yes. They can. But just as you can not make an extrovert out of an introvert, you will not be able to convince the perceiving person to become a neatnick who'll arrive on time.

The other occasion when perceiving types often get into difficulty in college is deadlines. Often a perceiving type has not put deadlines into his/her daily planner. S/he's had a syllabus, like everyone else, since the first day of class. However, mysteriously they only discover a project is due the day before, or the day of (yikes!) when s/he is in casual conversation with a classmate. Oftentimes s/he has keep his/her options open so long, that s/he hasn't moved an inch toward the project, paper or homework until it is too late. These are the folks who "cram" for tests the night before, never thinking ahead and planning for distributed study sessions. These are the folks that are knocking on your dorm room door at 3:00 AM wondering if you have any poster paper and magic markers, because s/he has a project due at 8:00 AM and s/he is just now starting it!

The world is made up about 50/50 of judging and perceiving types. There is no "good" or "bad" way to be. College tends to be run mostly by judging types who make deadlines and structure things in a timely way. When was the last time a professor told you, "Turn that assignment in whenever you feel like it"? But, perceiving types are needed too. They do great at jobs where fluidity and fast adaptation are necessary. They are the types who like to have their office in their car and set out on a day's appointments knowing they'll do something productive today, but have no clue what that something is!

Imagine a vacation planned by a judging type and one planned by a perceiving type. What would the judging type's vacation be like? How about the perceiving type's? If you can imagine this scenario, you have the concept of judging versus perceive conceptualized.

Why is this personality stuff important to me?

Understanding yourself better helps you understand what kinds of jobs you would be more likely to enjoy or hate. For example, someone with the ST combination (sensate, thinking), might enjoy working with numbers and consider the idea of being an accountant a good career choice. However, the opposite of the ST is the NF. Would an intuitive, feeling individual enjoy working as an accountant? Probably not as much as the ST. The ST individual is very detail oriented and would enjoy the job of being a "detective" where they'd be looking for a misplaced cent or two on a million dollar spreadsheet. The NF would more likely prefer to make a notation of "ESP," (error some place) and let it go. That doesn't work well in banks, auditing agencies, and other careers. So, understanding yourself, helps you understand what kinds of careers might be more enjoyable for you.

Understanding your personality also helps you understand some of your weaknesses. Every type has strengths, and every type has weaknesses. That's why there is not an advantage of any one type over another. If you understand where your weaknesses are, you can be aware of them and compensate for them. Many companies administer an MBTI or an equivalent type of personality inventory so they can use the information to build teams. Team building based on personality is helpful because you can select carefully to make sure that you have enough variety of type in your work group so that you have the maximum amount of creativity and practicality; that you have people who are into exploration, as well as individuals concerned with on-time delivery.

Right now you have some important pieces of information about college just from thinking about type. For example, much of what you have to do in college is to relate to and understand the communication of your professors. Think over the different people who you are taking classes from. Do you think the majority of professors are introverts or extraverts? (Remember, in order to be a professor, you must study things in great detail for many years.) If you said intraverts, you'd be correct. A higher proportion of professors are introverts. How does that affect your communication with them? Often it means that they are more comfortable with people one-on-one in the their office than in front of a whole group. It means that some don't have very much public speaking experience. It means that you may have to work hard to identify yourself as a person in trouble and needing some of their attention.

What else can you know about type that can help you in college? You can listen to your professors for cues. Do they talk as sensate or intuitive types? That is, is history or experience more important to them? If they are more interested in history (sensate) you might expect questions on a test to reflect that.

Another way you can use this information on type is to know yourself better. If you are a strong perceiving type, you may feel slightly uncomfortable in this judging world of college. Does that mean you shouldn't go to college? Absolutely not! Does it mean that you will be less successful academically? No. What it means is that you will have to adapt to this judging world and conform to it for a time, until you can graduate and be in more control of your everyday environment. It is your *choice* to do what is uncomfortable now, to pay off later in career options. While it is a *tendency* or a *preference* to keep your options open, if you are a perceiving type, it isn't a necessity. You can choose to do what you must to get that degree, even if it is slightly uncomfortable now and again.

And, don't forget that your parents, your friends, and your boss has a personality too. Perhaps knowing what you now know about personality explains why your mom goes ballistic when you come in five minutes late? Maybe knowing what you know now, explains why your girlfriend thinks you're not very emotional, and appear uncaring at times? If you understand personality more, you can understand others, as well as yourself.

Where can I learn more?

There is much, much more to know about personality type than can be explicated in these few pages. If you are interested in reading more about personality, consider reading one of the following books:

Please Understand Me, An Essay on Temperament Styles, by David Keirsey and Marilyn Bates. Prometheus Nemesis Book Company, P.O. Box 2748, Del Mar, CA 92014 (619-632-1575).

Gifts Differing, Isabel Briggs-Myers (with Peter Myers). Consulting Psychologists Press, 1980, ISBN 0-89106-011-1 (pb) 0-89106-015-4 (hb).

Type Talk. Otto Kroeger and Janet M. Thuesen. Bantam Doubleday Dell Publishing Group, Inc. (Tilden Press also mentioned.) ISBN 0-385-29828-59.

Type Talk at Work. Otto Kroeger and Janet M. Thuesen. ISBN 0-385-30174-X.

People Types and Tiger Stripes. Gordon Lawrence. Available from Center for Application of Psychological Type, Gainesville, Florida. ISBN 0-935652-08-6.

A Quick Overview of Type
Implications of Psychological Type

I(ntroverted)

Introverted people get their energy from solitude. These people recharge their internal "batteries" by being alone. Introverts don't see being alone as being a problem. They prefer being alone at time. They want to be with people too, but it's actually essential for them to have some time alone in order to keep themselves energized and ready to meet new challenges. Introverts are about 25 percent of the population. Introverts compose a larger portion of the population here at GT than you would have found in your high school class. So, if you are an introvert, you may feel more comfortable here where there are a higher number of introverts like yourself.

(I)N(tuitive)

We've already used the "I" for Introverted, so we use the second letter, "N" to stand for intuitive. Intuitive people have a n innate "radar" that helps them know what other people around them are feeling. Intuitive people have a "gut" sensation about why they select something. Intuitive people can look at someone and "know without a word being spoken" if that person is sad, happy, upset, etc. Intuitives are also forward thinking. They are concerned with the future and sometimes spend a lot of time daydreaming about how they can get from here to there. Intuitive managers will want to know, "Where do you envision yourself being in five/ten years"?

F(eeling)

People who make decisions based on a preference for feelings often see things in a global way. These individuals may come away with "impressions" of what a place was like (Pat's place was sort of mauve all over.). They often arrive at mathematical answers without necessarily knowing the individual steps of how they arrived at the answer. When in an intense feeling state their palms will become warm and they are more likely to perspire. There can be conflict between feeling people and thinking people, because often the feelers believe that thinkers are unfeeling. This is not true. Thinking types don't exhibit the overt signs of emotion (sweaty palms or flushed face) as frequently as feeling types, but Thinking types do feel.

E(xtraverted)

Extraverted people get their energy from being with others. These people recharge their internal "batteries" by being in the company of others. Extroverts are about three-fourths of the population, and because there are so many of them, they often don't understand why introverts would choose to be alone! Extroverts can enjoy time alone too, but they get their energy from being with others and can, for instance, get so charged from being with others at a party, that they can't retire-- they find other things they want to do. Extraverted people are more open to new opportunity, more innately able to go out and meet others enthusiastically.

S(ensate)

Sensate people are very oriented toward data-driven decisions. When making a decision this person wants to collect data and base the decision on "cold, hard facts." This person can, at times, be perceived by others (Intuitives) as a roadblock in the decision-making process, because this person will often want to put off making decisions until more data is collected. This person uses all his/her senses to taste, touch, smell and feel the world around him/her. Sensate people have an appreciation for history and will often evaluate the efficacy of an approach based on how well it worked in the past. Sensate managers ask you to, "Tell me your job history"? These are people who may judge you based on your GPA in college or hire based on past performance.

T(hinking)

Thinking people make decisions based on analysis. They want to take many factors into consideration and use that as the basis for a forthcoming decision. Physiologically, when a Thinking person becomes emotional, they do not manifest the same outward signs as a Feeling person and can be accused of being "cold" or "unfeeling," when, in fact, they do feel, they just don't show it as visibly. Dry palms and a "cool" outward appearance do not indicate a lack of feelings. Memories of places are often very detailed with color, objects and dress.

J(udging)

People who have a preference for making decisions based on Judging, are not necessarily judgmental. In this case, Judging is a preference for closure. What does that mean? Well, if I tell you "I'll be by on Friday," is that OK? Judging people would have a preference for closure, so would likely ask, "What time"? Judging people represent about fifty percent of the population. They are often time-conscious and are concerned about being prompt. Schedules are meant to be kept, due dates are important and will appear in appointment books. The due dates of papers and work assignments are meant to be kept.

Overview

There is no right or wrong way to be. You can't be a wrong personality type. The combinations of letters merely reflect back to you information about, when forced to make a decision, which preference you commonly use to make your decisions. This inventory is only about 80 percent accurate. You may not identify strongly with what your score suggests. If you feel strongly that you belong in a different personality type, then you probably do.

Extraversion and Introversion are actually genetically determined (that's the only continuum that is). Infants display this tendency right from birth. Other elements change over time and circumstance. When relating to others, like roommates, friends and instructors, keep in mind, that no matter what your preference is, if the other person comes from a different personality type (s)he may not place the same importance on some aspect of life that you do. This is not good or bad, it just is. And, you may wish for all the world that (s)he would make your life easier by changing to suit you, but it doesn't happen that way. People with a strong Perceiving score are often late and live with a certain level of chaos around them. If you are strong Judging type and value organization and timeliness, you won't be able to change your roommate to be more like yourself. Give up and accept who they are. It will save a lot of conflict. If your significant other is a strong Feeling type (this continuum is the only one that shows a trend influenced by gender--about 60 percent of women are Feeling types and about 60 percent of men are Thinking types) and you are a

P(erceiving)

People who have a preference for making decisions based on Perceiving are not necessarily better at perceiving. In this case, Perceiving is a preference for keeping things open. What does that mean? Will, if I tell you, "I'll be by on Friday," is that OK? Perceiving people would be fine with that. If they are there, OK. If you miss them, no big deal. Perceiving people operate on their own time schedule and are not pressured by social norms or the time values of others, consequently these folks are often late to functions, dates, or turning in papers. Arbitrary time schedules (like course syllabi) do not act as "alarms" for Perceiving types.

strong Thinking types, this does not mean that you are "irrational" in how you make a decision--though a strong Thinking type often wants to know on what analytical basis you came to your decision. The Feeling person doesn't necessarily know, (s)he just has a "gut" feeling which is right for them. Just because the strong Thinking type makes a decision based on analysis, doesn't make the outcome of that decision more likely to be "right" or "wrong." If you find yourself trapped in these kinds of conflicts, stop and look at the personality of both individuals and remember, you can't change him/her. Work with what you've got. Accept that individual where they are. Save yourself a LOT of stress.

There are 16 possible combinations of the four continuums. Your combination is just as good as anyone else's. Each of the 16 combinations has strengths and weaknesses. If you can come to understand your strengths, they you have a great team. Be alert to these personality influences and you can be smarter about interviewing on jobs, happier living with your roommate, develop new ways of understanding your parents and more.

If you have any questions about the implication of this instrument, please talk to your instructor. We want you to feel that you have learned something about yourself and how to relate to others. If there is information in here that you do not understand or which you want to learn more about, your instructor will be happy to give you more information.

	Sensing with Thinking	Sensing with Feeling	Intuitive with Feeling	Intuitive with Thinking
Introverted & Judging	**ISTJ** Serious, quiet, earn success by concentration and thoroughness. Practical, orderly, matter-of-fact, logical, realistic and dependable. See to it that everything is well organized. Take responsibility. Make up their own minds as to what should be accomplished and work toward it steadily, regardless of protests or distractions.	**ISFJ** Quiet, friendly, responsible and conscientious. Work devotedly to meet obligations. Lend stability to any project or group. Thorough, painstaking, accurate. May need time to master technical subjects, as their interests are not often technical. Patient with detail and routine. Loyal, considerate, concerned with how other people feel.	**INFJ** Succeed by perseverance, originality and desire to do whatever is needed or wanted. Put their best efforts into their work. Quietly forceful, conscientious, concerned for others. Respected for their firm principles. Likely to be honored and followed for their clear convictions as to how best to serve the common good.	**INTJ** Have original minds and great drive which they use only for their own purposes. In fields that appeal to them they have a fine power to organize a job and carry it through with or without help. Skeptical, critical, independent, determined, often stubborn. Must learn to yield less important points in order to win the most important.
Introverted & Perceptive	**ISTP** Cool onlookers, quiet, reserved, observing and analyzing life with detached curiosity and unexpected flashes of original humor. Usually interested in impersonal principles, cause and effect, or how and why mechanical things work. Exert themselves no more than they think necessary, because any waste of energy would be inefficient.	**ISFP** Retiring, quietly friendly, sensitive, modest about their abilities. Shun disagreements, do not force their opinions or values on others. Usually do not care to lead but are often loyal followers. May be rather relaxed about assignments or getting things done, because they enjoy the present moment and do not want to spoil it by undue haste or exertion.	**INFP** Full of enthusiasm and loyalty, but seldom talk of these until they know you well. Care about learning, ideas, language, and independent projects of their own. Apt to be on yearbook staff, perhaps as editor. Tend to undertake too much, then somehow get it done. Friendly, but often too absorbed in what they are doing to be sociable or notice much.	**INTP** Quiet, reserved, impersonal. Especially enjoy theoretical or scientific subjects. Logical to the point of hair-splitting. Interested mainly in ideas, with little liking for parties or small talk. Tend to have very sharply defined interests. Need to choose careers where some strong interest of theirs can be used and useful.
Extraverted & Perceptive	**ESTP** Matter-of-fact, do not worry or hurry, enjoy whatever comes along. Tend to like mechanical things and sports, with friends on the side. May be a bit blunt or insensitive. Adaptable, tolerant generally conservative in values. Dislike long explanations. Are best with real things that can be worked, handled, taken apart or put back together.	**ESFP** Outgoing, easygoing, accepting, friendly, fond of a good time. Like sports and making things. Know what's going on and join in eagerly. Find remembering facts easier than mastering theories. Are best in situations that need sound common sense and practical ability with people as well as with things.	**ENFP** Warmly enthusiastic, high-spirited, ingenious, imaginative. Able to do almost anything that interests them. Quick with a solution for any difficulty and ready to help anyone with a problem. Often rely on their ability to improvise instead of preparing in advance. Can always find compelling reasons for whatever they want.	**ENTP** Quick, ingenious, good at many things. Stimulating company, alert and outspoken, argue for fun on either side of a question. Resourceful in solving new and challenging problems, but may neglect routine assignments. Turn to one new interest after another. Can always find logical reasons for whatever they want.
Extraverted & Judging	**ESTJ** Practical realists, matter-of-fact, with natural head for business or mechanics. Not interested in subjects they see no use for, but can apply themselves when necessary. Like to organize and run activities. Tend to run things well, especially if they remember to consider other people's feelings and points of view when making their decisions.	**ESFJ** Warm-hearted, talkative, popular, conscientious, born cooperators, active committee members. Always doing something nice for someone. Work best with plenty of encouragement and praise. Little interest in abstract thinking or technical subjects. Main interest is in things that directly and visibly affect people's lives.	**ENFJ** Responsive and responsible. Feel real concern for what others think and want, and try to handle things with due regard for other people's feelings. Can present a proposal or lead a group discussion with ease and tact. Sociable, popular, sympathetic. Responsive to praise and criticism.	**ENTJ** Hearty, frank, decisive, leaders in activities. Usually good in anything that requires reasoning and intelligent talk, such as public speaking. Are well-informed and keep adding to their fund of knowledge. May sometimes be more positive and confident than their experience in an area warrants.

273

Potential Pitfalls of the Types at Work

	Sensing with Thinking	Sensing with Feeling	Intuitive with Feeling	Intuitive with Thinking
Introverted & Judging	**ISTJ** • May overlook the long-range implications in favor of day-to day operations. • May neglect interpersonal niceties. • May become rigid in their ways and thought of as inflexible. • May expect others to conform to standard operating procedures and thus not encourage innovation.	**ISFJ** • May be overly pessimistic about the future. • May not be seen as sufficiently tough-minded when presenting their views to others. • May be undervalued because of their quiet self-effacing style. • May not be as flexible as the situation or others require.	**INFJ** • May find their ideas overlooked and underestimated. • May not be forthright with criticism. • May be reluctant to intrude upon others and thus keep too much to themselves. • May operate with single-minded concentration, thereby ignoring other tasks that need to be done.	**INTJ** • May appear so unyielding that others are afraid to approach or challenge them. • May criticize others in tideal. • May iculty letting go of impractical ideas. • May ignore the impact of their ideas or style on others.
Introverted & Perceptive	**ISTP** • May keep important things to themselves and appear unconcerned to others. • May move on before prior efforts bear fruit. • May be too expedient, conserve efforts, and take shortcuts. • May appear indecisive and undirected.	**ISFP** • May be too trusting and gullible. • May not critique others when needed, but may be overly self-critical. • May not see beyond the present reality to understand things in their fuller context. • May be too easily hurt and withdraw.	**INFP** • May delay completion of tasks because of perfectionism. • May tryt o please too many people at the same time. • May not adjust their vision to the facts and logic of the situation. • May spend more time in reflection than in action.	**INTP** • May be too abstract and therefore unrealistic about necessary follow-through. • May over-intellectualize and become too theoretical in their explanations. • May focus overly on minor inconsistencies at the expense of teamwork and harmony. • May turn their critical analytical thinking on people and act impersonally.
Extraverted & Perceptive	**ESTP** • May appear blunt and insensitive to others when acting quickly. • May rely too much on improvisation and miss the wider implications of their actions. • May sacrifice floow-through to the next immediate problem. • May get hooked by materialism.	**ESFP** • May over-emphasize subjective data. • May not reflect before jumping in. • May spend too much time socializing and neglect tasks. • May not always finish what they start.	**ENFP** • May move on to new ideas or projects without completing those already started. • May overlook relevant details. • May overextend and try to do too much. • May procreastinate.	**ENTP** • May become lost in the model, forgetting about current realities. • May be competitive and unappreciative of the input of others. • May over-extend themselves. • May not adapt well to standard procedures.
Extraverted & Judging	**ESTJ** • May decide too quickly. • May not see the need for change. • May overlook the niceties in working to get the job done. • May be overtaken by their feelings and values if they ignore them for too long.	**ESFJ** • May avoid conflict and sweep problems under the rug. • May not value their own priorities enough because of a desire to please others. • May assume they know what is best for others or the organization. • May not always step back and see the bigger picture.	**ENFJ** • May idealize others and suffer from blind loyalty. • May sweep problems under the rug when in conflict. • May ignore the task in favor of relationship issues. • May take criticism personally.	**ENTJ** • May overlook people's needs in their focus on the task. • May overlook practical considerations and constraints. • May decide too quickly and appear impatient and domineering. • May ignore and suppress their own feelings.

274

Sensing with Thinking	Sensing with Feeling	Intuitive with Feeling	Intuitive with Thinking
ISTJ Steelworkers, Dentists, Police Supervisors, Police and Detectives, Auditors, Accountants, Electricians, Engineers (Mechanical), Technicians, Teachers (Trade, Industrial & Technical), Mathematics Teachers.	**ISFJ** Nurses, Teachers (Preschool, Speech Pathology and Therapy), Librarians, Archivists, and Curators, Public Health Nurses, Elementary School Teachers, Physicians (Family & General Practice), Bookkeepers.	**INFJ** Priests and Clergy, Educational Consultants, Physicians (Pathologists), English Teachers, Art/Drama Teachers, Psychiatrists, Social Workers, Professors, Marketing Personnel, Social Scientists.	**INTJ** Attorneys, Scientists, Chemists, Researchers, Engineers, Systems Analysist, Judges, Photographers, Professors, Psychologists, Social Scientists, Electrical and Electronics Technicians, Administrators, Writers.
ISTP Farmers, Air Force Personnel, Mechanics and Repairers, Engineers (Electrical & Electronic), Steelworkers, Dental Hygienists, Service Workers, Mechanics, Secretaries (Legal), Military Personnel, Corrections Officers, Carpenters.	**ISFP** Storekeepers, Clerical Supervisors, Dental Assistants, Bookkeepers, Carpenters, Radiologists, Secretaries (Legal), Waiters/Waitresses, Medical Assistants, Physical Therapists, Recreational Specialists, Sales Agents, Police & Detectives.	**INFP** Psychiatrists, Editors, Research Assistants, Artists, Entertainers, Agents, Journalists, Psychologists, Religious Educators, Social Scientists, Clinical Laboratory Technologists, Counselors, Art/Drama/Music Teachers.	**INTP** Chemists, Scientists, Writers, Artists, Entertainers, Computer Programmers, Lawyers, Systems Analysts, Biologists, Journalists, Psychologists, Pharmacists, Respiratory Therapists, Pathologists.
ESTP Marketing Personnel, Police and Detectives, Carpenters, Sales Clerks, Auditors, Craft Workers, Farmers, Laborers, Community Health Workers, Restaurant Workers, Computer Specialists.	**ESFP** Child Care Workers, Receptionists, Mining Engineers, Factory and Site Supervisors, Cashiers, Designers, Preschool Teachers, Coaches, Respiratory Therapists, Aeronautical Engineers, Medical Secretaries.	**ENFP** Journalist, Rehabilitation Counselor, Art/Drama/Music Teachers, Research Assistants, Psychologists, Resident Housing ASsistants, Musicians and Composers, Computer Operators, Actors, Social Workers.	**ENTP** Photographers, Marketing and Sales Agents, Journalists, Actors, Systems Analysts, Credit Investigators and Mortgage Brokers, Psychiatrists, Chemical Engineers, Mechanical Engineers, Researchers.
ESTJ Teachers (Trade and Industrial), Food Service Managers, Bank Officers and Financial Managers, Factory and Site Supervisors, Sales Representatives, Judges, Insurance Agents, Brokers, and Underwriters.	**ESFJ** Medical Secretaries, Hairdressers and Cosmetologists, Receptionists, Dental Assistants, Religious Educators, Nurses, Retail Trade Clerks, Office Managers, Radiological Technicians, Bookkeepers.	**ENFJ** Priests and Clergy, Actors, Art/Drama/Music Teachers, Writers, English Teachers, Optometrists, Counselors, Resident Housing Assistants, Physical Therapists, Dental Hygienists, Library Assts.	**ENTJ** Attorneys, Administrators, Managers, Marketing Personnel, Computer Specialists, Personnel and Labor Relations Workers, College and Technical Administrators, Educational Consultants, Biologists.

Occupations Attractive to Individual Personality Types

For more information on personality and job choice, read Myers, I.B., and M. H. McCaulley. (1990). Manual: A Guide to the Development and Use of the Myers-Briggs Type Indicator, Consulting Psychologists Press, Inc., Palo Alto, CA.

Appendix 4

Campus Computing

Since the Information Age is based on the Computer, you must know you way around one if you are to be a successful citizen of the 21st Century. This doesn't mean you need to be a computer scientist, but computerphobes will not have a bright future. With each passing year, more of you grew up with a computer in your home, if not in your room. A fair number of you are hackers. Most of you have used computers to do word processing. Some of you, however, have not. This is certainly no crime, but it will be a major roadblock to your success if you don't catch up quickly. Here is what every college student needs to know:

1. Word Processing. MicroSoft Word and WordPerfect are the most widely used programs, so you should know one or both of them. Most professors expect papers to be printed out rather than written in long hand. You also should keep your resume on a disk. It makes updating it very easy. All business letters should be word processed and printed out.

2. The InterNet (See below.) There are many resources available to you on the internet, but e-mail is probably what is most important. E-mail is for all practical purposes a requirement on most campuses. Some professors make assignments, post their syllabi, and schedule appointments exclusively on e-mail. It's also a great way to schedule meetings with your friends, make organizational announcements, and learn what events are happening on your campus. Through the internet, you can also access your campus library (as well as other campus libraries), find out which companies have internships available, apply for a job, and gather information about virtually anything on the face of the earth.

3. Spreadsheets. If you're studying science, engineering, or business, you'll need to learn a spreadsheet. Lotus 1-2-3, Excell, and QuatroPro are three that are widely used. A spreadsheet enables you to manipulate numbers in rows and columns and can also be useful for the average student in making presentations.

4. Mac vs. PC. It's helpful if you are familiar with the two principal types of personal computers: those manufactured by Apple with its operating system and those which use the DOS operating system. With the advent of Windows 95, this distinction becomes less important, but it's probably a good idea to be "ambidextrous."

5. Access. Know where the computer clusters are and when they're available. Unless you're a hacker, get to know a user-friendly student assistant whose job it is to help the rest of us through the maze of computer resources which alternately help us and drive us nuts.

6.   Open your computer account as soon as possible. You won't be able to access campus network without opening your account.

An Introduction to the Internet

Today, anybody who keeps up with the news is bombarded with talk of surfing the 'net or getting hooked up to the information superhighway. All this excitement is due to something called the internet. The internet is an extremely large network of computers all over the world that allows any computer connected to the internet to exchange information with any other computer that is also on the internet. This allows the people to send their friends electronic messages, or e-mail; talk to their friends live (well, at least type to their friends); find information on practically anything known to man; and countless other things.

It all began in 1969 with the dawning of the cold war. With the threat of a nuclear war hanging in the air, the Department of Defense saw a need for a decentralized computer network that could withstand parts of itself being destroyed without losing functionality. With this in mind, the government commissioned the Advanced Research Projects Agency to build what was known as ARPANET. Soon after this network was established civilians started using it as well. Gradually other networks adopted the standards used by ARPANET and began hooking themselves to each other and the ARPANET. It didn't take long before the original ARPANET was but a small neighborhood of these other networks, and the internet was born. Eventually, the Department of Defense dropped out of the picture leaving the main supporter to be the National Science Foundation. Now everyone from colleges to high schools and even elementary schools are getting connected to the internet and causing it to grow exponentially. The number of servers between 1986 and 1995 grew from 10,000 to 1.7 million, and there is no indication of a decline in this growth.

Now the internet is **ubiquitous** in colleges and universities and the corporate world is also catching on to the trend. Obviously, then, it is becoming increasingly important for an educated person to know the essentials of how to use the internet.

UNIX

Currently, the majority of users access the internet through what is know as a shell account. These are text-based interfaces (You see words, not ikons or pictures) on a computer running what is known as UNIX or a similar operating system. So, obviously, you should have a basic familiarity with UNIX if you are going to access the internet.

The basic concepts of the UNIX environment are probably familiar to anyone who has ever used a computer. In order to execute a command, you simply type in the command and hit *enter*. You just have to remember to be careful about the case of the command since UNIX is case-sensitive. The main problem comes in knowing the name of the command. In order to find out this UNIX has a special command, *man*. This command allows you to find out information on any other command in UNIX. For example, if you want to find out more information on the *man* command, just type:

man *man*

and hit the enter key and you will see information about that command. If you want to find out information about a particular topic, you can type

man -k *topic*

this will give a list of man pages on that particular topic from which to choose. So if you wanted to find a command to find a file, you might try

man -k *find*

and you would be given a list of commands that you can check out individually by using *man* to find out what each one does.

The file structure of UNIX is probably also familiar to anyone with a passing familiarity with computers. UNIX arranges its files into folders called directories. Each directory can contain as many directories and files as the user wants. For example, suppose you have a directory structure given by the following:

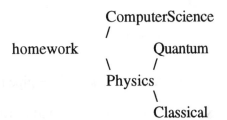

Now, suppose that you are in the homework directory and want to go to the Quantum directory.

Then you would type

cd *Physics/Quantum.*

The directories are separated by a /. If you wanted to go to the previous directory you would type

cd ..

The two periods are a special notation meaning to go to the directory containing the directory you are currently in, called the father directory. If you were in the Quantum directory and wanted to go to the ComputerScience directory then you could type:

cd */homework/ComputerScience.*

The initial backslash tells UNIX to go to the main directory that contains all other directories, called the root directory, before going to the other directories. Other useful commands to know to manipulate files and directories include:

-       **more** *this*: displays the file this.

-       **cp** *this that*: copies the files this to the file that

-       **mv** *here there*: moves the file here to the file there. The difference between this and *cp*, is that *mv* does not leave the original file where it was.

-       **rm** *this*: erases the file this. *rm* does not normally ask you to confirm whether or not you really want to erase the file, so use it very carefully.

-       **ls**: lists the files in the current directory

-       **mkdir** *this*: creates a directory named this

-       **rmdir** *that*: removes the directory named that if it is empty. Otherwise you will need to use rm to erase the files in the directory first.

Two other invaluable things to know in UNIX are the wildcards and the pipe key. The pipe key is used to pipe the output from one command into another. So for example if we wanted to find all commands related to directories we could execute the command:

man -k directory.

Most likely, this will scroll by too fast to read. In order to allow you to page through the output of the command at your own pace, you could type

man -k directory **/ more**

where \ is the pipe key and directs the output of *man* into *more*. Wildcards are even more useful. They allow you to perform an action on all files in a particular directory or a subset of those files. Let's say you wanted to delete all the files in a directory. To do this you could execute *rm* on each of these files individually or you could go into the directory and type

rm *

This would remove all the files from the directory you are currently in. Just make sure this is really what you want to do before you do it, however, as there is no way to recover the files once they are erased. You could also type

rm *phlit

if you wanted to remove all files beginning with phlit.   The asterisk essentially allows you to specify all possibly combinations of letters. So m*p would specify all possible combination of letters and numbers beginning with m and ending with p. The question mark is also a wildcard, except that it can only specify one character. So, for example, if you wanted to view a file that is called mop but can't remember whether it was called mop or map, then you could simply type

more *m?p.*

E-Mail

Probably the most widely used part of the Internet is electronic mail, abbreviated e-mail. E-mail is quite similar in concept to regular mail. It allows you to send text-based messages to other people who are also on the internet. Unfortunately, unlike regular mail, you cannot (in general) send graphics or other things that you might like to send through regular mail. The upside to this is that electronic mail normally takes less than a few minutes to reach someone. So it is much faster than regular mail and you do not have to worry about paying postage.

In order to send someone e-mail, one first has to know their address, just like regular mail. An e-mail address is quite different from a street address, though. It normally looks something like this:

eb81@prism.gatech.edu

or

locke@broach.gt.ed.net.

This first part of the address (*eb81* or *locke*) is the username of a particular person and the other part is the name of the server on which the user has his account.

Once the person's address is known, then one can send them a message. The most commonly used program for this is ELM. To use elm, simply type in *elm* at the command prompt (We're assuming you're in the campus computer cluster. If you have trouble, ask for help.), and you will see a screen similar to this:

Mailbox is '/var/spool/mail/locke' with 11 messages [ELM 2.4 PL23]

```
 1  Apr 11 jason                 (31)  Re: LETTING GO(READ LAST)(FWD)
 2  Apr 11 Mark Noel             (46)  Re: Congrats, Meeting, Etc.
 3  Apr 11 Demosthenes           (55)  My new road
 4  Apr 11 Jeff F.               (34)  Re: Congrats, Meeting, Etc.
 5  Apr 11 Nikhil Manohar Kam    (64)  (CHI) GT Tour Friday
 6  Apr 12 Women's Student Un    (44)  WSU mailing list
 7  Apr 12 Chuck Chung           (80)  (USA,AK) ACTION ALERT: Alaska (fwd)
 8  Apr 13 Andy James            (45)  Tabling Tuesday
 9  Apr 13 Demosthenes           (35)  Re: meeting and more
10  Apr 13 Deomsthenes           (26)  Your man at his finest
```

```
     |=pipe, !=shell, ?=help, <n>=set current to n, /=search pattern
a)lias, C)opy, c)hange folder, d)elete, e)dit, f)orward, g)roup reply, m)ail,
   n)ext, o)ptions, p)rint, q)uit, r)eply, s)ave, t)ag, u)ndelete, or e(x)it
```

Command:

It's commands are pretty self-explanatory. To mail someone a message you can type *m*. It will prompt you for a subject for the message, the address of the person you want to send it to, and if you want to send it to anyone else. The subject of the message will let the person receiving it know what it is about. This can be very important if you want a response when the person you are sending it to gets a large volume of e-mail (as many people do). When it prompts you for the address of the person, you need to type in their e-mail address and you can follow it by their name in parenthesis if you would like. If you want to send copies of the message to other people, you can type in their e-mail addresses when you are so prompted.

After you have gone through all this, you will be put into a text editor. Normally, this will be either pico or vi. Pico is the simplest to use, so beginners should probably use this one. To check to see which one you are using type *o* when at the main screen in elm. This will allow you to choose a different editor if yours is not pico.

In pico, the main commands are displayed at the bottom of the screen. You can simply type in your message and then when you are finished hit the control key and x. You will be asked whether you want to save. You need to answer yes to this and when it prompts you with a filename, just hit enter again without changing anything. This is very important as otherwise you will just send someone a blank e-mail. After you have saved, elm will prompt you as to what to do with the message. You can either hit *s* to send it or *f* to discard it.

After you have sent people e-mail, people will begin to send e-mail to you, too. If you wish to read a message you have received, you can highlight it with your arrow keys and hit *enter*. If you wish to respond to a message, you can highlight the message and then press *r*. This will prompt you for information similar to that prompted for a new message, but it will also ask whether you want to copy the message. This allows one to quote the message he is responding to so that the person he is responding to can know which message one is responding to.

After this you will be returned to the main screen and you can either quit by pressing *q* or you can send another message.

Mailing Lists

Once you can read e-mail, another thing you can do is subscribe to some of the countless mailing lists out there. These are services which allow discussions of specific topics over e-mail. For example, many of the student organizations have a mailing list devoted to keeping its members informed of its activities. Other mailing lists might be devoted to discussions about the sciences or literature. With many of these lists, you can contribute to them just like everyone else.

Subscribing to most mailing lists involves sending e-mail to an address like list-request@somewhere or listproc@somewhere with the phrase SUBSCRIBE LIST YOURFULLNAME where LIST specifies the list you wish to subscribe to. This does vary from list to list, though. Some lists want you to put this line in the subject while others want it in the message itself. Generally, you should put it in both and it will ignore the one it doesn't want. So for example, if you are really interesting in expanding your vocabulary, you could send an e-mail to wsmith@wordsmith.org with SUBCRIBE YOURFULLNAME in the subject. In this case you don't have to specify the name of the list since there is only one list served from that address.

Once you are subscribed, you will receive through your e-mail account all the messages that are posted to the group. And if you want to add something to the list and that particular list allows contributions, you can do it by just sending e-mail to the list like you would to an individual. Just remember that many other people are receiving this mailing list, and make sure that your contribution is worthwhile.

If you ever want to unsubscribe from the mailing list, you can send e-mail to the same e-mail address that you subscribed by except with the subject or message containing the command UNSUBSCRIBE LIST YOURNAME where LIST is replaced by the name of the list. In our previous example, you would send e-mail to wsmith@wordsmith.org with UNSUBCRIBE YOURFULLNAME in the subject header.

USENET

Another popular part of the internet is Usenet, or the newsgroups. This is like an extended form of e-mail where everyone who wants to can read and respond to what you have to say and you can read and respond what everyone else has to say. It's like a very extended, and sometimes rowdy, conversation.

The Usenet is divided up into many thousands of newsgroups. Each newsgroup is normally devoted to a single topic or a group of topics. Some newsgroups may get over a hundred posts a day and some are lucky to get a single post a day. The various posts are normally divided up into "threads" each consisting of a single subject. If you have an interest, there is probably at least one newsgroup devoted to it.

Newsgroups are divided into a few major divisions according to the type of topics discussed:

- **alt**: Anything and everything is discussed in these groups but unfortunately access is not allowed by all internet providers

- **bionet**: biology

- **biz**: Business

- **comp**: computers

- **misc**: Miscellaneous

- **news**: News about usenet

- **rec**: Games, sports, recreation.

- **sci**: science

- **talk**: talk about current, normally incendiary, topics such as politics, abortion, religion.

There are also regional newsgroups such as the git or ga newsgroups which are not carried by all sites.

Examples of some newsgroups are comp.os.linux.advocacy, which is devoted to advocating the Linux operating system, and rec.humor, which is devoted to humor. All newsgroups are specified by a main category and successively narrower categories, each separated by periods.

To access newsgroups, you have to have a program to do so. Normally, you use rn, trn, tin, or nn. The most commonly used and widely available of these is trn so we will focus on that. To start trn, you can just type *trn* at the command prompt and hit *enter*. If you want to quit at any time you can type *q*.

trn is a fairly simple program, but it can take a while to get used to it and learn all the commands. It can be divided into three levels:

1. **Newsgroup selection level**: Allows one to select a newsgroup to read. This is the level in which rn starts.

2. **Article Selection level**: This will list the articles in the newsgroup the user selects and allow   the user to read any article he selects.

3. **Paging Level**: This is where the user actually reads the article he choose.

Now all this may seem a bit complicated at first, but it is easier than it sounds.

When you first enters trn, it has to set up your account so that you can use it. This is all done automatically, so you don't need to do anything here. Next it will ask the you whether or not you want to subscribe to a bunch of newsgroups. Type *N*, and it will skip all of these. You can always decide later to subscribe to them, and it will take forever if you go through them all. After it goes through all this, you will be given a prompt like this:

`====== 83 unread articles in news.announce.newusers -- read now? [+ynq]`

This means that rn has automatically subscribed you to the group news.announce.newusers, an introduction to the USENET for novices. You can read this group now by pressing *y*, going directly to the first article, go into the article selection mode by pressing *space* or +, or skip the group entirely by pressing *n*. It will prompt you this way for each newsgroup that you are subscribed to that has unread articles in it. This level is called the newsgroup selection level. Other useful commands to know at this level are:

- **g** *name*: goes to the newsgroup specified by name. It also allows you to subscribe to different newsgroups.

- **l** *pattern*: searches for newsgroups that match the pattern. This can be the full name of a newsgroup of part of a name. For example, if you wanted to find a group about physics, you might try entering l physics. This should give you a list of all the newsgroups with physics somewhere in the name. You can then go to the newsgroup of your choice with the g command.

- **p**: goes to the previous newsgroup.

- **c**: allows you to catch up with a newsgroup. It marks all the articles as read. This is useful when you haven't read news in a while and have too many articles to read.

- **u**: allows you to unsubscribe from a newsgroup you don't want to read anymore.

Once you decide to read a newsgroup, you can enter it from two different levels. If you press + or *space*, you enter it through the article selection mode. This allows you to choose the articles you want to read instead of just reading them all. Or if you press *y*, you enter directly into the first unread article.

If you did the first, you will see a screen like this:

news.announce.newusers   34 articles (moderated)

a Aliza R. Panitz	1 How to find the right place to post (FAQ)
b Dave Taylor	2 A Guide to Social Newsgroups and Mailing Lists
Dave Taylor	
d Mark Moraes	2 Usenet Software: History and Sources
Mark Moraes	
e Mark Moraes	2 What is Usenet?
Mark Moraes	
f David Alex Lamb	1 FAQ: How to find people's E-mail addresses
g Chris Lewis	1 How to become a Usenet site
i Mark Moraes	2 Welcome to Usenet!
Mark Moraes	
j Joel K. Furr	2 Advertising on Usenet: How To Do It, How Not To Do It
Joel K. Furr	
l Brad Templeton	2 Copyright Myths FAQ: 10 big myths...copyright explained
Brad Templeton	
o Mark Moraes	2 Emily Postnews Answers Your Questions on Netiquette
Mark Moraes	
r Mark Moraes	2 A Primer on How to Work With the Usenet Community
Mark Moraes	

-- Select threads (date order) -- Top 55% [>Z] --

You can select articles by typing their letter, and then read all of the selected articles by hitting *space*. If you want to read a single article or thread, you can highlight it and then press *enter*. Pressing *space* without selecting any articles allows you to just read all the articles.

Once you start reading an article, either by pressing *y* at the newsgroup selection level or by the article selection level, you can page through it by using *space* or go back a page by pressing *b*. If you don't want to read the whole article you can go directly to the next one by pressing *n*, or to the previous one by pressing *p*.

If you need help at any level, you can press *h*, and will get a list of commands that you can use at your current level.

Once you have read articles for a while, you may want to begin to contribute your own ideas and ask your own questions. You should only post to a newsgroup after you have been reading it for awhile and are sure that what you have to say is appropriate to the newsgroup. Otherwise you risk getting "flamed." These are nasty responses sent to people who do not follow the conventions of the particular newsgroup (among other things).

Once you are sure you know your post will be appropriate, you can post by hitting f or F in the paging mode. If you are responding to a another post, F will copy it so that you can let people know what you are responding to. After you type this, it will bring you to your default editor so that you can compose your message. Then just type in the message, save it and exit, and it will be posted.

The World Wide Web

Probably the most popular part of the internet after e-mail is the World Wide Web, normally referred to as the Web or the WWW. The Web is a system where users can access hypertext documents, called pages, with inline graphics, sound, videos or just about anything imaginable. These pages all contain connections, or links, that you can follow to other pages or other information. For example, a page about a foreign language could allow you to click on a phrase to hear it spoken aloud or a page about an artist could allow you to click on the title of a work to see it.

The most popular browser for the Web is Netscape. With this program, all you have to do is click on a link and you will automatically follow it. Links are normally differentiated from the rest of the document by appearing in blue. If any text is blue or any picture is surrounded with blue, it is normally a link. This rule is not hard and fast, however, so in general if it looks like a link, then it is one.

A person can find practically anything he wants to know on the web, the only problem is finding it among the many millions of pages out there. To do this, you can use what are known as search engines. These let you type in a few keywords describing what you want to find out about and then return a list of web sites that have relevance to the keywords. To get to one of these, you can types in the URL, or the address, in the Go To window of Netscape. A few of the more popular search engines and their URLs are listed below.

Webcrawler: http://www.webcrawler.com

Lycos: http://www.lycos.com

Yahoo: http://www.yahoo.com

Telnet

Another useful service you can use over the internet is telnet. With telnet you can log into a remote computer and access libraries and databases or run programs remotely on a more powerful computer. To connect to a remote computer you would type:

telnet *nyx.cs.du.edu*

In this case we are telnetting to nyx, but you would replace this by the address of the computer you wish to connect to. Unfortunately, if you want to connect to a remote computer, you have to have a login name and a password.

FTP

Another widely used service is FTP, or file transfer protocol. This allows you to transfer files from one computer to another. To use this, all one does is type

ftp *name*

where name is the address of the computer you want to transfer files to or from. This time, when it asks you for a name, however, you can type anonymous and it will allow you to login and download files. Some common commands use in ftp are:

- **get** *something nothing*: copies the file named something to your computer and names it nothing. If you don't specify the second file name, it assumes you want to keep the original name.

- **put** *nothing something*: copies the file named nothing on your computer to the remote computer into a file named something. If the second file name is not specified, it keeps the original name. This will not work on sites where you do not have permission to upload files.

- **cd** *dir*: changes to the directory called dir. cd .. is a special case of this used to change to the father directory.

- **ls**: lists the files in the current directory

- **ascii**: changes the transfer mode to text mode. It is very important for the transfer mode to be set correctly when transferring files as otherwise the data will be messed up. Use this transfer mode to transfer pure text files only. Files from most word processors contain formatting information and so should not be transferred this way.

- **binary**: changes the transfer mode to binary mode. You should use this mode when transferring programs, text with formatting information, pictures, and most other things.

Some of you may be snoozing because this is all ancient history for you. Others may be in panic mode, thinking, "How can I ever remember all this?" Relax. Computers are very fast, but very simpleminded machines. You are smarter than they are. You learn how to use a computer the same way you learned to drive or play tennis -- by driving and playing tennis. Don't try to memorize command in this appendix. Do take this appendix to a computer and refer to it as you begin to master the number two tool of the Information Age. What's the number one tool? Hint: it's located between your ears!

One final point we'd like to make has to do with access. How do you find computers available for your use? We believe it's a definite advantage for you to own one. We also think it's advantageous to own a printer. Laser jets produce documents that look quite good, and they're relatively inexpensive. We also know that many of you can afford neither computer nor printer. If you can't, there's no use in bemoaning the fact. Find out where the clusters are on your campus and when they are in least demand. Don't wait until the last minute to finish some project that requires a computer and expect one magically to become available. Chances are good that your classmates are also finishing up projects and fighting over the same limited pool of computers.

Appendix 5
Should I get an Advanced Degree?

===
LAW SCHOOL
===

Admissions:
The most important factors are:

1.   Grades.
2.   LSAT Scores

Other factors that influence admission:
3.   Personal qualifications and accomplishments
4.   Ethnic group, gender, and geographic diversity
5.   Graduate or professional school record
6.   Letters of recommendation
7.   Relationship with law school (Your chances are better if the library is named after one of your parents.)

LSAT Facts:
Since 1982 a writing sample has been a part of the LSAT. Reading comprehension, analytical reasoning, evaluation of facts, and logical ability are also tested. In 1983-84, 89 percent of students took the test once, 11 percent took it twice, and 0.4 percent took it three or more times. You can cancel scores before they are reported, but the law schools are notified that you have been exposed to the LSAT. Law schools tend to average scores of repeat test-takers. (Information taken from the 1985-1986 PRELAW HANDBOOK: The Official Guide to U. S. Law Schools.)

How to Get In:
If you decide to go prelaw in college, contact your school's prelaw advisor early on. Join the prelaw club if there is one. Get hold of guides to the LSAT and to Law School. They're full of good information and sound advice. Remember, entrance into a better law school depends on grades and LSAT scores. GPA and LSAT depend on your verbal skills and reasoning ability. Can you read well? Rapidly and with comprehension? Can you write well? With clarity and ease? Are you an analytical thinker? If not, we suggest you think twice about a legal career.

The Job Market for Lawyers
The 1994-95 *Occupational Outlook Handbook* projects there to be a faster than the average growth in the need for lawyers through the year 2005. Although jobs for lawyers are expected to increase rapidly, competition for job openings should continue to be keen because of the large numbers graduating each year. The willingness to relocate may be an advantage in getting a job. In addition, employers increasingly seek graduates who have advanced law degrees and experience in a particular field such as tax, patent, or admiralty law. Graduates of less prominent law schools will have to struggle. So will those with undistinguished academic records.

Books to Read:
Barron's Guide to Law Schools
Barron's Guide to the New Law School Admission Test
Getting Into Law School by Amy Shapiro & Sandra W. Weckesser, Philadelphia; W. B. Saunders Co., 1979
Prelaw Handbook: The Official Guide to U. S. Law Schools by the Law School Admission Council

Admissions:

The most important factors are:

1. Grades.
2. MCAT Scores

Other factors that influence admission:
3. Personality and character
4. Place of residence
5. Career plans
6. Recommendations
7. Interviews
8. Being a member of a disadvantaged minority group

Fewer than 10% of those applicants who were admitted had GPAs below a 3.0.

MCAT Facts:
There are six subtests:

1.	Reading	4.	Chemistry
2.	Quantitative	5.	Physics
3.	Biology	6.	Scientific Problem Solving

From: Medical School Admission Requirements, 1983-84, Association of American Medical Colleges

How to Get In:
The big problem is getting through the door. Good grades from a good school is obviously the key. Master the skills presented in chapters 2 and 4 of this book as soon as possible, preferably by yesterday. Latch onto your pre-med advisor early on. Organic Chemistry and Human Anatomy will probably be your biggest academic hurdles. Unless you're an unusually strong student, we recommend auditing these two courses before you take them for credit. If you're week in math, get tutorial assistance. A few low grades can torpedo your plans. And don't forget, you'll be tested on Physics and Math on the MCAT.

Finally, we advise having an alternative career plan in the event you don't make it into medical school. There are many medically-based careers such as physician's assistants, physical therapists, respiratory therapists, and so forth .

The Job Market for Physicians
The 1994-95 *Occupational Outlook Handbook* projects there to be a faster than the average growth in the need for physicians through the year 2005 due to continued expansion of the health industry. Job prospects are good for primary care physicians such as family practitioners and internists, and for geriatric and preventive care specialists.

Books to Read:
Getting Into Medical School by Donald J. Solomon, Philadelphia, W. B. Saunders Co., 1979.
Barron's Guide to Medical, Dental, and Allied Health Science Careers
Medical School Admission Requirements, Association of American Medical Colleges, 2450 N St., N.W., Washington, DC 20037-1131.

Admissions:
The most important factors are:

1. Grades.
2. GMAT Scores

Other factors that influence admission:
3. Your accomplishments or experience at work, in the military, or in campus or community activities
4. The overall quality of your application and recommendations
5. Intangibles such as your motivation, maturity, and leadership abilities, as suggested by a variety of information

GMAT Facts:
A four-hour test assessing:

Quantitative -- Basic mathematics, quantitative reasoning, problem solving, graph interpretation

Verbal -- Reading comprehension, writing ability, analysis of situations

How to Get In:
To get into a top school, you need top grades. But graduate programs in business tend to weigh practical experience more heavily than do most other graduate programs. Therefore, co-ops and those with internships or career-related summer work will be at an advantage compared with those who have had no significant work history at all. Having clear career plans also counts in your favor. Read the basic books on how to get into an MBA program and go for it.

The Job Market for MBAs
The 1994-95 *Occupational Outlook Handbook* projects there to be a faster than the average growth in the need for managers through the year 2005. Companies are moving toward employing more consultants for management than ever before, having trimmed many from their corporate payrolls. As a consequence a high percentage of MBA are now self-employed. There is a rising need for individuals with a technical background, such as engineering or biotechnology, combined with an MBA. Despite projected rapid employment growth, competition for jobs is expected to be keen in the private sector.

Books to Read:
Barron's Guide to Graduate Business Schools
The Official Guide to MBA, Graduate Management Admission Council
The MBA Career: Moving on the Fast Track to Success by Eugene Bronstein & Robert Hisrich, Barron's Educational Series

Admissions:
The most important factors are:

1. Grades.
2. Graduate admissions test scores

Other factors that influence admission:
3. Letters of recommendation
4. Appropriateness of undergraduate degree
5. Interview
6. Evidence of creative talent

Admission Tests:
Graduate Record Exam:

General test: Seven 30 minute sections designed to measure verbal, quantitative, and analytical abilities. Think of it as the SAT for college students.

Subject tests: There are 17 different areas, ranging from biology to Spanish. Each test lasts 170 minutes.

Miller Analogies Test:

Requires the solution of 100 intellectual problems stated in the form of analogies.

The GRE and the MAT are the most widely used, but there are also:
Dental Admission Testing Program
NTE Program Tests (formerly National Teacher Examinations)
Optometry College Admission Test
Pharmacy College Admission Test

Read the catalog for the program you are interested in carefully to determine which examination is required for the program and college you desire to attend.

The Job Market

It all depends on your field. A PhD in electrical engineering will have many more options to choose from than a PhD in Classics. Some fields require a doctorate. In others, the terminal degree is a master's. Some schools are professional -- dental, optometry. Some are research -- you're trained to conduct scientific or scholarly research. If you want to be a researcher, it may be less important for you to attend a prestigious school than to study under a famous scholar.

Books to Read:

Graduate Professional Programs, An Overview 1985, Peterson's Guides
(Also look at the Peterson's Guide specific to your field of interest.)
The Gourman Report (provides ratings of the top schools)

Appendix 6
PSYCHOLOGICAL TESTS

In this class you're expected to take some psychological tests. Why? Because self-knowledge is crucial for your success, and testing is one path to self-knowledge. You can't choose the right major or plan a solid career unless you know yourself. You can't be a good leader or an effective team member without knowing yourself. Even friendship depends in part upon self-knowledge.

Defining clear goals, is possible only through self knowledge. Psychological tests can help you know yourself better. They are not the only source of information about who you are, nor are they infallible. But they CAN help. When you know more about yourself, you will be better able to make informed decisions about the goals and objectives you select for yourself. You will be better able to choose a major, if you haven't already; to help you understand your roommate, your parents; and very possibly, that special someone in your life!

You might even compare psychological tests to a medical check-up. A medical exam takes time, costs money, and sometimes even seems like an assault on your dignity what with the pinching and probing and drawing of blood. But after it's all over, a good physical can help to identify what ails us as well as how we're healthy.

We hope we've sold you on the idea that the tests and surveys you take as a part of Psych. 1010 can be helpful to you. Here's some ways you can get the most out of them:

1.   Be curious. A student was once asked if he realized that ignorance and apathy were the two biggest barriers to learning from psychological tests. The student's response: "I don't know and I don't care." Why in the world would you not want to learn more about yourself unless you have a burning desire to keep yourself in the dark? Use this opportunity to learn as much as you can about what makes you tick.

2.   Understand testing. Psychological tests are designed to measure some aspect of you. They are neither magic nor perfect. In fact they vary in how accurately they do their job. Part of this is attributable to the fact that the psyche is harder to measure than the body. Tests can be more or less **reliable** -- a psychometric term referring to stability. If I measure you in January and again in June, and it's granted that you haven't changed, your scores should be similar. Tests can also be more or less **valid**. Validity is another psychometric term that has to do with what the test actually measures. If a test suggests that you are more resilient, for instance, then you should be better able to tolerate stress

than a less resilient individual.

3.   Understand the particular test. Make sure you know the purpose of the test, what it claims to measure, and how that factor is relevant for you. For example, the Strong Career Interest Inventory does NOT measure your aptitudes or abilities. *It does NOT tell you what you're supposed to be.* It DOES measure your interests and shows how they compare with the interests of people who are typical of various occupations. It DOES suggest the sorts of occupations you'd likely by compatible with.

4.   Reflect on the results. Do the results confirm my picture of myself, or is there a substantial discrepancy? Are the test results off, or is it my own self-estimate? Or both?

5.   Gather additional information. Take additional tests. If you have additional questions arrange to speak with the teacher of your section. Or arrange for an appointment with a counselor in the Counseling Center and bring your results with you for an in-depth interpretation. Ask your roommates, friends, professors, advisors, peer leaders, parents, etc. how THEY would assess you on a particular issue.

6.   Consider acting on the information. For example, if you're majoring in engineering and your interests turn out to be very different from most engineers, you should think about why it is you want to be an engineer. It's true, there are a few successful engineers whose interests are rather different from most other engineers, and maybe you're one of them. It's also true that many students go into a field that doesn't fit them well and suffer because of it. Make sure you're the former and not the latter.

Glossary

anachronism--n. 1. The representation of something as existing or happening at other than its proper or historical time. 2. Something out of its proper time.

aversive--adj. Causing avoidance of an unpleasant or punishing stimulus.

demographics--n. (used with a pl. verb). Demographic data used especially to identify consumer markets. Demography: the study of the characteristics of human populations, as size, growth, density, distribution, and vital statistics.

denizen--n. An inhabitant, resident.

epochs--n. 1. a. a particular period of history, especially one considered remarkable or noteworthy. b. a notable event that marks the beginning of such a period. 2. Geol. A unit of geologic time that is a division of a period. 3. Astron. an instant in time that is arbitrarily selected as a point of reference.

indigenous--adj. 1.Occuring or living naturally in a particular area or environment; native 2. Intrinsic; innate.

millennium--n. pl. millenniums or millennia. 1. a span of one thousand years. 2. a thousand year period of holiness during which Christ is to rule on earth. 3. a hoped-for period of joy, serenity, prosperity, and justice.

mitigate--v. to make or become less severe or intense; moderate.

noxious--adj. 1. injurious or harmful to health: noxious chemical wastes, 2. injurious or harmful to the mind or morals; corrupting: noxious ideas.

prolific--adj. 1. producing offspring or fruit in great abundance; fertile. 2. producing abundant works or results.

sartorial--adj. 1. of or relating to a tailor, tailoring, or tailored clothing.

savvy--adj. 1. practical and perceptive.

tomes n. 1. one of the books in a work of several volumes. 2. a book, especially a large or scholarly book.

ubiquitous--adj. Being or seeming to be everywhere at the same time, omnipresent.

7/15

Three Ages (Eras) of Civilization

John King Hsu

B-9

Era: _Agricultural_

Ideal level of education: _Farming_

Era: _Industrial_

Ideal level of education: _Mechanical, Blue Collar_

Era: _Technology_

Ideal level of education: _College or higher – pencil pusher_

Seven Principles of This Age: Examples: Implications for Me: Educational Implications

1. _Knowledge is Power_

2. _Diversity_   _willing to move_

3. _____

4. _____

5. _____

6. _____

7. _____